LJ 8208

372.623 Graves, Donald H.
GRA
        Write from the
        start

DATE		

41 X 11/99 ✓ 12/00
45 X 10/05 ✓ 3/06

LJ
1695

WRITE FROM THE START

DONALD GRAVES &
VIRGINIA STUART

WRITE FROM THE START

**TAPPING
YOUR CHILD'S
NATURAL
WRITING
ABILITY**

E. P. DUTTON | NEW YORK

Published in the United States by
E. P. Dutton, a division of New American Library,
2 Park Avenue, New York, N.Y. 10016

"My Father's Neckties" from *Our Ground Time Here Will Be Brief*
by Maxine Kumin. Copyright © 1977 by Maxine Kumin.
Reprinted by permission of Viking Penguin Inc.

Excerpt on pp. 150 and 151 from *What Makes Writing Good:
A Multiperspective* by William E. Coles, Jr., and James Vopat.
Copyright © 1985 by D.C. Heath & Company.
Reprinted by permission of the publisher.

Excerpt on pp. 20–23 from *Language, Learning and Education*
by C. G. Wells.
Copyright © 1985 by NFER—Nelson Publishing Company, Ltd.

Library of Congress Cataloging in Publication Data

Graves, Donald H.
Write from the start.

1. English language—Composition and exercises.
2. Reading readiness. 3. Children—Writing. I. Stuart,
Virginia. II. Title.
LB1528.G79   1985   372.6'23   85-6993

ISBN: 0-525-24347-X

Published simultaneously in Canada by
Fitzhenry & Whiteside Ltd., Toronto

W

DESIGNED BY MARK O'CONNOR

10 9 8 7 6 5 4 3 2 1

First Edition

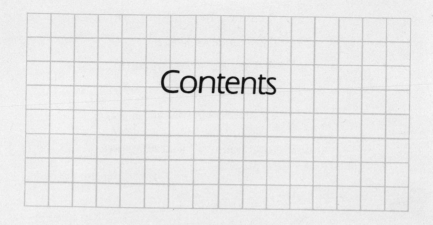

Contents

Acknowledgments

Many children, teachers, parents, researchers, school administrators, and professors have contributed to this book. First, we must thank the teachers who took the time to discuss their experiences as writers and writing teachers. A number of them also shared their thoughts on working with young writers at home, and some invited us into their classrooms to observe and talk with their students. These teachers include Connie Bataller, now of Drew Model School, Arlington, Virginia; Pam Bradley of Mast Way Elementary School, Lee, New Hampshire; Barbara Campey, now of Mount Austin Primary School, Wagga Wagga, New South Wales, Australia; Sue Clancy of Tatton Primary School, Wagga Wagga, New South Wales, Australia; Kathy Diers and Mary Anne Byrne of Webster Elementary School, Manchester,

New Hampshire; Lila Edelkind of Public School 152, Brooklyn, New York; Judy Egan, now director of The Children's Place, Canterbury, New Hampshire; Mary Ellen Giacobbe, now finishing her doctorate at Harvard University; Judi Hilliker of Oyster River Elementary School, Durham, New Hampshire; Marita Maes of Gossler Park Elementary School, Manchester, New Hampshire; Kathy Matthews, now completing her master's degree at the University of New Hampshire; Carolyn Reynolds and Mary Dietz of Briarcliff Elementary School, Shoreham, New York; Phyllis Tashlik of Manhattan East School, Harlem, New York; and Karen Weinhold of North Hampton Elementary School, North Hampton, New Hampshire.

We are especially indebted to Nancie Atwell and Susan Stires of Boothbay Region Elementary School, Boothbay Harbor, Maine; Ellen Blackburn, now of Edward Devotion School, Brookline, Massachusetts; Linette Moorman of Public School 152, Brooklyn, New York; Jo Parry of Reservoir East Primary School, Reservoir, Victoria, Australia; Dale Paul of Barton Graded School, Barton, Vermont; Susan Porter of Stratham Memorial School, Stratham, New Hampshire; and Jan Roberts of Mast Way Elementary School, Lee, New Hampshire.

The children who contributed to the book are far too numerous to list, but we appreciate all their help. Special thanks go to the following children, who shared their thoughts, or their writing, or both: Brandon Aamen, Sam Aaronian, Stefanie Adams, Paul Agakian, Robert Baumiere, Jr., Holly Bergeron, Scott Brown, Parks Christenbury, Nicole Ciancarelli, Birger Dahl, Daniel Donovan, Teena Eggleston, Amy Eldridge, Melissa Finemore, Amy Flemming, Megan Frazer, Lauryl Green, Emily Holmes, Nickie Houle, Nathan and Meg Hubbard, Cassie James, Jarek Jaroslaw, Sonja Kingston, Jalil Lynch, Greg Manship, Kasey McGarrigle, Nathan and Justin Merrill, Debbie Nichols, Jill Perrault, Aerica Pratt, Sarah Pruitt, Adi Rule, Jeannette Santos, Bobby Schimoler, Amanda Shepard, Susie Sible, Greg Snicer, Anne Stires, Nick and Alex Tornow, Glen Watt, Jonathan and Hillary Wentworth, and Pierce Woodward, plus all the children of Jan Roberts's 1982–1983 third-grade class at Mast Way Elementary School in Lee, New Hampshire; all the children of Ellen Blackburn's 1983–1984 first-grade class at Great Falls

School in Somersworth, New Hampshire; and all the children of Kathy Diers's 1983–1984 third-grade class at Webster Elementary School in Manchester, New Hampshire, originators of the June Series books.

In addition, we have learned from comments made by the following parents: Peg Aaronian, Carolyn and David Allen, Nancy Bergeron, Betsey Burton, Sissel Dahl, Sandra Finemore, Elinor Green, Van Gsottschneider, Val James, Ed and Heather McGarrigle, Joyce Vining Morgan, Peg Nichols, Gretchen Ramsay, Dick Talbot, and Jennifer Wilson, among others. Becky Rule and Joan and John Tornow were especially helpful.

We thank the following school administrators for their remarks: Richard Anderson, Principal, Wading River School, Wading River, New York; Martin Brooks, Principal, Miller Avenue Elementary School, Shoreham, New York; Roberta Charlesworth, North York Board of Education, Toronto, Ontario, Canada; Mike Deineke, Joan Leslie, and Marilyn McNeil, Teacher Consultants, North York Public Schools, Toronto, Ontario, Canada; Mark Goldberg, Assistant Principal, Shoreham-Wading River High School, Shoreham, New York; Elizabeth Johnson, Quebec Ministry of Education, Quebec, Canada; Jane Kearns, Writing Coordinator, Manchester Public Schools, Manchester, New Hampshire; John Lowy, Principal, Mast Way Elementary School, Lee, New Hampshire; Jean Robbins, now Principal of Oyster River Elementary School, Durham, New Hampshire; and Herbert Shapiro, Principal, and Marilyn Savetsky, Assistant Principal, Public School 152, Brooklyn, New York.

A number of researchers and educators who work with teachers have also made important contributions to the book. These include Garth Boomer, President of the Australian Association for the Teaching of English; Lucy Calkins, now Associate Professor at Teachers College, Columbia University, New York; Bryant Fillion, Professor, Fordham University, New York; Barbara Kamler, now Lecturer at Riverina College for Advanced Education, Wagga Wagga, New South Wales, Australia; Mary Maguire, Director of Student Teaching, McGill University, Montreal, Quebec, Canada; Thomas Newkirk, Director of the New Hampshire Writing Program; Susan Sowers, now finishing her doctorate at Harvard University; and Gordon Wells, now Professor at the Ontario Institute for the Study of Education, Toronto, Ontario, Canada. For her extensive interviews with Cassie James, special thanks go to Marilyn Woolley, now Lecturer at Melbourne College of Advanced Education in Carlton, Victoria, Australia.

We have been fortunate to have a number of willing and perceptive readers, starting with Leslie Wells and Jerret Engle, our editors at Dutton. Ruth Clogston, Jane Hansen, Lorri Nielsen, Candice Stover, and Nancy Walz all made helpful comments on various parts of the book. Anne Holmes read the manuscript with a mother's, as well as an editor's, eye. We are particularly indebted to Donald Murray, who read with his usual speed, acuity, and sense of perspective.

Ruth Hubbard takes on nearly every role listed above— parent, teacher, researcher, teacher trainer, reader—and she gave us invaluable help in every one of those roles. Dori Stratton not only spent hours and hours typing, but also helped in many other ways. Lorraine Merrill, Eve Varrieur, and Katharine Wentworth offered moral support and shared their experiences as mothers and teachers. Paul Farrell provided much-needed distraction on hot, humid days when the computer went haywire.

Virginia Stuart would also like to thank several people who contributed a great deal to this book indirectly. Her parents, James and Lorraine Stuart, have always shown great respect for children and faith in their abilities. Former high-school teachers Bill Thorndike and Elizabeth Brady made her want to write more and helped her to write better.

Most of all, she is grateful to her husband, John Hill, who helped with the book at every stage, providing sound judgment, useful suggestions, unfailing support, and a seemingly endless supply of patience.

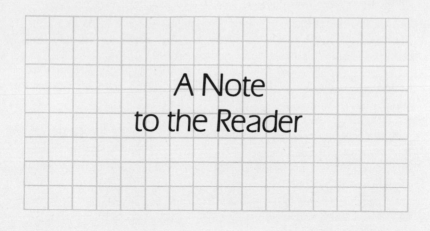

A Note
to the Reader

This book shows what happens when teachers and parents realize that every child can write. It comes out of the experiences of many children, parents, teachers, and researchers around the globe, all of whom have felt the influence of a seminal research project directed by Donald Graves. Although the book is the result of a collaboration, the two authors have chosen to preserve their separate voices. Virginia Stuart tells the story of the children who have discovered the joys of writing, and the parents and teachers who have helped them make that discovery. Drawing on his years of experience as a researcher, educator, and parent, Donald Graves adds a running commentary as that story unfolds. His remarks appear throughout the book, indented and in italics.

WRITE FROM THE START

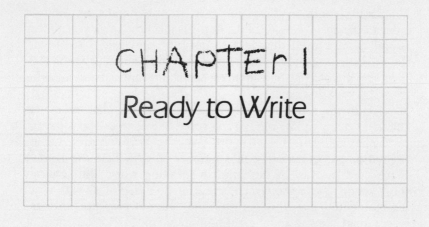

CHAPTEr 1
Ready to Write

One day a four-and-a-half-year-old named Emily called to her parents, "Look. I made a word! I spelled *SIR* with my blocks." Her parents looked down and saw *S-G-H-Y-R*. They had an important decision to make in a matter of seconds. Emily had shown that she understood the purpose of the written word. She knew that words have meaning, letters make words, and at least some of those letters correspond with the sounds of words. She wanted to write and had taken the risk of trying it on her own. Her parents had two choices. They could point out all that she knew: how to place letters from left to right and how to sound out the first and last letters. Or they could say, "That's not how you spell *sir*." In short, they could encourage her to keep trying or convince her, and themselves, that she wasn't ready to write.

Recognizing the significance of this occasion as another first, like her first tooth, her first spoken word, or her first step, Emily's parents chose to congratulate her. "Look how well you did at sounding out these letters all by yourself," they said. "You heard the *s* and the *r* sounds." They knew that the elementary school in their town would also recognize her ability and desire to write from the very first day.

Emily was ready to write. And so are all the children in our school systems today, ready to surprise themselves and a parent or teacher with what they can do. Over the last few years, a quiet revolution has taken place in a number of schools in the United States and the rest of the English-speaking world. Students in these schools have shown that they can do much more with writing than adults ever thought possible, without pressure, threats, or cajoling. Now, a second revolution has begun in the wake of the first. More and more parents like Emily's are learning how to give their children a chance they themselves never had, both at home and at school. This book is about both revolutions. It documents the first in order to strengthen the second.

Emily's parents and the teachers at their local school are still unusual. Most adults think children can't write until they can read. But children can learn to write the same way they learn to talk, by going through a series of ever-improving approximations of what adults do. When children write first, reading comes more easily. A first-grade teacher reports that her entering students have a much better grasp of phonics now that the kindergarten teacher has dropped phonics exercises and allows her students to write instead.

A teacher named Kathy Diers from Hooksett, New Hampshire, discovered how naturally reading follows writing in her own home. Her son, Terry, was attending a pre-first-grade readiness class in which the children were able to start writing before they could read, by sounding out spellings as best they could. They were not being given any drills, worksheets, or standard lessons in phonics. One evening in November, Diers was at the stove when a scene around the corner in the family room caught her eye. Her husband, Ken, was on the couch, reading the newspaper, and Terry had just walked over to a shelf full of children's books. He seemed to be thinking aloud. "Now let's see," he said. "I should be able to read one of these." Kathy froze, and her eyes met Ken's. He held a finger to his lips.

After scanning the shelf, Terry selected a favorite book, sat down, and proceeded to start reading. When he was stumped, he went to his father for help with a word. Out in the kitchen, the smell of burning cauliflower brought Kathy's attention back to the meal she was making.

Most adults think children can't write until they successfully complete spelling, punctuation, and grammar exercises. But children can best learn these skills in the context for which they were intended: writing. One fourth-grader from Boothbay Harbor, Maine, had been labeled "learning disabled" in writing because he repeatedly failed to punctuate and capitalize correctly in classroom exercises. The usual prescription for such difficulties is more of the same: off to the "resource room" for more drills. The teacher in this little boy's resource room, however, had a different approach. She let him write. He wrote about fishing, his rabbit, and a lost contact lens. He wrote poems about happiness and mustangs. He wrote letters to the town manager and the principal of the school. Now that he needed to make his meaning clear, he had a reason to punctuate and capitalize, and so he did.

Most adults think children can't write without assignments, pictures, "story starters," or even word lists to get them going. More and more teachers are discovering otherwise. In an inner-city school, where teachers may be even more likely to question their students' own resources, one teacher dared to allow her second-graders to write from their own ideas. She immediately received this memo from a little girl in her class.

to: Mrs. L. Moorman
from: Sonja
Dear, Mrs. Moorman
I wood like to make books about animals, insects,
Babys, all kinds of books.
When I grow up I will be a authr.
and a authr is someone who likes to write books.

Equipped with ideas and enthusiasm, Sonja was ready to improve all her writing skills.

Above all, most adults think children don't want to write. But children want to make sense of the world around them, and writing can help them do that. Through writing, children can discover new ways of thinking, seeing, listening, and reading. They can learn about themselves and find their own writing voices. A few lucky children discover these things on their own. But most don't. The adults around them neither encourage nor expect them to do so. Now a number of teachers and parents are changing their expectations and their approaches to helping children write. They know how to respond to children's writing and how to create an atmosphere conducive to learning at home and at school. Their children show their desire to write in many ways. Some of them write during their free time at school, at recess, and even at home in bed. A fourth-grade teacher has found that she doesn't have to push her students to write anymore; now it's hard to stop them after an hour. And a seventh-grade teacher is thrilled to have students coming in before school to work on their writing. In the classrooms he has studied or visited, Donald Graves has found that children want to write, for their own reasons.

> *More and more children are seeing themselves as writers, seeing that writing helps them live today, even though they may be no more than six years old. When they discover the rewards of writing, some children even talk about wanting to be writers when they grow up.**

All these parents, teachers, and children have felt the influence of a research project on children's writing directed by Donald Graves at the public elementary school in Atkinson, New Hampshire, from 1978 to 1980. Together, the teachers and researchers at Atkinson developed an unusual method of teaching writing. The results were remarkable.

In one first-grade classroom, the children composed thirteen hundred original little books in one year and "published" the best four hundred for family, friends, and classmates to read. Many children began to revise their work of their own accord. Some fourth-graders would occasionally go through as many as ten drafts before they were satisfied with a piece of writing. Unaware that children are supposed to have short attention spans, these

---

*Donald Graves's comments will be indented and italicized throughout the book.

students were able to spend up to an hour at a time working on writing and to maintain their interest in one piece over a period of several weeks. Even though the time for writing came out of time formerly spent on reading drills, the children's reading scores were as high as, or higher than, those of previous years. Yet these children were not under any pressure to perform. Their own will to communicate led them to talk, listen, read, write, and rewrite without deadlines.

A number of teachers in English-speaking countries around the world have adopted a similar approach and have seen it work in their own classrooms. This book shows the effects of this kind of approach at Atkinson and in many more classrooms, from Maine to Brooklyn to Australia. The children in these rooms come from different backgrounds and range in age from five to fourteen.

The book also shows how parents have been able to support or introduce similar methods in their children's schools and to apply the same principles in their own homes. As more and more parents and teachers learn about this approach, they will be able to create an atmosphere in which children can discover the rewards of writing for themselves. Within that atmosphere, children can develop their own topics and ideas, talk about their work, receive criticism, reflect, revise, and finally share their writing with classmates and relatives. For thousands of children, this process has already become routine. But in the vast majority of our classrooms, the teachers still aren't aware of it, and the children don't get a chance to try it.

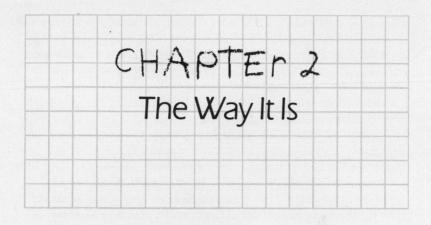

CHAPTEr 2
The Way It Is

Susan is teaching her baby to talk. As he lies gurgling in his crib, she speaks to him in a firm voice, "OK, now purse your lips and then bring your tongue down to the floor of your mouth as you blow out. Practice this sound: *Buh, buh, buh.*" As the child reaches for the bottle in her hand, he says, "Baw baw!" Susan frowns. "No, that's *bottle.* But first we must practice our *b* sounds. Now try again."

Ralph is teaching his daughter, Christine, to walk. With the child standing unsteadily next to him, Ralph is ready to begin. "Christine," he says, "before you try your first step, I want you to practice with your right foot. That one right there. Now touch it to the floor in front of you, toe first. Like this. Touch, lift, touch, lift, touch, lift."

The absurdity in each of these imaginary scenes is im-

mediately apparent. Yet for some reason, absurdity in our classrooms is harder to identify—perhaps because it is sanctioned by
experts. Amelia is a real little girl in a real first grade. She has long
red hair that she colors with orange crayon when she draws a self-
portrait. She is a spunky child who will respond openly to a
question when she feels like it and simply say, "That's top secret!" when she doesn't. Last year, in her pre-first-grade readiness class, Amelia had the opportunity to write every day. During
the year, she produced twenty-four booklets that averaged fourteen pages long. Her longest work contained 129 words.

When asked about the writing she does this year in first
grade, she hesitates. "We do have *hand*writing pages," she explains. "You have a big sheet of paper and a pencil." What do they
write on the sheets of paper? "The teacher tells us these words,
like *and, if, is; and, if, is.*" Do they write anything else? "That's
about it."

Michael attends first grade in another school. He loves to be
read to, and he loves to talk about his latest project, such as an
elaborate papier-mâché castle he made with his father. But he
doesn't like school.

The work Michael brought home during the first two weeks
of November may explain why he doesn't like first grade. During
that time, he traced 111 words, copied 50 more, and filled in 55
pages of worksheets. On the worksheets he was required to make
x's, draw lines between items, and color in pictures of objects
whose names began with certain letters. One day Michael's
mother visited his class. The children were all busily coloring in
mimeographed drawings. Since she had heard about the writing
children were doing in other schools nearby, she asked Michael's
teacher whether the children would be writing any original com-
positions. The teacher explained that there wasn't enough time
for writing.

Is the work done in Michael's and Amelia's classrooms in the
name of learning to read and write any less absurd than Susan's
and Ralph's approach? This philosophy of teaching prevents children in thousands of classrooms from finding out what they can
do with writing and what writing can do for them. It also creates a
climate hostile to the kinds of reading, writing, talking, and listening that help children learn.

Bits and Pieces

Virtually all children who are physiologically normal learn to talk on their own. Although a few parents actively try to "teach" children to talk, no teaching is necessary. In fact, children are fortunate they are not taught to talk by the same methods used in our school systems. If they were, we would have many more people with speech disabilities and problems.

The natural process of learning to talk provides a valuable model for learning. The model can be seen at work in any skill we learn without being taught: talking, walking, riding a bicycle, or jumping rope. All these processes have several things in common. Children have a clear purpose for learning each one and a clear goal to reach toward. Because they want to talk and walk, for example, children practice on their own. Babies make sounds like "buh, buh, buh, buh" for hours on end. One mother watched her daughter spend a straight half-hour pulling herself up to a standing position over and over again, no matter how many times she fell smack on her bottom in between.

That is not to say that parents don't play an important role in helping children learn to walk and talk. Parents provide models and encouragement. But there is no need to teach these skills in the pedantic sense, with drills and harsh correction. Children learn simply by trying and failing and succeeding. Adults help them a little, cheer them on in their successes, and ignore or make light of their failures.

Children often show their readiness to learn to read and write in a similar way. They begin by pretending, imitating adults. A third-grader named Danny says he can remember pretending to write by "scribble-scrabbling" on a piece of paper. At four, a little girl named Hillary loves to "read" books, telling the story and turning the pages. If encouraged, children continue to imitate adults in a series of efforts that soon approximate actual reading and writing. Many adults who know they learned to read before ever going to school, but can't remember how, followed this natural process.

Compare this language-acquisition style of learning with the component model adhered to in most schools. Beginning in the first grade, sometimes in kindergarten, children are blitzed with hundreds of mimeographed "skills" worksheets designed to prepare them to read and write. One mother was horrified to hear that her son was more than one hundred pages behind in his workbook. *Skills,* in the jargon of the component approach, are those minute units into which theorists have broken down words and sentences. When a skill is "mastered," a child can recognize and manipulate the unit in isolated exercises and eventually in actual text—or so the theory goes.

Thus, in order to learn how to read, children practice, hundreds of times, breaking down words into discrete visual and aural units: beginnings and ends and vowels and blends, among others. When faced with actual sentences, they are taught to attack the words in similar fashion, breaking them down into individual letters and groups of letters. Even once children are skilled at reading, teachers may continue to drill them on bits and pieces of words. One fourth-grader I know was dismayed by the phonics worksheets she had to complete. After all, she was reading on a sixth-grade level.

In writing, the *components* consist of letters, words, punctuation marks, and parts of speech. First-graders practice forming individual letters, copying or tracing models provided. Soon they graduate to words, which are also copied or traced at the start. When they are actually allowed to construct sentences, they are usually given a list of words to use, as if a sentence could be built from a kit. In subsequent years, they practice punctuating lists of sentences, to ensure that they will punctuate their own correctly when they do get a chance to compose. And to make sure they know how to put a sentence together right, they take sentences apart, labeling the parts of speech. Judging from the problems many students have with punctuation and grammar, an observer might conclude that grammar and punctuation exercises are relics of the past. But that is not the case. Many current texts and curriculums are filled with grammar and usage exercises.

More advanced writing assignments also reflect the component approach. For example, the typical elementary-school report requires children to go to the encyclopedia, extract many facts or bits of information—if not the words themselves—and put them back together again. These are a more sophisticated version of the writing-kit sentences first-graders assemble from lists of spelling words. Children can hardly be blamed if they get confused and use some of the words as well as the facts from the book. Many students are still confused when they get to college.

In a broader sense, the component philosophy pervades all levels and subjects in many of our schools. From first grade through college, the curriculum itself is fragmented. No effort is made to encourage students to draw connections between the content and techniques of different subjects. Within the subjects, emphasis on memorization and repetition of bits of material is the norm. First-graders must memorize the words on spelling lists just as college students stay up all night on the eve of a test to cram hundreds of facts into their brains.

The component model of learning is based on a seductive idea: to learn how to put something together, first you take it apart. This concept clearly works in the physical world of things and machines. People will often take apart mechanical objects, like clocks or toasters, in order to figure out how they work. Many of the things around us are built on assembly lines, after all, and on assembly lines component parts are progressively fitted together to make a whole. Unfortunately, humans and their mental processes don't work that way.

People no more learn how to jump rope by practicing isolated components of the process than babies are made by fitting together two arms, two legs, a body, and a head. Instead, would-be rope jumpers practice actually jumping rope, now missing it, now clearing it, until they get the rhythm of it. Once they have the hang of it, they may benefit from pointers on discrete parts of the process, but they will not practice jumping without the rope before they start.

The children in our school systems have to go through a lot of isolated rope swinging and jumping without the rope before they get a chance to jump rope. The components they work with are essential in many cases. An understanding of the letter sounds and sentence structure is as crucial to reading and writing as swinging and jumping are to jumping rope. But a growing body of research shows that children tend to learn language, oral or written, by moving from wholes to parts; they focus on meaning before mastering the fine points of form. Thus, a two-year-old who says "Sit chair" knows more about the meaning of words and the purpose of conversation than she does about prepositions. Yet there's no need to rush. She'll pick up prepositions in due time. Learning, like most things in the natural world, is a complex and integrated process. Purpose and practice and failure and success are all tied up together. Components, in other words, are best mastered in the context of an engaging and meaningful activity.

Drills on skills taken out of context cause several problems for teachers and students. To begin with, drilling and memorization often don't take. "When I first started teaching," a junior-high English teacher reports, "I would start with my worksheets. By the second year, I had abandoned grammar books. I used examples from the students' own papers, and even with that I found they could get the worksheet absolutely correct and sit down and write an essay as if they'd never learned it. I became convinced that the carryover was minimal, and there must be another way of handling this."

As Michael's mother discovered, the emphasis on components often prevents children from getting practice with reading and writing for the real-world purpose of communicating with other human beings. The curriculum may be so full of grammar exercises, for example, that the teacher can't find any time to spare for writing. In the average classroom, children spend 17 percent of their "reading" time filling in workbooks and skills sheets, according to a National Academy of Education Commission on Reading. Actual reading and writing assignments may be used more as a test of skills than as a means of conveying or receiving information. A special-education teacher confesses, "I used to teach reading with word lists and skill sequences. We would read stories and books *only* so that they would learn how to use context clues and so that I could check fluency and phrasing." Whatever the reason, many, many children get very little chance to write in school. A National Assessment for Educational Progress survey revealed that, on average, even high-school students had a chance to write only one day in ten.

Because the component approach preaches that children must master discrete components before attempting an actual act of reading or writing, it is easy for teachers to lose sight of the ultimate purpose of their students' activities. When a daring fourth-grader asked why she had to do a certain worksheet, her teacher replied, "Because it's part of the packet." If teachers lose sight of the goals, how can children be expected to do otherwise?

> *Many teachers believe that if they know where the part fits into the whole, that is the only requirement for working with the child on the isolated part. Or the assumption is that if the teacher knows where the part fits within the whole, the child does, too. In many cases, the teachers continue to ask themselves, "How do I motivate this kid?"*

In the component model, the end—learning to read and write—is meant to justify the means—drilling isolated skills. But in our schools, as elsewhere, the means too easily becomes the end. At best, the end is delayed; at worst, it is unappealing. Books filled with sentences like "Come, Laddie" and "Run, Jill" offer children little incentive to learn how to read. One kindergarten teacher, who reads her class lots of children's literature and poetry by writers such as Robert Frost, was pleased when one of her students sized up an older brother's first-grade text, a standard "basal reader." "What's the story in the book about?" the teacher asked the little girl. "There is no story," the child said. "It's just a lot of words." The words, of course, were carefully selected to match the component skills due to be mastered at any given point in the school year.

If they are unappealing to read, the readers also make poor models of writing. It may be fortunate that students in these classrooms see no connection between the writing they do and the production of textbooks. One researcher found that, unlike children who write, students in a component-oriented classroom did not even understand the meaning of the word *author.*

Because the means has become—or perverted—the end, many children schooled in this approach come to dislike the activities for which they're so arduously prepared. Through reading and writing, children can discover the thrill of vicarious experience, the catharsis of a good story, the pleasure of a reader's response, and the satisfaction of gaining knowledge. Yet few people besides linguists and grammarians can get excited about a diphthong or a preposition outside the context of a piece of writing.

When the teacher of a pre-first-grade transition class asked her students at the beginning of the year, "Who likes to write?" every hand went up. But it doesn't take too many years of filling blanks, copying words, diagramming sentences, and ending someone else's story starters before children decide writing is no fun at all. When another teacher asked her second-graders to produce a composition on why they liked to write, their groans were so loud that she decided to allow them to write on why they didn't like to write.

Overemphasis on components, however, does more than train children to dislike reading and writing. In denying them the opportunity to practice actual reading and writing, the method prevents children from using important thinking skills, such as organizing, analyzing, interpreting, and evaluating information. Instead, standard worksheets and tests ask children to fill in the blank or circle the correct answer.

> *It's hard to say what the effects of this fill-in-the-blank mentality are on students, except that they are encouraged to expect simple, one-step solutions to things. Most advertising and television programming reveals the same mentality. Just buy x, and your problems will be solved. All you need is one grand shootout at the O.K. Corral at high noon, and all this complex fuss will be over.*
>
> *Component instruction implies simple right or wrong answers for every issue we've got. But how do we discuss major issues in foreign policy, the beauty of a painting, or the problem of nuclear waste? It takes a lot of reading, writing, talking, and listening to address those issues. And students from first grade on up need to practice those skills.*

Given all its ill effects, it may seem curious that the component model persists. Our school systems themselves, however, are complicated mechanisms, full of vicious circles, all interlocking and turning each other like the gears inside a clock. These circles are spinning in the classroom, in the school administration, in the community, and in the education industry of publishers and testmakers.

First of all, textbook and workbook series using the component method are very simple to follow and teach. Many school systems adopt *scope-and-sequence* curriculums that specify the skills children should know, the order in which the skills should be learned, and the time when children should learn them. Once a district has adopted a scope-and-sequence curriculum, the next logical step is to purchase the textbooks, workbooks, and manuals that will help students and teachers follow the chosen path. The manual tells the teacher exactly what to do and when to do it. When it comes time to evaluate students' work, the teacher need only check things wrong or right and apply an appropriate sticker, smiley face, or phrase at the top of the page.

> *But there is another factor quite apart from philosophies and ease of application. Since the early 1950s, the educational publishing industry has been growing and growing in depth and scope. The industry has its own momentum. Enormous investments go into the publishing of a reading series. Systems that buy the reading programs make heavy investments in reading materials, in turn. And when systems make investments in materials, they make further investments in personnel. They hire people to use the materials that they have bought.*
>
> *In 1965, with the passing of the Elementary and Secondary Education Act, commonly called Title I, enormous amounts of money became available to schools. The investment went into visible things like people and books. If you have people and books, you have to use them. Literally billions upon billions of dollars have been invested in this approach to learning.*

The use of the scope-and-sequence curriculums as a yardstick for measuring all children provides another lucrative market for the industry. Children who do not master skills at the prescribed time and in the prescribed order are considered deficient and in need of remediation. Remediation requires a whole new set of materials and trained personnel.

Outside of, yet integrally tied to, the school systems and the publishing industry another monolithic industry grinds away. It is the test-making, -giving, and -grading business. Through national standardized tests, school systems are able to demonstrate their efficiency in drilling bits of information into students.

> *We have constructed a national testing system that assesses components. In an ordinary workbook, children take tests on component skills every day. The children read a paragraph and then cricle, draw a line to, or underline something. Later, the teacher corrects the work, and the children receive a grade or number of errors circled in red. These daily tests are a shadow of an annual test, such as the Stanford Achievement Test, in which the child is compared with other students in the country. And the annual achievement test is a shadow of the Scholastic Aptitude Test taken for admission to college. Although it is often claimed that scores on these assessments correlate with students' ability to handle larger blocks of material over longer periods of time, they in fact do not.*

In the March 1984 issue of *American Psychologist,* Norman Frederiksen, of the Educational Testing Service, cites research that refutes the argument that performance on multiple-choice tests reflect students' abilities to perform complex tasks. An analysis of the Graduate Record Exam Advanced Psychology Test, for example, showed that 70 percent of the questions measured only the ability to remember facts and formulas. Frederiksen believes that the multiple-choice format is to blame. In his own research, he converted tests of problem-solving skills into a multiple-choice format. On the original form of the test, the subjects were asked to write a series of hypotheses based on information provided—a task requiring the ability to reason and to produce a large number of ideas. In its multiple-choice version, however, it became largely a test of memory.

A growing number of educators have been questioning the benefits of the system of standardized tests used in this country. Like Frederiksen, these critics suggest that the increasingly pervasive tests have had a deleterious effect on the development of students' thinking abilities, not directly, but through the influence testing has on teaching.

The tests from first grade through the Graduate Record Exam all deal with small units of information which are circled or underlined. Because we test this way, we teach this way. And that is the tragedy.

A 1982 study made by the National Assessment of Educational Progress seems to corroborate the educators' fears. It revealed that while students' performance on tests measuring "basic skills" has risen over the past decade, there has been a significant drop in their abilities to perform tasks involving more complex thinking in all fields. The largest drop occurred in reading and writing.

Another important influence in our school systems comes from the computer. Perhaps computers, like guns, cannot be held responsible for the things humans do with them. But computers do lend themselves easily and well to the component approach. There are, of course, ways of using computers to allow children to learn skills in context. With Seymour Pappert's LOGO software, for example, children learn about geometry by programming the computer to draw shapes and designs. In a playful atmosphere, students collaborate with the teacher and with each other to explore different possibilities through trial and error. Word processors could easily be used to help children write. Children with coordination problems might find keys easier to push than pencils. And the ease with which text is moved, changed, and deleted might encourage children to accept revision as a normal part of writing. But too often computers are used to create video versions of worksheets and flashcards.

Behind all the pressures that push schools to use and be accountable for component methods, there lies the enemy—us. Many adults—including teachers, educators who train teachers, administrators, and parents—have come up through schools that used the component method. And we're OK. We graduates of the system find it very easy to take an "I turned out OK, they'll be OK" attitude toward education. If we want the very best for our children, however, we must scrutinize our own experiences and ask ourselves whether we can find a better way to prepare them for a future neither we nor they can imagine.

What Does This Have to Do with Me?

In his book *Mind and Nature,* biologist, anthropologist, and philosopher Gregory Bateson writes, "Break the pattern which connects the items of learning and you necessarily destroy all quality." Our school systems break not only the connection between the items of learning, but also the important connection between those items and the child asked to learn them. First-grader Michael is intensely interested in space, science fiction, buildings, dinosaurs, animals, and war. But his own interests and reasons for doing things, for wanting to learn, have no bearing on the work he does in school. He has little understanding of the purpose behind the endless mimeographed sheets that fill his days.

Like too many children at too many levels in our education system, Michael is, in effect, trying to put together a puzzle without having seen the picture on the cover. Even worse, he only has some of the pieces, and all of them are blue. As he goes through school, he will soon discover that the picture of the completed puzzle is in his teacher's mind, or manual. Only the teacher knows the purpose of all work, the meaning that links all components, the answers to all questions.

Our greatest problem is that we underestimate what children can do. We underestimate their will to make sense of themselves and the world around them. Children are curious and want their curiosity satisfied. But we don't know children, nor the interests that arouse their curiosity, nor the learning process well enough to know how to respond to them. We constantly try to trick them into learning things that have nothing to do with them. Most of our classrooms are reflections of what teachers do, not of what children do. If our classrooms are to be effective, they should be filled with stuff, the stuff of what children know and what they want to know more about. This is how children learn at home. And this is how they will learn when they have left formal education and are working on the job.

The idea that education must be meaningful—to students—is falling out of fashion rapidly. We are still living with the results of the sixties students' demand for "relevance" in their education. In too many cases, the result was a slackening in school requirements. The old and the classic were not just supplemented, but often replaced, by the new and the popular. In high schools, for example, courses like "Bachelor Living" made their way into the curriculum, and English teachers found themselves teaching Science Fiction in place of Shakespeare.

But *meaningful* doesn't have to be synonymous with *current, popular,* or *easy.* There are too many examples of inner-city, "disadvantaged" students enjoying the Oedipus plays and Shakespeare. When one mother read *A Tale of Two Cities* aloud to her children one summer, she found that all three of them, including her eleven-year-old, became involved with the story. Children in a second-grade classroom in one of the poorest areas of New York City have chosen to write reports on topics ranging from the supersonic transport to Vincent Van Gogh. In a classroom where teacher and student work together in a spirit of collaboration, they can usually find a common ground in which children are eager to learn many of the things that teachers are eager to teach. As hard as it is for a graduate of a standard curriculum to believe, in a certain atmosphere, children will swap grammatical tips as if they were baseball cards.

In order to strike up a collaboration, a teacher must uncover the knowledge and interests the children already have. In our school systems, however, teachers often focus more on what's in their own mind or manual than what's in their student's mind. Part of the problem stems from curriculums inflated with facts and skills that teachers feel compelled to instill into children. Nevertheless, the component approach is not entirely to blame.

It is no coincidence that this is a problem around the world— in Australia, England, the United States, and other countries. It is a human tendency to want to be in possession of more knowledge than people around us: "I know and you don't." The last thing we want is for someone to get information directly from a book without our help. When we teach,

*we don't want it to be wholesale; we want it to be retail. A
student of the Bible might say, "Go directly to Genesis, the
third chapter," which says man's sin is that he wants to be
God. We want to play God with children.*

The problem is perhaps most apparent in school conversations, which set the tone in a classroom and affect every subject, including reading and writing. Consider a conversation recorded in a first-grade classroom in Bristol, England, where researcher Gordon Wells made a study of language use and development. Like many children in British classrooms during the holiday season, a little girl named Rosie is making a gift for Mum out of an old Christmas card, a new calendar, and a bit of ribbon. The card Rosie has been given features a picture of Father Christmas skiing down a snowy mountainside. In the conversation, which Wells details in his book *Language, Learning and Education,* the teacher begins by asking Rosie questions about the picture.

TEACHER: *What are those things? Will you put it at the top?* (Pause.) *What are those things?* (She points to the card. Rosie drops something and picks it up.) *What are those things* (referring to objects on card)*? Do you know what they're called?* (Rosie shakes her head.) *What do you think he uses them for?* (Rosie shakes her head. Teacher speaks to another child.)

TEACHER: *What do you think he uses them for?* (She points at objects shown on the card.) *What do you think he uses them for?*

ROSIE: *Go down.* (She rubs one eye with the back of her hand.)

TEACHER: *Yes, you're right. Go on.* (Rosie rubs both eyes with backs of hands.) *What's the rest of it?*(She puts down the card.) *You have a little think, and I'll get the calendar for you. I think you're sitting on one.* (She points to calendar. Rosie takes calendar from teacher.) *Could you put some glue on the back there? He uses those to go down—is it a hill or a mountain?*

ROSIE: *A hill.*

TEACHER: *A hill. Yes. And what's on the hill?*

ROSIE: *Ice.*

TEACHER: *Yes, ice. They're called* skis. (Interruption while teacher attends to other children.) *That's lovely, and afterwards we'll put some ribbon.* (She points to calendar and looks at Rosie.) *What do you think the ribbon's for?*

ROSIE: *For Father Christmas.*

TEACHER: *Sorry?* (She bends closer to Rosie, looking into her face.)

ROSIE: (She looks away from teacher.) *For Father Christmas.*

TEACHER: *For Father Christmas?* (She straightens slightly from bending position and looks at card, pointing at it again with hand.) *If I—you want to put it up on the wall, you have a little piece of ribbon to hang it up by.*

With the exception of three instances, every question the teacher asks is what Wells calls a "display" question—that is, it is not a genuine question. The teacher already knows the answer; she simply wants the child to show that she knows it, too. Poor Rosie is not very good at producing the right answer.

The teacher asks Rosie to identify skis—which she has probably never seen before. Even though it becomes clear that Rosie doesn't know the answer and couldn't possibly guess it, the teacher repeats the question numerous times. Very often in class discussions, teachers will hold off children eager to provide a correct answer and deliberately call on children who don't know the answer. After Rosie fails to come up with the name of the objects, the teacher asks her what they're used for. With vigorous questioning and prompting, Rosie is barely able to approximate the answer that the teacher clearly has in mind. Then, when Rosie does answer the teacher's final question with some confidence, the teacher insists on negating Rosie's own purpose for applying the ribbon. Score three for the teacher, zero for the child.

Fortunately, there were two teachers in Rosie's classroom. On the very same morning Rosie made the Christmas calendar, she had a conversation with the second teacher while reading a book. Each sentence of the book begins with the phrase " 'I am tall,' said the ____."

ROSIE: (Rosie reads while the teacher points to each word with a pencil.) *"I am tall, said the—tower."*

TEACHER: *Chimney.*

ROSIE: *Chimbley.*

TEACHER: *It's a big factory chimney, isn't it?* (She points to picture.)

ROSIE: *I don't like—*

TEACHER: *There's a lot of smoke coming out of the top.* (She points to illustration with a pencil.)

ROSIE: *I don't like that one.* (She points at the illustration with her finger.)

TEACHER: *You don't like it?* (Rosie shakes her head.) *Why not?*

ROSIE: *I only like little ones.*

TEACHER: *Have you got a chimney in your house?* (Rosie nods emphatically.) *D'you have smoke coming out the top?* (Rosie nods emphatically.) *Mm?* (Rosie nods her head again. Teacher closes the book.) *What's underneath the chimney, then, that makes the smoke come out?*

ANOTHER CHILD: *I know. Fire.*

ROSIE: *Fire.*

TEACHER: *Mm? Is it? Is that a fire then? Which room's the fire in?*

ROSIE: *In the front one.*

TEACHER: *Is it? So it keeps you warm? Lovely.*

ROSIE: *And I got a bed.*

TEACHER: *Where's your bed?*

ROSIE: *'E's upstairs.*

TEACHER: *Anybody else got a bed in your room?*

ROSIE: *Carol's got a bed and Kelvin . . . and Carol.*

TEACHER: *Um hum. What about Donna?*

ROSIE: *Donna—we're sharing it.*

TEACHER: *You're sharing with Donna, are you?* (Rosie nods emphatically.) *Do you have a cuddle at night?*

ROSIE: *Yeh and I—when I gets up I creeps in Mummy's bed.*

TEACHER: *For another cuddle? Ooh, that's nice. It's nice in the morning when you cuddle.*

In this second conversation, Rosie seems like a different child, capable of responding in complete sentences, eager to contribute. Her physical actions alone show the change in her response to the teachers. In the first session, she rubs her eyes and looks away; here she nods her head emphatically more than once. Since the two conversations have taken place on the same morning, however, it's apparent that she hasn't changed. The only difference is in the styles used by her two conversational partners.

Instead of confronting her with a display question, this second teacher makes a comment about the task they are undertaking together. When Rosie offers her own comment on a picture in the book, the teacher draws her out. Nearly all the questions this teacher asks are genuine. Instead of trying to get Rosie to guess at answers she doesn't know, the teacher asks her for information that she does have: why she doesn't like big chimneys, where the chimney is in her house, where the different beds are, and who sleeps in them. Because she has information that the teacher wants, Rosie is able to speak with confidence.

In this case, two teachers talking to the same child on the same day have, because of their different styles, come away with two very different evaluations of the child's verbal ability. Teachers use display questions presumably to allow children to demonstrate their abilities. A child like Rosie, however, perceives that she has been asked to guess at something the teacher knows but she doesn't. The questions don't seem to have anything to do with her. As a result, she becomes intimidated, and, ironically, the very questions meant to expose her abilities disguise them. The teacher is left with a low estimation of the child, an estimation that may follow and influence Rosie through school and beyond.

Since most conversations in our classrooms more closely resemble the first teacher's example, most children like Rosie appear to have severe and very basic problems. As it happens, the children teachers most often describe as "nonverbal" are the same children considered to be "disadvantaged." One adminis-

trator in a poor urban area in the United States recently remarked, "I went into the kindergartens and found the children
absolutely nonverbal. They would shrug. This is 99 percent of
them." More than one researcher has found that children, like
Rosie, who appear to be "absolutely nonverbal" in school speak
quite fluently outside of school.

When learning revolves around the teacher's rather than the
child's mind, certain children are at a double disadvantage. Without any conscious effort, middle-class teachers naturally bring
into the classroom their middle-class ways of talking and approaching tasks. Children from different segments of society
come to school with their own ways of talking and interacting,
which may be quite different from middle-class habits.

In a study of several communities in one of the Carolinas,
Shirley Brice Heath found that children in a black working-class
neighborhood were treated differently in conversations at home
than working-class white children or middle-class children of
either race. The working-class black children became competent
speakers before they attended school, Heath reports in her book
Ways with Words. In fact, she found them to be more skilled than
other children in playing with language, able to produce rhymes,
alliteration, and repetition with ease. But these children were
seldom questioned by adults in their own community and virtually never faced with display questions. No wonder some children appear nonplused, if not nonverbal, when interrogated by
adults who always seem to have answers to their own questions.

Nevertheless, factors that aggravate the negative effects of
school conversation for some children must not obscure the effects it has on all children. Display questions that amount to oral
guessing games are to genuine conversation as worksheets are to
reading and writing. Like reading and writing, talking helps children learn. Yet a recent study of more than one thousand classrooms showed that teachers outtalk their students by a ratio of
three to one. In his study, Gordon Wells found that half the statements children made in school were in the form of incomplete
sentences. In short, teachers are getting more practice with oral
language than their students are.

The use of written language in schools naturally parallels the
use of oral language. It reveals the same unarticulated attitudes

toward children and knowledge—that is, that children don't know much and that knowledge comes down to them from on high. Both school talk and fill-in-the-blank exercises and tests also show a preference for certain thought patterns. Most school-work requires students to search for the one "right" answer, from the teacher or a book, in any given situation. Even opportunities for older children to make important connections and interpretations turn into guessing games instead of a mutual exploration of complex issues that can be viewed from more than one perspective. "And what does the elephant symbolize in this story?" a teacher asks. Past experience, tone, and wording all tell the students that the question has one answer, which the teacher knows and they must struggle to guess.

The repetition of that process hundreds of thousands of times effectively, if not intentionally, trains students to become convergent rather than divergent thinkers. *Convergent thought* seeks the safe and predictable answer, shunning all alternatives. *Divergent thinking,* on the other hand, leads people to dream up and entertain alternatives. Some situations require convergent thought. A set of complicated instructions for building a model should produce one interpretation and one result. But divergent thought is the foundation of creativity, the source of every new idea that has ever been conceived. As such, it is a handy tool for any human and one that should not be neglected in the classroom.

Classroom talk, reading, and writing share other limitations. Just as children have little opportunity to initiate conversational topics important to them, they have no choice in what they read. The implication is that their interests don't matter. Moreover, reading isn't something to be done in pursuit of knowledge or pleasure, but something that must be done to show the teacher what you know.

Writing assignments also ignore students' interests and purposes. In the lower grades, children are often asked to copy someone else's words or to use someone else's idea as a starter. In subsequent years, assignments may require them to write on someone else's topic, using someone else's knowledge, for someone else's reasons, and, in the worst cases, with someone else's enthusiasm.

Many classroom assignments require children to write on a

subject they neither know nor care about. At the same time, their audience of one, the teacher, invariably knows the subject well. These assignments put children into an unnatural position for any writer, let alone a beginner. In the real world, writers usually know more about, or at least have a different angle on, their subject than their readers do. Otherwise, there would be little point in writing.

Motivation is the mainspring of the school system. When it isn't wound, all the gears in the system stop and have to be forced into motion. Teachers give students tasks of little apparent purpose or meaning; the students act uninterested. Observing the students' lack of motivation, the teacher may have cynical beliefs confirmed: most children are lazy and don't want to work. In some cases, teachers confuse genuine motivation with "having fun" and conclude, like TV programmers, that fun means silly, trivial, and gimmicky. Hence, "aids" like Inflatable Mr. P and his friends appear on the scene to entice children to learn their letters. A vicious circle develops when the teacher gets a response to a gimmick and concludes that more are needed.

Unmotivated children tend to have a short attention span. As a result, the teacher must break up the day into short segments, just like the work in workbooks. The children get no opportunity to develop their ability to work on more complex and time-consuming types of tasks. Donald Graves, other researchers, and teachers have all found children willing to work long and hard on material that interests them. Neither research nor teachers are required, however, to prove something that common sense will verify. Few adults would want to spend hours pursuing knowledge of little purpose or interest to them. A seventy-five-year-old who lives in Manhattan and relies on public transportation and taxis would have little use for the names of the parts of a car engine. On the other hand, a sixteen-year-old lusting after a Corvette or a single parent looking for ways to save money might be eager to learn the same information.

Of course, many students do seem to be motivated to work. Despite the artificiality of most classroom conversations and assignments, they do well in our school systems by the prevailing standards. They get good grades and test scores. Sure, there are the Rosies, who have difficulty in finding a common ground between home and school, between their interests and the school curriculum, between their own goals and school goals. But no system, successful graduates tend to reason, can reach everyone.

It is true that children coming from some parts of society are at a disadvantage when making these crucial connections. In *Ways with Words,* Shirley Brice Heath reports that one of the significant differences between middle- and working-class children in the Carolina Piedmont communities she studied was the degree to which their experiences outside the school dovetailed with, or diverged from, school experiences. She noted that school field trips, for example, took middle-class children to places where they might be likely to go on weekends with their parents. In addition to these overlapping activities, she found that middle-class parents made attempts to draw parallels between schoolwork and home activities, whereas the working-class parents did not.

From the start then, middle-class children may be less likely than others to look at their school work and ask, "What does this have to do with me?" Nevertheless, bright to average middle-class students are likely to be harmed by the system in a different way than the less intelligent or the economically disadvantaged student. Those who don't fit in and don't do well may reject the system entirely. They rebel, refuse to work, or simply remove themselves mentally or physically from school. Their reaction may have unfortunate consequences for them in many ways. But in the meantime, these students sometimes maintain the integrity and ability to think for themselves that "good" students often sacrifice.

For many of the better students, the natural motivation for reading, writing, and learning about a subject has been replaced by the drive to get good, or acceptable, grades. It doesn't take children long to conclude that the way to get good grades is to figure out what the teacher wants. As they move through the system, much of their energy goes into continual attempts to do just that. When one of these students does unexpectedly poorly on an assignment, one excuse comes to mind, and mouth, as surely as a foot kicks when the knee is tapped: "I wasn't sure what you wanted."

Ed McGarrigle, a high-school English teacher who recently

left the profession, will never forget a class he taught during his final year. They were the "best" students the school had to offer, college-bound seniors. Their behavior in McGarrigle's writing class might best be described as "slavish." As he remembers it, "They copied everything you said, everything you did. You could see there was no thinking going on." In short, they had one thing in mind: " 'The grade—I gotta get the grade. And I know if I give back exactly what is given to me, that's what I'll get.' And they didn't realize that writing isn't like that. That something had to come *from* you."

Motivated by grades and skilled at getting them, some students have difficulty with writing outside of prescribed exercises. McGarrigle found his students particularly resistant to revision. He describes their attitude as follows: "There's nothing to rewrite because you aren't even thinking about coming up with a different thought or a different perspective on it, or any more specific references or detail. 'This is what I thought you wanted—not what I *thought,* but what I thought you wanted. If you want it rewritten, that's like coming up with another whole guess at second-guessing what you wanted.' And they're never really thinking for themselves at all."

CHAPTEr 3
Wrong from the Start

The vast majority of first-graders have no problem when asked to write on the first day of school. Their "writing" ranges from pictures to scribbles to letters to words. But the children believe they can write, and in most cases not one child will ask, "What should I write about?" Adults, on the other hand, do have trouble believing that children have the ability to write and something to write about. An Australian kindergarten teacher confesses that she thought a professor was joking when he suggested that she allow her students to start writing on the first day of school.

Unfortunately, it doesn't take long for a teacher's doubts to rub off on the children. A second-grade teacher was able to see the results of different teachers' attitudes in one class. Half her children had come to her from a standard, component-oriented first grade where the teacher had used pictures as "starters." The other half had come from a classroom where children wrote every day on topics of their own choice. When the teacher asked the class to write on the first day of second grade, she got two very different reactions. The children who were used to writing on their own were excited and ready to begin. The children from the other class were clearly disturbed. "What do you mean, write?" they asked. "I can't write." "What do you want us to write about?" "Where's the picture?"

Learning to Fail

For most children, first grade signals the start of a long decline in self-confidence. In 1980, eleven teachers at Boothbay Region Elementary School in Boothbay Harbor, Maine, made a survey of their students' attitudes toward writing. One of the questions the teachers asked was "Are you a writer?" or "Do you know how to write?" The teachers were surprised when 76 percent of the entering first-graders said yes, they could write. (In other schools, nearly 100 percent of first-grade classes have been known to answer yes to the same question.) But the third- and fourth-graders were less confident. And only 40 percent of the fifth-, seventh-, and eighth-graders considered themselves writers.

Soon the teachers at Boothbay discovered that it didn't have to be that way. Through the Boothbay Writing Project, directed by junior-high teacher Nancie Atwell, they began to examine and modify their own teaching methods. When the teachers asked their students the same question at the end of the school year in 1982, 90 percent of their students from kindergarten through eighth grade answered with a resounding yes.

But many students aren't so lucky. They grow less and less confident of their own abilities with each year they spend in school. By the time they reach college, their self-doubts are firmly entrenched. In many college courses, students need not worry. Some professors will continue to feed them tiny bits of information to be memorized for future tests; others will assign writing topics complete with focus, main idea, and format. Students who attend a school where freshmen write weekly on topics of their own choice may not perceive their good fortune immediately. One student pleaded with his instructor, "I can write anything, if you just tell me what to write about. Or give me a form. Do you want a comparison?" Considerable time must be spent at the beginning of the semester convincing many students that they do know something and they do have something to say.

While component exercises squeeze writing out of the school day and convince children that reading and writing are a bore, a whole host of factors combined convince children that they couldn't and wouldn't write, even if they had a chance. The effect is unintentional but nonetheless systematic: our schools wring the self-confidence out of children. And self-confidence can be as critical to successful learning as motivation. Schools destroy self-confidence in numerous ways. The component approach is, again, partly to blame.

> *This approach to teaching gears itself to the deficit model of learning. According to this model, students don't know very much and therefore can only handle tiny components. Teachers often ask, "How am I going to teach kids that can't do simple things like this?" Or "My gosh, how can I teach him to write if he can't even write a single sentence?"*

With such theoretical underpinnings beneath their curriculums, it is not surprising when teachers develop negative attitudes toward children's abilities. At the same time, teachers' attitudes and expectations are extremely important since they are so easily transmitted to the children themselves. As children become older and more convinced of their inabilities, their own doubts both reflect and reinforce their teachers' negative attitudes. In 1980, 60 percent of the entering fifth graders in one teacher's class said no, they weren't writers. At the same time, someone gave the teacher a suggestion: Why not allow her students to choose their own topics? Her initial response was, "But they won't have anything to write about unless I get them started."

If it is the negative theory underlying the component approach that helps convince teachers children don't know much, the actual application of the method ultimately convinces many children. Standardized tests, designed to put nearly half of all children below "grade level," contain ambiguous questions and trick answers. Worksheets, exercises, and tests are based on a right-or-wrong view of information. In the average school day, children face many opportunities to be right or wrong, on paper or in conversation with the teacher. Since the assumption is that there is only one right answer and many wrong ones, children soon discover that it is very easy to be wrong.

> *The underlying message is "Someone else knows—you don't." The underlying message is that your information is only valuable if it fills someone else's blank.*

It doesn't take children long to get the message. And once they get it, the effects may be lasting. Children who are wrong too many times in the early grades, who are considered failures because they don't fit the prescribed norm in scope-and-sequence curriculums, may never recover in their own eyes or in the eyes of the school system.

Of course, as every schoolchild knows, fear of failure can be a motivator in itself. But psychologists specializing in achievement motivation have found that people motivated by the desire to achieve perform better than those driven by fear of failure. To instill positive achievement motivation, many psychologists recommend an environment of warmth and encouragement, an environment in which more emphasis is placed on rewarding success than on punishing failure. Attitudes toward the causes of success and failure are also important. When children are convinced that they themselves—rather than the teacher or the wheel of fortune—have the power to determine whether they will succeed or fail, they are more likely to develop a positive attitude toward their own abilities. The component-oriented system, with its hundreds of ways to be wrong and its refusal to grant children the right to collaborate in setting their own goals, is hardly designed to bring about a positive form of achievement motivation.

A positive desire to achieve is also healthier than fear of

failure. At least one study has shown that people with a high fear of failure tend to have more psychological problems than other people. Again, we hardly need experts to tell us that failure and fear of further failure can cause emotional disturbances. It doesn't feel very good to be wrong all the time. Add to that feeling the boredom of filling out endless sheets that seem to have no connection with your own interests. On top of all that, you can't express your feelings. You're not encouraged to talk or write about your world or your frustrations. What do you do? You probably misbehave. When you do, what were perhaps simply low opinions of your ability in your teacher's mind become fused with negative emotions.

Wrong from the Start

Much of our school system, with its all-pervasive components approach, is unintentionally designed to set children up for failure and all the bad feelings and expectations that accompany it. The problem, however, goes beyond the component approach. It goes beyond that human desire to feel that we know more than the other guy, even if the other guy is just a kid. Within the whole curriculum, children are often made to feel worst about their ability to read and write. Once again, the cycles children get caught up in swing far and wide outside the school system into society as a whole.

A little boy I know used to pronounce *l* like *y,* as in "yittle red riding hood." But he, like all children, wanted to learn to talk like grown-ups. And so, he eventually corrected himself. His parents teased him lightly about it once in a while. But he was not regularly corrected or made to feel bad about his temporary mispronunciation. No one worried that he would still be saying "yittle" at thirty.

Parents seem to be naturally inclined to respond to beginning talkers in a positive way, thus speeding their progress. As beginning writers and readers, however, children are treated quite differently. A mother hears her nine-month-old son producing the first *Mm mm* sound that could possibly be interpreted as *Mama.* She laughs and kisses him, saying, "Mama! Mama!" to show that his attempt to communicate has been successful. Five years later she arrives at his kindergarten on another important day. He has written his first words: "I LOVE MOME." Her first response: "*Mommy* is spelled wrong."

A first-grader I met explained why she didn't like reading. As she spoke, she was in constant motion rocking back and forward in her seat, fiddling with a horse chestnut she had brought to school. "My babysitter gets mad at me," she said, "because I don't sound out the words and I don't know what they mean." As a society, we allow children to learn to speak by trial and error. But when it comes to reading and writing, we expect them to be right the first time.

Afraid that their children will have permanent problems with reading and writing, parents put pressure on teachers and administrators. The clamor for more teacher "accountability" usually translates into testing, which translates into emphasis on components. The already negative tone of the component approach is compounded by a sense of panic, both within and outside the walls of the school.

> *When students have a hard time learning, teachers can either blame the children or blame themselves as professionals. I think we can see panic on both sides of the question.*

Even if they weren't already inclined by their own experience and beliefs to do so, teachers under pressure feel compelled to sniff out every error. Often the crusade takes on moralistic overtones. In one classroom, a teacher displayed a new commandment, framed and engraved on parchment in Biblical-looking calligraphy: "Thou Shalt Not Write Incomplete Sentences." As is often the case, the teacher's gospel was misleading. Professional writers as well as students often use incomplete sentences to good effect. But more important than its inaccuracy is the tone of the message. Having red-inked every error, a conscientious teacher may feel absolved of responsibility for a child's inability to grasp the "basics." While the teacher feels better, however, the child feels worse.

> *Most of us have been taught that we are unworthy of putting*
> *words on paper. We have been punished for our sins.*

First-grader Amelia, the redhead who is required to write "and, if, is; and, if, is," describes the pressures she feels when writing in school. For her, the hardest thing about writing is making "perfect, perfect, perfect, perfect, perfect, perfect, perfect, perfect, perfect, perfect, perfect, perfect handwriting." Spelling also has to be "perfect."

Why are first attempts at writing and reading received so harshly? At least part of the answer is that our society is obsessed with reading and writing. And why shouldn't it be? Recent reports on the status of our educational system reveal that one-fifth of all American adults and 13 percent of all American seventeen-year-olds are considered functionally illiterate. And many who are considered literate still have difficulty with various aspects of writing.

The reaction of parents and teachers to the problem is not inexplicable. Most parents and teachers don't realize that a child's first written *MOME* is as transitory as his oral *Da Da,* if not more so. Because of the way the school system has been structured, neither parents nor, in many cases, teachers have had a chance to see the normal process of learning to read and write as it parallels other normal processes like learning to talk or walk. Recent studies by Donald Graves and other researchers have shown how that process unfolds. The research has given an increasing number of teachers and administrators the confidence to allow children to follow a more natural course of learning in their classrooms.

Parents and teachers have seen the cycle of failure and how it perpetuates itself, so it's only natural that they try to prevent it from beginning. Unfortunately, their anxious efforts to prevent problems too often create them. Many of the adults who teach children or who criticize teachers are not experienced writers themselves. Their teaching and criticism often reflect their own misunderstandings as to what makes good writing. Correct spelling, punctuation, and grammar will generally make a good piece of writing more effective. But far too many teachers treat the conventions as their first, foremost, and, in some cases, only concern in a piece of writing. This attitude not only gives children a warped view of the qualities of good writing; it makes unrealistic demands on them.

Even Hemingway rewrote passages as many as thirty-nine times. How can we ask a child to "get it right" on the first try, down to the placement of every comma on a first draft or the pronunciation of every syllable on a first reading? Children soon discover that lurking in and around every sentence are more chances to be wrong than there are pages in a workbook. Their inability to stave off all those errors on the first try starts many children on the downward spiral toward failure and the low self-concept that leads to more failures.

Of course, there are always a number of students who, for reasons relating to genes and upbringing, can learn to produce relatively flawless prose without much effort. They don't get the negative feedback that leads to the failure syndrome. In one sense they are lucky, but once again, they may not emerge from the system unscathed. Students like these are continually praised for their lack of errors, rather than their original ideas, strong supporting evidence, vivid details, apt wording, or effective organization. In fact, these writers may have none of the above, but because they have no mistakes, they still do well. They, too, become convinced that good writing is simply error-free writing. Because they have always been "correct" on the first try, they may also have had little experience with accepting and learning from mistakes. Mistakes and failure are seen as things to be avoided at all costs.

Often these students have no inkling that something is amiss in their work until they reach college. The news hits them hard in the form of their first *C* on a piece of writing. Some professors have seen students burst into tears over the trauma of receiving an *A* − .

When it comes to the painful effects of schooling, some graduates, successful or not, lack sympathy. In fact, many believe they had it worse than children do now and actually recommend a return to the hard old days. "The teacher had a chart that she would pull down," a librarian told one researcher. "It had the alphabet and syllables. We'd have to line up and pronounce them.

If we got it wrong, she rapped us with the pointer. She could tell among all the voices who said it wrong." After a pause, the woman added, "I wish they had pointers like that now."

Learning to Whimper

At a school open house, one father was pleased to read a piece his son had written about a trip to the ocean. Glowing with pride, he turned to his wife and said, "Gee, this is a beautiful story." The glow began to dissipate, however, as the couple thumbed through the papers written by their son's classmates. All the children had beautiful pieces about a trip to the ocean. The same information, the same words, just rearranged. The piece was not an expression of the unique and wonderful child they knew. It was about as different from the next boy's writing as a Dodge is from a Plymouth.

In another first-grade class every child, including a little boy named Julian, "wrote" the following lines, copying from a workbook:

This is our school.
We like to write.

This workbook has given the children a poor model of writing, teaching them the fine art of making the obvious statement and mouthing the empty sentiment. Most first-graders, including Julian, could do better on their own. The sentences are false in purpose, tone, and fact. (Few children in classrooms like these like to write.) The writing certainly doesn't sound like Julian, or any real person, for that matter. In short, the writing in classrooms like these lacks the quality writers call "voice."

Voice is the imprint of the person on the piece. It is the way in which a writer chooses words, the way in which a writer orders things toward meaning. As writers compose, they leave their fingerprints all over their work.

It is the voice in a piece of writing that conveys a sense of the writer's personality. In fiction, voice is one of the qualities that make a character or narrator convincing. A writer's voice can even give a business memo flavor and technical writing a touch of humanity.

Voice is integrally connected to word choice. A strong voice and apt wording keep readers reading for little sparks of surprise and humor. Only *Joy of Cooking* would introduce directions for beating an egg thus: "To describe the beating of egg whites is almost as cheeky as advising how to live a happy life." Writing in the traditionally understated *New Yorker,* film critic Pauline Kael consistently turns out lines like this one: "Those who are susceptible to this sort of movie [*Love Story*] may not even notice that Ali McGraw is horribly smug and smirky, though if you share my impulses, whenever she gets facetious you'll probably want to wham her one." An engaging voice will hold readers who might normally dismiss a piece of writing because of its subject matter. Readers who have little interest in the movie in question, or who always disagree with Pauline Kael, may read her reviews just for the bracing quality of her voice.

Since anything written by a human will presumably bear the stamp of its author, or at least of another writer imitated by the author, it is probably impossible for writing to be "voiceless." But writers often use the term to describe writing that sounds as if it came out of a machine. Or, like Julian's exercise, it may have a false ring to it. Either way, voiceless writing is likely to be dishonest or devoid of meaning. (Other sentences Julian has been asked to copy include "Our school is good!" and "People do many things.") For the writer, a strong voice usually signifies authenticity, either in an artistic sense or in a personal sense. People who write with their own voices are people who are not afraid to say what they mean.

The worst problem we see in college writing is the paper in which "nobody's home." We do this to students. We do it to them in school by having them write about things they know nothing about. Worse, we have them write about things they don't care anything about. The writing is for only one person, the teacher. It's written "To Whom It May Concern."

Then there's just the way we criticize what people put on paper. Time after time after time, writers are reminded of what they don't do well, not what they do well. So they have no turf. They have no language. They only make mistakes; they only have poor handwriting or poor spelling. To protect themselves, they invest nothing in the piece.

One of the reasons adolescents give you the grunt-and-shoulder-twitch routine is so that they can't get hurt. Writers who put their voices into their work and say what they think can really get hurt by severe criticism. So gradually, from first grade on, we start to knock children's writing voices out of them. By the time they're seniors in high school, they whimper, or talk in a monotone, or say nothing—just generalities. Generalities are nice insulation against insult.

If poor students produce skimpy, voiceless writing out of self-defense, more skilled writers are likely to go on the offensive. They can produce prose in volume, imitating the scholarly voice that they are convinced the teacher wants. Other students shun academic locutions without being any more genuine. One freshman wrote: "Everybody gives gifts during their lifetime, but not enough people give the most important gift of all—the gift of life." The voice seems to come straight from the advertising world, a kidney-association brochure to be exact, rather than the flesh-and-blood student who wrote it.

"Basketball can be viewed in many ways," began another freshman English paper. The sentence could have been a direct descendant of "People do many things." Give Julian a few more years of writing exercises, and he will soon be capable of producing papers that don't sound like him on his own. But give him a chance to write on his own topics in his own words under the guidance of a teacher who knows something about writing, and he will soon be discovering his own meanings and his own voice.

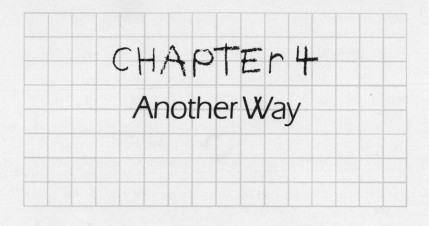

CHAPTEr 4
Another Way

In the fall of 1978, Donald Graves, Susan Sowers, and Lucy Calkins set out to do something that had never been done before. Writing research was a relatively new branch of educational inquiry to begin with, but research on children's writing was particularly rare. Following the lead of Janet Emig, a Harvard University researcher who had made a case study of twelfth-graders, Graves had studied several second-grade writers in 1973. Now he and his associates planned to observe sixteen children extensively over a two-year period. In addition to analyzing their finished work, the researchers would observe and question the children as they wrote.

At the public elementary school in Atkinson, New Hampshire, sixteen entering first- and third-graders were selected to represent a variety of abilities, and their parents were asked to sign a release form. The form stated that there would be "no substantial change in my child's learning experiences" as a result of the study. Although the statement was made in good faith— Graves was performing a "descriptive" rather than an "experimental" study—nothing could have been further from the truth. In the end, the study had a profound effect on the chosen classrooms and all the people in them.

Parents, teachers, children, and researchers all embarked on the project with different expectations. The parents were mildly curious. The children going into the first grade believed, like virtually all children going into the first grade, that they were quite capable of writing already. Unlike the vast majority of their peers in traditional classrooms, they would not be disillusioned. The third-graders were old hands, practiced at figuring out what the teacher wanted. They didn't realize that the teacher's wants were about to change. The teachers themselves had consented to put up with live-in researchers, but they were suspicious. They expected to be told how to do things.

Graves and his associates expected to find a common pattern of development among the children. There were bound to be differences and idiosyncracies, but Graves's proposal for the project stated that "the more important variables will be developmentally consistent from child to child." The curriculums used in many schools assign language skills to certain levels taught in a rigid sequence: commas one year, quotation marks the next. The problem as Graves saw it, was that both the sequence and timing in these programs were invariably out of whack because they were based on research that focused more on methods of teaching than patterns of learning. Although much time and money had been spent plotting the normal stages of development followed by beginning talkers, little had been done on the development of beginning readers and writers. Since school curriculums imposed an artificial sequence and most parents had also been sold on the dissect-and-drill method, children rarely got a chance to follow a natural progression when learning to read and write at home or at school. Graves hoped to map out the sequence children naturally follow as they learn to write, so that teachers would know what to expect and when to teach certain skills.

"Writing time," the event the Atkinson researchers were prepared to spend hours observing, happened infrequently at first,
and it usually lasted a mere fifteen minutes. Graves needed to
watch children in the process of writing, but they were hindered
more than helped by their well-meaning teachers in the beginning.
Laden with spelling lists, workbooks, and assignments, the children were admonished to watch for errors before they even began. When they did try to form sentences from word lists, the
paper they were given to write on in one class was too small.

The teachers were disheartened, as well. Their students'
writing was disappointing, and when they asked for advice,
Graves would often as not answer one question with another. He
didn't want them to worry about "doing it right" by his standards,
and he believed that teachers, like children, learn best when
urged to find their own answers.

One day first-grade teacher Mary Ellen Giacobbe took her
class to visit an apple orchard. The next day, she made a list of
words for the children to use in their writing. When a bright little
girl named Allison produced garbled syntax, Giacobbe went to
Graves in despair. "Why would Allison write like this?" she
asked. "She doesn't talk this way." Graves quickly pointed out
the things that Allison *could* do: writing from left to right and
spacing between words. When it came to her sentence structure,
however, he provided no easy answer. He asked Giacobbe what
she thought. She went home convinced that the researchers, who
naturally knew all the answers, were holding out on the teachers.

That night the thirty-mile drive back to the University of
New Hampshire was typical for Graves and his associates. They
were weary. They were tired of trying to milk writing data from
math and spelling lessons, and they wondered whether the project would ever amount to anything.

Six to eight weeks into the school year, several events dra-
matically improved the quantity and quality of the children's writing and thus the researchers' data. After some thinking, Giacobbe
had some ideas about possible causes of Allison's unnatural
wording. A trip to another school confirmed her suspicions. At a
researcher's suggestion, she visited a classroom where children
were free to write whatever they wanted by making up or "inventing" the spelling of words they didn't know. Excited by their

work, she read some of it to her own students the next day. Their
reaction surprised her. One boy stood up and announced, "That's
cinchy! We can do that." Apparently piqued, the children started
writing. They wrote about whatever they wanted to, in their own
words.

From that day on, topics were as varied as the children who
chose them. "Our Trip to the Apple Orchard" was replaced by
"Woody Owl," "Chemicals," "The Gerbil's Upstairs," and "The
66,000 Mile Space Flight." The children were not only doing
much more writing, but their pieces were longer. A little girl
named Cathy, along with every other child in the class, had written two lines about the trip to the apple orchard: "I like apples
and the apples are delicious and juicy. I like my kite." As soon as
she was free to choose her own words, however, she wrote a
seven-page booklet called "All About Animals." Many of the
other children went from one-liners to six pages. Even though
they didn't know how to read or spell words conventionally,
they had no fear of trying. One little boy promptly tackled *tyrannosaurus*. In the meantime, Allison's wording became more
natural.

Children in a third-grade class, wiser in the ways of school,
were not as responsive at first when given free choice of topics.
Without an assignment to guide them, they responded to the new
challenge of figuring out what the teacher wanted by relying on
old assignments from memory. Thus, they wrote things like "My
Life as a Pencil." But then their teacher brought in a set of x-rays
and wrote the story of her operation on the blackboard. Soon
after, the children branched out into many topics drawn from
their own knowledge and experiences.

A third breakthrough occurred when the researchers and
teachers discovered the reason behind the children's reluctance
to revise. In his six-page book on dinosaurs, first-grader Greg
drew a large brontosaurus and underneath it wrote, "Brontsaurus
[Brontosaurus] may have stayed in grops [groups]. Brontsaurus
was a plant eater." When his teacher asked why they stayed in
groups, he said, "To protect the little ones, of course." But that
information wasn't in the book, the teacher observed. Carl
pointed to the two lines of writing cramped at the bottom of the
page and said triumphantly, "There's no room!" He and the

teacher found a blank space at the top of the page, where he wrote "to perteckit (protect) the little ones," which he connected with an arrow to the line about staying in groups.

This incident and others like it taught the researchers that first-graders had aesthetic objections to revision, which requires cross outs, insertions, and arrows. The third-graders, used to being admonished about neatness, simply needed the teacher's permission to be messy on early drafts. Once the teachers changed their attitudes, the children started rewriting.

Throughout the two years, the three researchers observed the children and asked them questions designed to expose their grasp of certain writing concepts. Before long, however, the teachers recognized that the same questions got the children to think and thus made excellent teaching questions. Emulating the researchers' attitudes toward students and teachers alike, the teachers became less authoritative. They stopped hushing the children during writing time and often paused beside a child's desk to ask questions like "Where could you put that information if you wanted to add it?" or "What are you planning to do next?"

Before long the children were using the same sorts of questions with each other. "Which story is your favorite?" they would ask. "Why?" As they developed their own standards of good writing, they also offered suggestions to one another. "You need more details," one third-grader prompted a friend. "Did your mother scream? What did her eyes look like?"

The classrooms had settled into a new routine in which children and teachers talked, read, and wrote together. Following certain guidelines, each child was free to consult friends, the teacher, or a researcher during writing time. A writer might ask for advice on choosing a topic, for example, or narrowing its focus. The teacher would check on each child's progress from time to time, but the children could often approach the teacher when they needed help. As a piece of writing developed, the author might read it aloud to a small group of classmates or the whole class. The listeners could comment or ask questions as the writer called on them. The exchange of questions and answers would sometimes lead to revisions.

After four or five "books" had accumulated in a child's folder, the teacher might sit down with the child to discuss the work and select the best piece for "publication." The book would be typed with conventional spelling and punctuation and then bound in stiff cardboard sewn with dental floss and covered with wallpaper. A biographical note, "About the Author," was added, and the finished book might be read aloud to the whole class before it was placed in the class library. Then other children could take it home to read and share with their families. A library card inside the cover provided a record of the names of children who had borrowed the book throughout the year.

Although this outline generally held true, there were exceptions at every turn. Sometimes a child grew tired of a piece of writing or decided it was not worth finishing. In such cases, the piece might be abandoned or temporarily laid aside. Occasionally, a child might produce two books worthy of publication right in a row. Another might hit a slump and write a series of six books that weren't suitable for publication. At any given moment, the children were in all different stages of writing, and the course of no two books was just alike.

In the meantime, the success of the project had become visible in many ways. Tests and interviews showed that the children in the project classrooms had a better understanding of the use of various punctuation marks than did children from neighboring classrooms where punctuation drills prevailed. The researchers also found that the children spent approximately 30 percent of their writing time reading their classmate's or their own work. So even though the teachers had replaced reading drills with writing, it was not surprising when reading scores were as high as, or higher than, they had been in previous years. But teachers also noticed a difference in their students' reaction to what they read.

Two years before the research project had begun, second-grade teacher Judy Egan had presented some of her favorite children's books to her class. In the middle of the lesson, one little boy announced, "This is boring!" and the faces of his classmates expressed their solidarity with his sentiment. Hurt but determined, Egan left the books out in hopes that the children would come to them of their own accord. But she was never satisfied with their appreciation of literature.

During the second year of the project, she tried again. She had already read several of Tasha Tudor's books to the class when she chose to read *Corgiville Fair.* After she'd finished, at least fifteen hands shot up. "Look at all the detail—the corgis are all dressed up," said one child. "This story isn't true," said another, "but some of hers are." The whole class wrote admiring letters to Tudor. "I love you," wrote one child, "because you're a great illustrator and writer." But many of the letters also had a writer-to-writer tone. "How long does it take you to write?" one asked. "Do you really use the butter churn you wrote about?"

Egan concluded that the main difference between the two classes lay in the amount of writing they did. Her children now wrote so much that they naturally appreciated their reading more. Unlike many young children, they were aware that books were written by people. Of course, it helped that the books they were reading, genuine children's literature as opposed to basal readers, sounded as if they had each been written by a real person rather than an anonymous committee. Their teacher had also helped them realize that those people, grown-up authors, were going through much the same process that they as young authors were. After she had thought about the change in her students, Egan did something that showed how much she had changed in two years—she wrote about her discovery, in an article that was later published. Encouraged by the researchers, she and other teachers in the project had started to write, too. Some of them met regularly to discuss their writing with each other.

During the second year of the project, both Egan and Giacobbe replaced their basal readers with trade books, real children's literature. The two teachers were using fewer and fewer worksheets and exercises. But they were also nervous. No teacher wants to cheat her students of needed "skills" or antagonize parents. When Giacobbe announced her intention of eliminating basal readers to a group of parents, they gasped in unison. After she had searched her soul, her records, her students' test scores, and her memory, Giacobbe reported to Graves that she had been teaching the same skills children normally get from worksheets through their writing. Egan also worked hard to demonstrate accountability. Throughout the year, she gave the children all the tests from both the spelling text and basal readers she had used in the past. Although the children had had no exposure to the readers or the lists of spelling words usually provided for study, Egan found that they were testing as well as, if not better than, children in previous years. When she gave the year-end spelling test, nineteen of the twenty-one children performed on or above grade level. She, too, concluded that the children were picking up skills in the context of reading trade books and writing and reading their own books. In subsequent years, Egan and Giacobbe continued to use the same teaching methods, and their students continued to test well. At the end of the school year following the study, for example, 82 percent of Giacobbe's first grade scored on or above grade level on a reading test.

In the end, the children at Atkinson had surprised the researchers nearly as much as they had surprised their parents and teachers. These children had proved themselves to be far more capable than adults had expected in many ways. Just before the study had begun, a prominent researcher in the field had flatly stated that children below the fourth-grade level were incapable of revising their work. At Atkinson, half the first-graders demonstrated their ability to revise. In most scope-and-sequence curriculums, quotation marks are arbitrarily assigned to, and thus taught in, the fourth grade or even later. At Atkinson, one-third of Mary Ellen Giacobbe's first graders used quotation marks in their writing, simply because she took the time to show them how when they needed the marks for dialogue. Perhaps most astonishing was the sheer quantity of written work the children voluntarily produced, as good a sign as any of their motivation. In Giacobbe's first grade, the children produced thirteen hundred, five-and six-page "books" in one year and "published" four hundred of them.

Nearly a year after the classroom phase of the study was completed, Graves sat down to draw up his conclusions for his final report to the National Institute of Education. It was then that he faced his original goal of specifying a natural sequence that teachers could follow in place of the artificial schedules imposed on them. But the data had surprised him. He and his associates had documented a number of patterns as the children learned to arrange words properly on the page, compose silently, spell correctly, and manipulate information. Nevertheless, the researchers had also found exceptions to every rule.

Despite similarities, the children were amazingly different from each other. The more you gather data on people, the more different they become—not more similar. In the paint industry, scanning electron microscopes are used to reveal subtle differences between weathered paint samples. To the naked eye, two samples may look identical. But under the microscope, they look as different as silk and tweed. In the same way, an intensive observer of children sees those differences that another person might miss.

The important thing in teaching is to rejoice in the differences, not to despair. That was a major shift for me as a researcher. In research, we're always trying to generalize from one subject to another. Unfortunately, that process forces me to try to make people more similar. The real task is to help people see the differences within themselves as potentially beautiful. As a researcher, though, I can't see the differences until I understand how people are the same. The similarities provide a foil for the differences.

In my final report, I translated my conclusions into classroom practice:

Many similarities were seen among the children when they wrote, but as the study progressed, individual exceptions to the data increased in dominance. In short, every child had behavioral characteristics in the writing process that applied to that child alone. It is our contention, based on this information, that such variability demands *a waiting, responsive type of teaching.*

Amy made internal revisions, "thinking through" several drafts without making many changes on the paper. Andrew made progressively fewer revisions, while Brian wrote more and more. . . . One teacher may see revision as worthy of a classroom mandate and remain unaware that Amy revises internally. Another teacher may not realize that although Brian revises extensively on most drafts, today may not be a good day to ask him to revise. Teachers who respond, who follow what children say and do, will be able to see differences among writers and to help the individual child write.

Together, the teachers and researchers at Atkinson had developed their own method of teaching writing and the beginnings of a new approach to teaching reading. Many of their techniques and attitudes had been adopted before. Maria Montessori, for example, had documented the use of invented spelling among factory workers' children in Rome as much as sixty years earlier. Writing "conferences" between teacher and student had been used in some college and high-school courses. And there have always been a number of teachers—Robert Frost was one—who allow students to write on topics of their own choice.

But the Atkinson project brought together many of these features for the first time in elementary classrooms, documented the results, and made them available to teachers in plain English, a language apparently unknown to many research writers. Because he knew that many teachers had an aversion to research, Graves had made a commitment to make his results accessible to them from the start. Over the course of several years he, his associates, and the teachers at Atkinson all wrote numerous articles drawn from the research, and eventually two books came out of the project. The researchers and teachers involved also began conducting workshops for other teachers.

It didn't take long for the media outside of education journals to pick up the story as well. National Public Radio, *Time, Psychology Today, The New York Times, Better Homes and Gardens, Family Circle,* and the Associated Press all reported on the developments at Atkinson. By the second year of the project, the school was deluged with hundreds of visitors, eager to see the classrooms in action. The guests pumped teachers, researchers, and children for information. "Just one more question, and then I'll leave you alone" was the refrain that rang in Mary Ellen Giacobbe's head at the end of a visitors' day in her classroom.

All in all, thousands of teachers in the United States, Australia, Canada, and England have been influenced by the work done at Atkinson. More than twenty teachers who were not part of the original Atkinson project have been interviewed for this book. Only four of these teachers have studied with Graves. The others have perhaps heard him speak, read his articles, and read his book *Writing: Children and Teachers at Work.* In many cases they have studied the teaching of writing in courses or summer institutes that are not connected with him. Yet all have witnessed in their own classrooms many of the things that happened at Atkinson.

Every one of these teachers has developed a unique blend of techniques and approaches, but all would agree on certain principles. The methods they use differ from those in the average classroom in two important ways. First, these teachers differ from most in their understanding of how children learn. Their classrooms have the air of a workshop in which children are free to write, talk, read, and listen—all within definite guidelines. Second, these teachers view writing itself differently. They see it not so much as a subject with many facts and formulas to be memorized as a craft to be practiced under the guidance of an experienced writer.

CHAPTEr 5
A Society of Learning

Every day before lunch, a first-grader in Ellen Blackburn's class reads aloud to the whole class. These sessions reveal the children's enthusiasm for reading and writing and learning. The students all pursue their own interests when they read and write. But they also read and write for each other and with each other. Blackburn has high expectations, not just for individuals, but for the class as a group. Without the help of the group, individual children cannot reach their full potential as writers.

In a good classroom, the space is shared, responsibilities are shared, reading and writing are shared, experiences are shared, and, above all, learning is shared. The teacher works very hard to help the children develop their ability to capitalize on their collective power for the common good.

On the day I visited Blackburn's class, the children created a fantasy together, combining their own knowledge of the real world with the imaginary world of a storybook. Their joint version of the story was unique; no one child could have produced it alone. It began when a little girl named Nickie announced the name of the book she had chosen to read, *Mouse Soup,* by award-winning children's author Arnold Lobel. There were several hundred books to choose from, including about two hundred of the children's original "published" pieces. Nickie had been working on the stories in *Mouse Soup* during silent-reading time for several days, and she wanted to share one of those stories with the class.

Several other children had already read the story she had picked, and one little boy couldn't help giving away a bit of the plot. "Yup, that's the one!" he announced. "And it's gonna get deeper and deeper!" Nickie started the story about a mouse that had the misfortune of walking beneath a falling beehive. Once the hive had landed on his head, the bees announced their intention of setting up housekeeping there: " 'We like your ears,' said the bees, 'we like your nose, we like your whiskers!' " Nickie read the lines with expression, and the children giggled. When the lines were repeated a few pages later in a typical children's book refrain, the children chanted with her: " 'We like your ears,' said the bees, 'we like your nose, we like your whiskers!' " Meanwhile, the clever mouse had invited the bees to his own home, but he headed straight for a swamp.

"I know what's going to happen," said one little boy. His pronouncement was echoed by several "me too's," but the foreknowledge seemed to enhance rather than diminish the children's enjoyment.

"He stepped into the mud up to his knees," Nickie continued. " 'Here is my front door,' said the mouse. 'Oh yes!' said the bees.' "

"It's really mud," one child interjected.

"I bet it's nice and soft," added another.

"And it's nice and warrrrrm," a little girl exclaimed.

"I love it!"

"Nice and dirty!" said a little boy. "I'd like to go swimming in it."

"I only would like to go in it with a bathing suit," Nickie concluded, steering the group back to the story. She continued to read, and her listeners continued to comment, until the bees had flown off, and the mouse had gone home for a bath. Then the children gave Nickie a round of applause.

Vital Connections

In component-oriented classrooms, children are expected to learn in an intellectual context of fragmentation and a social context of isolation. Teachers like Ellen Blackburn strive to provide social and intellectual connections for children from first grade on up. They believe that children learn when they share knowledge with one another and when they see the links between their own lives and their schoolwork.

The sharing of space, responsibilities, experiences, and stories gives children a common bond. Shared humor and a spirit of playfulness strengthen the bond and offer relief from the serious business of learning. Blackburn consciously develops this bond by incorporating the stories children tell, read, and write into daily discussions and by reminding the class of their experiences together. One day a little boy questioned the wording in something he had read; he didn't agree that Michael Jackson should be called a "hero." After the group of children at the writing table had discussed the meaning of the word, Blackburn reminded them of a previous occasion. "Remember the rainy day a little while ago," she asked, "when we stayed in from recess and you all made microphones with Tinkertoys and pretended you were Michael Jackson?" "Yeah," said the children clustered around her. "I remember when I was the drummer," a little boy said.

Most important, an atmosphere of sharing motivates children to read and write for each other. Unlike their component-oriented counterparts, these classrooms are places where people read and write to communicate, not just to practice skills. In Blackburn's class, the children spend much of their time reading and writing and talking and listening. They write notes to each other and the teacher; they write books to share with the class and a journal to share with the teacher. Choosing among several hundred books in the classroom, they read alone, with the teacher, and in front of the whole class.

Blackburn teaches in a mill town that, despite the boom and bustle of growth in surrounding towns, seems to be locked into a progressive economic decline. Often, not one of her students' parents will have a college degree. Some of her students have not been read to much at home. Yet by the end of the year, they love school, largely because they love to read and write. The children often choose to read or write during their snack time in the morning. As one little boy in the class put it, "If you didn't know how to read, you'd miss a lot of good stuff."

A little girl named Jill explains that she likes to read what she has written to a group of children and the teacher so that "other people will know what I write." She is particularly delighted that her best friend often chooses to read her stories during independent reading time. As for reading in front of the whole class, that's fun, too, "so that they all know that I know how to read." They liked what she read last time; she could tell because "they said, *'Jump, Frog, Jump'* with me when I read it."

As important as the links between readers and writers in a room like Blackburn's is the overlap between the children's schoolwork and their own lives. The freedom to read and write about things that interest them strengthens their motivation and their ability to make intellectual connections. When they pursue their own interests, they are able to learn by building upon things they already know, making connections between new information and old.

Whenever there's a connection made between old knowledge and new knowledge, that's where the new growth is. Those are the green shoots out of the old stock, the shoots that will bear fruit. But it takes a fair amount of pruning to get new growth. The dead wood comes when children pay attention to what they think the teacher wants instead of what, in fact, they see.

Blackburn works hard to strengthen and capitalize on the vital connection between the written word and the children's own world, real and imaginary. She often finds that link in the stories the children tell when they read or write, true stories mostly, about their experiences. Because the children know that she enjoys stories and because they have a group identity as writers, readers, and storytellers who can take off on a flight of fantasy about mud, they share stories all day long.

On the day Nickie read the story about the mouse and the bees, she also read a story about a mouse that was irritated by chirping crickets. When she was done, a forest of hands sprung up. After the children had commented on things they liked about the tale, it seemed that nearly everyone had a story to tell about an experience with an unwanted insect. Soon the anecdotes escalated to bats and rodents. Rather than squelching the children's enthusiasm, Blackburn took advantage of it. After telling her own story about an experience with a bat, she explained how bats navigate without sight. She asked the children to reconsider their assumptions about insects. "Are bugs always a nuisance?" she asked. "What if there weren't any bugs in the world? What else wouldn't be here?" The children came up with numerous answers from spiders to snakes, and Blackburn carried the idea further up the ecological chain to humans.

In that session, Blackburn had allowed the children to show what they already knew about insects before she added to that knowledge. She challenged them to expand their existing framework for understanding the world around them to accommodate new information. She does the same thing with the children's writing. After one little boy had written a piece about dinosaurs, she suggested he write another piece, this time as if he were there in prehistoric time with them. Much of the fiction her students write is, like some of the best adult fiction, a hybrid of fantasy and fact.

Children as Teachers

Roxanne, a black second-grader, lives in an inner-city school district where educational expectations are generally not high. Many of the families are on welfare, and a number of her classmates are the children of immigrants who do not speak English. But Roxanne, like her classmates, likes to write because reading her own writing in front of the class gives her "feelings." After she has read her work to the class, she has the opportunity to call on other children who have questions about what she has written. "When they raise their hands," Roxanne explains, "I feel like I'm the teacher."

In a classroom where learning is shared, teaching is shared. And as any teacher will attest, nothing helps people clarify something they've just learned more than trying to teach it to someone else. The art of making children feel, and act, like teachers lies in helping them to know what they know, showing them that they do know something worth sharing with others.

> *I can challenge children who think they know a lot, much more than children who shuffle and think they know nothing. I'll say, "So you think you know a lot about submarines? I'll bet you can't handle this one." And I fire a good question about submarines.*
>
> *When children see themselves as knowledgeable, they are able to solve problems and act independently of the teacher or other children. We are working very hard to produce the independent learner. We also want children to feel confident to say, "I don't understand your question." Children who can do that will not stew in ignorance for very long. They save themselves and their teachers days and weeks of wasted teaching time.*

When it comes to making someone feel like a teacher, writing is the perfect activity. It is in the natural order of things for writers to teach—inform, convince, and entertain—their readers, the natural order of things outside of school, that is. If Roxanne had written her sentences with words taken from a spelling list, had all her errors highlighted in red ink, and then read her work to the class, she would probably not have felt like the teacher. And her classmates would not have been moved to ask questions about a set of sentences just like their own. Fortunately, Roxanne is expected to find her own topics most of the time. Writing on subjects she knows about, she begins the whole process from a position of strength. When hands start waving in the air after she has read her work, she knows her audience wants to congratulate her and ask her questions. She learns more about what she knows as she writes, and the good "feelings" she gets at the end will inspire her to find more things to write about and learn about.

The first step in making children feel like teachers is believing that every child has a story to tell, knowledge to share. Everyone's an expert at something, usually many things. Often teachers have to begin by acting as if this were true; it is hard for them to accept the premise without evidence. Teachers who have been using display questions and story starters may believe they actually have evidence to the contrary.

A teacher has to want to learn from children. That's the most important thing. I can show that I want to learn from them by listening and, above all, by waiting for their answers. I have to look straight into the eyes of those kids without wavering. They know I really want to know their answers for my sake and theirs. When I get an answer, I confirm what the child knows and use the information. Sometimes in the course of teaching I'll stop and tell the class what I have learned. It's useful for me, and it's useful for them. I'm always implying that there's so much more that I could tell, or that I don't even know about, that everyone is learning from minute to minute.

In Sue Clancy's kindergarten in Wagga Wagga, Australia, one little boy wrote about the swans he was raising at home. In his piece, he mentioned that the cygnets' feathers had started to come in and their beaks had begun to turn red. Clancy was surprised. "Oh, I didn't know," she said. "What color were the cygnets' beaks when they were born?" Neither the teacher nor the other children in the class had realized that black swans with red beaks started life gray all over. "Oh, dear, that's interesting," the teacher told the child. "You're telling me lots of things I didn't know."

Children who have been labeled learning disabled are all experts, too, and more in need of feeling that way than other children. Too often, children who fail at classroom exercises devoid of context and meaning are sentenced to more of the same, singled out, and banished to the "resource room." Although it would seem that children who have trouble with component work need a meaningful context for their work even more than other children, students in most resource rooms never get to the context. At the same time, the stigma attached to these children intensifies, beginning with their initial failure, their separation from the rest of the group, and the embarrassment of having to do things over again. All that is enough to convince the children themselves that they don't know much. Teachers and school records label them learning disabled, enough to convince any adult that they don't know much.

A number of resource-room teachers are now taking a different tack. One fourth-grader in a resource room at a New Hampshire school wrote several pieces about her trip to New York. Since she was a competitive swimmer, she also wrote a piece on how to swim. It so happened that her teacher was also an expert swimmer and thus a poor judge of how easily a beginner might follow the child's instructions for the different strokes. So a nonswimmer in the room, a real sinker, read her book and went through the motions she described. At the same time that he was graphically demonstrating that the girl had knowledge to share, his misunderstandings pointed the way to revisions. The little girl concluded her book with a quiz for her readers. The nonswimmer, of course, was an expert in other fields, including soccer, basketball, and science fiction.

Although these special-education teachers have had surprising success with their students, classroom teachers who take the same approach often find that they don't have to send children out of the room to begin with. At Boothbay Region Elementary School, where sixteen out of twenty-three teachers use writing to make children feel like experts, the resource-room teacher reports that referrals of children with writing problems have dropped to zero from the sixteen writing classrooms. Teachers in the other classrooms continue to send her children. That is not to say that language disabilities have disappeared from the sixteen classrooms. Some children still have problems with handwriting, spelling, and syntax. But in classrooms where teachers emphasize the positive, these children are able to write with the rest of their class and to work on their problems in the context of things they have chosen to write. At the same time, their self-confidence never suffers the blow of ostracism that can sometimes occur even within a self-contained classroom. As one junior-high teacher puts it: "When you're doing 'individual needs,' and one kid is having the book read to him because he can't read, or he's listening to a tape recorder up back with earphones, or he's taking a watered-down version of the test or the worksheet, not for one moment does that child not know that he is different. But with writing there's no singling out of the child. He's doing exactly what everyone else is doing. Sure, maybe he's writing three sentences and the kid next to him is writing twenty. But that's all right because the kid next to him may not be the brightest kid in the class. Maybe he's just more fluent."

In fact, a teacher's respect for every child's knowledge may be even more important with older students. Schooling and the self-doubts of maturity often conspire to convince children that they don't know much and that no one would be interested in what they do know. "At twelve years old," says the junior-high teacher, "the thing you know best is yourself. But you don't *think* you know anything. So it's a self-discovery: 'Yes, I do know things that no one else in here knows about or knows as well.' "

Learning from One Another

Teachers seem to bequeath certain phrases from one generation to another like heirlooms. Once acquired, the treasured phrases are used over and over: "Do your own work, please." "I hear lips!" Admonitions like these contribute to an atmosphere of isolation and competition. Teachers often use them in the belief that children who are allowed to talk while they work will learn less. Time will be wasted in discussions of last night's TV show,

teachers fear, and if the topic of discussion actually is schoolwork, the information shared may be incorrect.

But teachers find that they like to hear lips when the lips are
saying things like "Wanna know how to use apostrophe *s*?"
That's what one little girl said to another in a conspiratorial tone
as Linette Moorman's second-graders settled down in a circle at
the front of their Brooklyn classroom for a "share session."
Moorman has found that children who have an emotional and
intellectual investment in their work will sometimes talk about
apostrophes in a spare moment.

If children reading their work to a class play the role of the
teacher, then both their classmates and the real teacher—whose
hand will go up at the end, too—are the students. Whether listening to a classmate's story or talking to one another in individual or
group conferences, children learn from one another in a variety of
ways. First, they gain a lot of facts and insights from their classmates' books, which are invariably on a wide variety of subjects
from rainbows to death. Since the children write on topics they
know or have studied, the information exchanged is likely to be
accurate.

> *One day in a first-grade classroom, I overheard five boys*
> *vying for center stage to show how much they knew. The*
> *children were seated at desks facing each other, and they*
> *were supposedly writing. But they were more like five old*
> *ladies at a quilting bee or five old fishermen mending their*
> *nets. Their mouths were going as fast as their hands, and the*
> *conversation had nothing to do with the words that were*
> *going down on the paper. Within fifteen minutes, they went*
> *through a stream of topics. First they discussed recent mo-*
> *tion pictures, soccer teams, and the best way to name a*
> *soccer team. Then they moved on to fish: hammerhead*
> *sharks, piranhas, barracudas, giant squid, stingrays. They*
> *listened to one another only in order to outdo their friends*
> *with examples of the largest fish or the sharpest teeth.*
>
> *You might say this is an example of poor listening. But*
> *I've seen those boys use good listening habits in other set-*
> *tings. In one sense, they did demonstrate good listening by*
> *the way they sustained the subject. Nevertheless, the social*

situation was one of vying for supremacy in information, and that will go on through doctoral dissertations and beyond.

Many would view their discussion as a waste of time, something "off-task" and not related to learning. But never have I seen children develop classification systems for size, sharpness of teeth, or ferocity more quickly. And that's what learning is—developing frameworks for understanding information. Taking the one thing you know and finding out about three other things that you didn't realize were related. You have to change your mental framework to accommodate the new information.

Children who are allowed to teach one another learn a valuable lesson in the process. They discover that people, even peers, can be good resources. Their friends offer not only factual information, but also ideas and suggestions on how to do things. Because the children spend a lot of time writing and thinking about writing, they become expert at assisting one another in a variety of ways. Students from kindergarten through college get ideas for topics when they read their friends' writing. Children swap ideas because they need ideas. They talk about punctuation marks because they want to make their writing clear. Since punctuation can also add punch to a piece of writing, strengthening the voice, children sometimes get excited about it. Exclamation marks have been known to spread through a classroom faster than the chicken pox.

Children, like all writers, need advice on techniques to use when they get stuck. In Mary Anne Byrne's special-education resource room at a school in Manchester, New Hamphshire, the children read a lot of poetry. By Thanksgiving one year, a fifth-grader was writing her own poems, and she had discovered her own technique for getting started on them. Once she had chosen a topic, she would brainstorm a list of related words. Then she would look for rhyming words and synonyms that would fit in with her meter. She showed other children in the resource room how they could try the same method.

In some instances, children take a lesson from a peer more easily than from the teacher. Susan Porter was teaching a split class of first-graders and pre-first-grade transition students at a

school in Stratham, New Hampshire, when she observed two
children working together. Although it was late in November, a
transition student named Caleb was still drawing elaborate pictures without words during writing time. Porter described the
scene in a journal she kept for a course on teaching writing:

> Caleb had drawn the cover page of his latest book: *The Garfield
> Book.* It was a very elaborate picture and he had spent a long time
> on it. He obviously wanted to talk about it, because once he
> realized he had [my teacher's aide] Terry's ear, he just went on and
> on. . . . When Caleb was done, he sat back and looked at her
> expectantly. Terry quietly asked him what he planned to do with the
> writing piece next. Caleb said that he thought he would do some
> more about Garfield and how he likes to tease the dog and other
> cats.
>
> At this point, Ginger, who was sitting across the table from
> Caleb, leaned over and said, "Yeah, Caleb, but if Ms. Porter and
> Mrs. G. weren't here to talk about it, how would anyone know it
> was about Garfield?" Caleb just sat there and said he didn't know,
> so Ginger said, "Well, you have to start to write some *words!* And
> don't worry, they don't have to be perfect." So Caleb picked up his
> pencil and Ginger started to help him spell "Garfield." It was so
> *slow,* but she stuck with it and went *over and over and over* the
> word with him until he had this: GRFEELD. Then she said, "There,
> see, now you can do it!" Caleb, looking a little dazed, though also
> pleased with himself, just nodded.

Ginger had actually had more success with Caleb than Porter
herself. "Caleb is a transition student, and very immature emotionally," Porter explained in her journal. "Every time I've tried
to help him write words, he's clammed up completely. But he was
able to work with Ginger. And was he proud of himself! As we
were cleaning up today he was walking around showing everyone!" Although Ginger was playing a guiding role with Caleb,
children can also criticize one another in a painless, matter-of-
fact tone. "Deb, where are your periods?" one child asked
another in a first-grade room.

Students may become so skilled at helping one another with
their writing that they can even help their teachers. When Nancie
Atwell wrote an article about her research on topic selection, she

read a draft to her class of eighth-graders at Boothbay Harbor. First she told them her concerns: "I'm just worried that it's not convincing. I'm always afraid somebody's going to say, 'You liar. Kids don't really do that.'" Her students had a suggestion. "You need to beef it up with quotes," they said. To provide her with raw material, they spent a half-hour talking about the importance of free choice in topics. Atwell took their advice, and their quotes, and was pleased with the result. Her students, no doubt, were pleased with themselves.

Of course, children, like adults, are not infallible, and some of their information is erroneous, some of their advice better left untaken. Yet recognition of that fact is a valuable lesson, as well. Any writer who tries to incorporate every suggestion received will wind up in a muddle. Choices must be made.

A nine-year-old named Cassie likes making those choices. The daughter of a crane operator and a homemaker, she seems to have an opinion on everything. Marilyn Woolley gathered a number of those opinions as part of a case study of several children in Jo Parry's classroom in a suburb of Melbourne, Australia. When classmates comment on a piece of writing, Cassie explains, "You aren't only getting one side of the story. You have to choose. If you go to one person they might say they don't like your story or that part isn't right. But you can go to another person and they might say that's great or something. You just learn more because instead of copying off the board and only have one person teaching you, you're getting your brain working more."*

Listening Writers

The little girl sitting in the chair at the front of the room was shy. She spoke softly and with a slight lisp. Not one of the better writers in the class, she had written a piece that was long and rambling. By the time she finished reading, I realized my mind

*Cassie's comments here and elsewhere come from interviews quoted in a master's thesis Marilyn Woolley wrote at the School of Advanced Education at La Trobe University in 1984.

had wandered, and I had missed large sections of her story. But then the other children raised their hands. Their specific questions and detailed comments revealed how deeply attentive they had been. When children are picking up valuable information and tips from each other, they develop good listening skills in the process.

If things are working well, the teacher is working on two kinds of consciousness. The teacher helps children to establish their own voices and their own funds of knowledge but also shows how individuals, when gathered together, can become a group force for good. There is always a tension between the individual and the group. That will never end. But both forces need to be recognized as a teacher helps children to listen to their own voices, as well as the voices of others in the room.

Unless we have learned to listen to ourselves, it is difficult to hear other people. Writing helps us listen to our own voices, as inconstant as they may be. It also gives us a sense of who we are and what we know. When I have a sense of my own territory, my own unique area of expertise, then it is easier for me to begin to understand the territories of others. This is not to say that all writers are great listeners. But writers who regularly share their work with others can become better listeners.

Teachers who want to help young writers become good listeners start by giving their classes plenty of time to practice. Children begin to learn the etiquette of listening when teachers establish a way for speakers to take turns. But if children learn to take turns without understanding the reason for listening, then taking turns is meaningless. Teachers must show constantly that they listen because they need to learn from the children, and the children, in turn, need to learn from one another. Once children learn the structure that enables them to be courteous, their statements are not misunderstood. Then writers and readers can be very frank with each other.

In most conferences and class discussions, the authors read their work aloud. Some teachers ask the listeners to respond first by telling the author what they heard. The attempt to match what was written with what was heard is an education in listening in itself.

Although children in these classrooms become adept at listening closely, they are not mere passive receivers of information. Following the teacher's lead, they ask questions after listening. Often they allow the writer to direct the conversation. "What do you need help with?" they ask first. But most of their questions fall into two categories: content questions and process questions. *Content questions* are reader-to-writer questions about the experience or information underlying a piece of writing. These questions show the writer what the readers want to know more about and what they're confused about, vital information to someone ready to revise.

When a fourth-grader read a draft of his piece about a trip on an airplane, his classmates asked him several content questions: What happened? Did you get your luggage? Were you unhappy when you didn't find your luggage? But they also asked several *process questions* about the actual procedure of writing and evaluating the piece: What are you going to do next? What do you think the main part of your story is? These are writer-to-writer questions, which get the writer talking and thinking about judging and improving the work.

By learning to listen, children learn to help themselves become better writers. Every writer needs to hear various kinds of responses from readers. In an early draft, writing consists of a whole series of untested assumptions. It's like singing with headphones on. You think you are singing along with the music, and then you hear someone else do it and realize how often other people sing off-key when they have headphones on. Thus, children need to know when they are writing off-key. Then they can shift from writing just for themselves to writing with their ears unplugged and their eyes wide open.

The questioning that goes on in these classrooms is clearly a help to the child being questioned. The children are constantly being challenged to think, to stop and look again at what they have written. But the questioners benefit, as well. Eventually, they learn to turn around and ask themselves the very questions they ask of others. Young children tend to talk to themselves when they revise, allowing adults nearby to eavesdrop on the process. "Now I need to look at the end," one little girl said aloud to herself. "Do they know it was a squirrel that meowed?"

Over and over again, children reviewing their own work ask themselves what "they" will understand or enjoy. This process gives them a head start on an important part of learning to write—anticipating their readers' reactions. They are able to revise with a reader in mind, whereas many older people, in college and beyond, continue to write prose marked by a self-centered lack of concern for readers.

In narratives, the classic result is often called a "bed-to-bed" story. A writer eager to tell all about an exciting trip to the zoo, for example, begins the piece with the alarm going off in the morning and ends with the light going out at night. In the end, the alarm receives equal weight with the escape of the apes. In expository writing, the result is often poorly organized material, or perhaps an unnecessary narrative explaining how the writer found the information and arrived at the conclusions presented. A report on sea urchins, for instance, simply lists everything the writer knows on the topic, with no evidence of a controlling idea or purpose that connects the information. Or perhaps the report begins with the writer's first climb up the library steps.

Of course it is natural for young children to write self-centered narratives and "all about" books. And older writers working on a first draft can safely ignore potential readers. But the problem comes when an older writer fails to reconsider and revise the material in light of readers' needs and interests. Children who are allowed to talk about their writing have an audience that is immediate and concrete in the form of peers and a teacher always willing to listen and question. Used to switching back and forth between roles of reader and writer in a matter of seconds, these children can learn to write with their readers in mind.

A fourth-grader named Teena wrote a classic bed-to-bed

story about her trip to New York City. She included twenty-five events, giving equal space to her family's visit to the United Nations complex and a trip back to the hotel room to change their clothes. Since writing, and sequencing in particular, has been a struggle for Teena, this piece in itself was an accomplishment. But when she shared her draft with other writers, one small part of her story drew a reaction every time. That was the part about her carriage ride in Central Park. In a group conference, the other children drew her out on the subject, and in response to their interest, she wrote a new eleven-page book called *My Carriage Ride.* Here is an excerpt from the middle of the piece, just as the ride begins:

> So we hopped in. Then we took off. The guy said, "There was this man from Texas who gave me this tip. It was a big tip. He was a nice guy you know." Right off I knew he was hinting for a tip.
>
> In the middle of the ride he said, "I used the tips to buy my horse some carrots, sugar canes, and hay." When he was saying that, his horse stopped to eat some of the fresh green grass. The guy started to whip the horse with his reins. Then a boy came by on a bike saying, "Don't whip the poor horse!" (When the guy was bragging how nice he is to the horse!). . . .

Building Tolerance and Respect

The same process that helps children empathize with their readers helps them empathize with their classmates. Empathy is important in writing classrooms. Whether the subject is rocks or divorce, writers who care about their work take a risk in showing it to other people. Children must learn not only to listen but to respond with care.

> *When children respond to a piece of writing by first saying what they heard, they are showing that they understand what the author knows. In short, we are constantly striving to sit where the author sat when the author wrote. It also helps*

that the children know what it is like to be sitting in that chair, reading their work to the group. If in the course of a year, a child has sat in that chair six times, the child knows, in part, what it is to be that person sitting there now.

These students are constantly putting themselves through the mental gymnastics required to view their own work from someone else's point of view and to view someone else's work as if their own. The swapping of roles, and chairs, allows for an intellectual meeting of minds, but it also gives children lots of practice in looking at things from the other guy's point of view.

Many teachers have been surprised at the sensitivity children display in reacting to one another's experiences. A little girl in a third-grade class wrote about her parents' divorce in a piece that seemed to come from the heart. The book ended with this paragraph: "I am going to live with my mom soon. My mom has a judge and my dad has a judge too. When my mom got divorced from my dad she wanted to get divorced because she didn't like him any more. My mom still loves me just as she loves my sister. The End." When the little girl read her book to the class, the response was warm. One little boy raised his hand and said, "I really think it's great that you would share that because it's a very personal thing and you shared. Some people would be ashamed of a divorce in the family."

Writing even helped at least one child overcome one of the crueler traditions of childhood. When a very sensitive second-grader discovered that he had to get glasses, he worried that his classmates would tease him and call him "four eyes." He wrote a humorous book about his fears and read it to the group. The class laughed with him, enjoying the book, and the following week, when he appeared with his new glasses, not a soul teased him.

The more children listen to each other, the more they learn about their similarities and differences. A fourth-grade teacher uses divorce as an example. When a child shares a piece of writing about first-hand experiences with divorce, others in similar situations are thrilled to find out they're not alone. " 'It's just like that when I visit my father,' " a listener will comment afterwards, according to the teacher, " 'and he gives me stuff I don't know if I should take. He gives me food my mother says I shouldn't eat.'

For other children, who come from the perfect little home with Mom and Daddy and two little kids," the teacher adds, "it's good to see that there are other ways to live than Daddy coming home at night with a kiss for Mommy."

Children learn to respect one another in spite of their differences because their teachers work so hard to show that everyone has something worthwhile to contribute to the group. In classrooms where worksheets prevail, the children all do the same thing at the same time, and invidious comparisons are easily made. Children are considered smarter than others simply by virtue of how much they get "right" or "wrong." Reading groups reinforce those lines between fast and slow learners. But in classrooms where children read and write according to their own abilities and interests, every child has a chance to stake out an area of expertise and to receive recognition from classmates.

Like everyone else, the outspoken Australian nine-year-old named Cassie James has her strengths and her weaknesses. She suffers from asthma. Yet despite her slight build and occasional trips to the hospital, she hardly seems sickly. In fact, she wrote about her affliction in part so that the children in her class would understand it and realize that she was "not really sick." So knowledgeable is she on the subject that her classmates sometimes call her "Dr. James." Cassie and her classmates live on the outskirts of Melbourne in an area where nearly half the families receive government assistance and few of the homes are privately owned. Their teacher, Jo Parry, works hard to develop her students' respect for one another's knowledge and skills. Cassie describes how her teacher has encouraged the children to recognize and benefit from one another's abilities: "Miss Parry matches up people. Like if someone wanted some help with drawings in their publishing, Miss Parry would say straight away to go to Michael or someone else, and if they needed any humour she might say come to me or to go to Sam, and if they needed any information, Jason was good with information so Miss Parry might say go to him. . . . Kim knows how to work a dictionary quite well and so does Sam. Sam helps me with some things and I help her with some things."

Parents who volunteer to help out in classrooms like Cassie's notice the democratic atmosphere immediately. A New Hamp-

shire mother who typed the published books in a third-grade
classroom was surprised and pleased by the atmosphere she
found there. "It's been a nice way to get to know the other children in the class and their experiences and outlook on life," she
says. "Everyone's special, and at that age they so easily slip into
who's in the best reading group and who's in this and that. But
now they appreciate each other and the variety of experiences
they all have." She knows they appreciate one another because
her daughter "doesn't just take out books written by her best
friends. They seem eager to read everybody's books."

A Sense of Belonging

Imagine a classroom full of twenty or thirty children and one
teacher. The teacher is quietly talking with one child at the back
of the room. The other children are not under direct supervision
at the moment. In fact, they are free to talk and move about the
room. What are they up to? Depending on the age of the children,
you might imagine anything from fistfights to spitballs to discussions of last night's TV shows.

> *Many adults fear that permissiveness will lead to chaos.
> Their fears are well founded. Giving children freedom with-
> out limits invites psychic anarchy. The result can be more
> harmful than an overly restrictive environment. One of the
> problems of permissiveness is that children are allowed to
> make too many choices. With too many choices, a child loses
> sight of the logical outcomes of decisions. But the child also
> fails to realize that a choice made haphazardly destroys the
> choices of others. A child who suddenly decides to read
> aloud on a whim may disturb three friends working nearby.
> Children who live in an anarchic room are terribly self-
> centered because they never have to consider other children
> or the teacher.*

A teacher who wants to give children the freedom to work
together and make their own decisions must establish a predict-

able environment. Against the background of a familiar routine, children can concentrate on more important intellectual problems. Guidelines for proper behavior also preserve the teacher's own sanity. They give the teacher freedom, too—the freedom to spend valuable time alone with individual children. The rules are designed to protect, and eventually foster respect for, everyone's rights.

> *There are rules for use of space, materials, and time. Usually, only a certain number of children may use a given area of the room at one time. Supplies and materials are kept in set places so that children can find what they need and solve mechanical problems on their own. Children know the overall guidelines for listening and responding to someone else's work. And a variety of classroom responsibilities rotate among the children. The teacher also has a very predictable way of using time, running the day, and responding to the children.*

Of course, children don't always learn to take responsibility for their own behavior overnight. When students first come to school or move from a more rigid classroom into a less formal one, they need time to adjust. "That inner control isn't theirs yet," a second-grade teacher said of one of her classes early in the year. But once that period of adjustment is over, children often surprise visitors with their independence and maturity. When I visited one inner-city elementary school, I found the children talking and writing in any position that pleased them, sprawling flat on the floor or sitting in pairs at the bottom of a long coat closet running the length of the room. As I moved about the room, I was surprised to see that everyone was working. Even the conversations in the coat closet were serious discussions of writing.

Unfortunately, classrooms do not run by rules alone. If they did, schools would have far fewer disciplinary problems than they do today. Respect for rules, and ultimately for other people, comes only when children take pride in their classmates, their room, and their work.

Children who share their opinions, their joys, their embarrassments, and their sorrows have a lot invested in the group. They are proud of each other. When I visited Public School 152 in Brooklyn, I met a group of four third-graders, including a black girl, a black boy, the son of Polish immigrants, and an Irish Catholic boy. The children had been classmates the year before in Linette Moorman's room. For half an hour they reminisced about the things they had written in second grade. Jalil described a humorous story he wrote about the time his mother rescued her two children by leaping into a car as it rolled out of control down a hill. "His mother's a policewoman," Danny added afterward, with an unmistakable ring of pride in his voice.

Eighth-grade teacher Nancie Atwell feels that a change in her own behavior has had a lot to do with a recent change in her students' behavior. "It can be a nasty age, thirteen and fourteen," she reports, "but the nastiness stopped. There's a real sense of cohesiveness, and part of that is my own role in the classroom. I don't have to stand in front of the classroom and when somebody gets out of line use sarcasm to bring them back in, because I'm moving. I'm *everywhere* in that classroom. I've got a little dinky chair from the primary room, and I'm *covering* that classroom. So my conversations with them are quiet and one to one, or just in a small group talking. I feel that by moving, I'm drawing them in. I'm making it a group by the way that I'm moving."

Physical things, like arrangements of desks and chairs, do set the tone in a classroom. In one first-grade classroom, I found the children, just in from recess, quietly seated at their desks in rows all facing in one direction. Some of the children had their heads down. Taped to each desk was the occupant's name card, neatly printed in a teacher's handwriting. A wide gulf of carpet separated the children from the teacher's desk and the blackboard at the front of the room. On one side of the room, a bookcase held a few textbooks. The wall above was sparsely decorated with four or five mimeographed clowns that the children had colored in.

In Ellen Blackburn's first-grade classroom, the scene is quite different. Her classroom has the feel of an artist's studio, without easels or canvases, or a playground, without slide or swings. It is a kind of educational funhouse, broken up into contained areas that dispel the institutional air that fills most classrooms. You get the feeling that you never know what you'll encounter around the corner: a large cage housing a litter of guinea pigs, a bathtub filled with pillows, a full-length mirror, a handmade display case full of the children's own books. The walls are lined with several hundred books as well as records, tapes, and the children's original artwork.

After recess, the children talk to each other and the teacher as they filter into the room. A board at the back of the room assigns the children to the different tables in the room at different times of the day. So they all know where to go, whether to the listening, reading, writing, math, or science area. There is no teacher's desk as the focal point of the room. Blackburn generally sits at a kidney-shaped table with a small group of children or moves around the room.

> *Ellen Blackburn's room says, "People learn here, including the teacher."*

The room is as much the children's as it is the teacher's. A sign on the door, lettered and spelled by a child, reminds people not to run in the school: "KLEP KLPE THU RNING UTSD" (Keep, Keep the Running Outside). Blackburn has never asked the children to put up signs—they just appear. The children are all familiar with the classroom routines. When it is time for reading aloud, they put away their work and head for the rug at the front of the room, as if called by some silent signal. In many ways, the children make the classroom work. They are responsible for a number of duties: taking lunch and milk counts, feeding animals, and cleaning up. A second board at the back of the room tells the children who's assigned to the various tasks each day. On the day I visited, a little boy appeared at my elbow with a clipboard and asked whether I wanted to have milk at snacktime. Then he hustled off, as businesslike and self-important as a maître d'. Another little boy was showing off the purple cabbage he had brought for the guinea pigs.

Perhaps most important of all, children behave because they have an emotional and intellectual investment in their own work. It interests them. Misbehaving prevents them from attending to that work.

When children are first given choices, they often do make too much noise. But the noise ceases to be a problem because the three children who are bothered can successfully remind the noisemakers that they aren't abiding by the rules and are affecting other people's work. These children are negotiating all the time, and they are used to solving these kinds of problems, without the immediate direction of the teacher. Teachers in these rooms often say something like "Well, that didn't work. What's another way to do it?" "Oh, there's too much noise here this morning," a teacher might tell a group of children. "What seems to be causing the problem?" The children respond, and the teacher asks another question, "Well, how can we solve that one?" It's not just her problem, it's theirs because they can't do the work she assumes they want to do. You see, if it's her work, then the noise bothers her, but if it's the children's work, the noise bothers them. In short, whose space is it? It's ours, not mine.

As any parent or teacher knows, nevertheless, even the best-laid guidelines and strategies are subject to sabotage. In school, the sabotage usually comes from the rear of the room, where troublemakers tend to migrate. But for these children, writing offers more than a chance to take responsibility for their own work, more than an engrossing task. Writing gives them a way to get one of the things they crave most: attention.

Most behavior problems are problems of self-worth. I don't know where I fit with the teacher or with other children in the class. Writing, though abstract, is more concrete than reading because of the product that the child comes up with. It is concrete evidence that I know and that I am. When children can talk to each other as they compose, when they can hear and read each other's writing, they have both oral and visible evidence of what each knows.

The wonderful thing about writing is that it is the poor man's instant replay. A child can go over the same sentence, the same story, the same pictures again and again. A book published in November can be replayed in January and again

in March and again in May. The fact that Gregory knows
something about robots in November is up for examination
and affirmation by the class from November through June.
Furthermore, there on the sign-out card for the book is a list
of the names of children who have checked out Gregory's
book on robots from November through June. Outside of
school, Gregory can continue to read his book and get re-
sponses from others on the bus, in his own home, or at his
relatives' house during holidays.

Teachers can usually spot the class troublemakers during the
first week of school. Linette Moorman describes a typical example: "He was boisterous, he was unruly, he was loud. No proper
classroom behavior. He was walking around pounding on other
children. He was taking people's things away—anything he could
take—literally stealing things. And when I looked at him I said,
'He's going to be a tough one.' "

Along with the rest of the class, the boy started writing right
away. His first piece was so jumbled, Moorman couldn't decipher
it. But he read it to her and said, "This isn't very much."

"That's all right," she said. "We can always make it longer."
Together, they did. Later that day, the boy came to her and said,
"You said we were going to write stories and make books. . . .
Can I make a book about myself?" A month later he had rewrit-
ten three or four pieces and displayed them on the bulletin board.
"He wants to make corrections," Moorman reports, "and he
wants to put them up on this board. It's very important that his
work goes on the board. And he has really turned around."

As is often the case for such children, this student's best
days were the days when the class wrote. In fact, Moorman has
learned to use writing as a kind of first aid on the other days.
When restless children come to her and say, "I can't do the work
on the board," or "I don't want to do the work on the pages," she
says, "Well, maybe you would like to work in your journal and
then later you could go back to this." "And then we'll take their
journals out for a while," she explains. "But they're not up and all
over the room sticking pencils in other children, which is the
behavior this boy would be exhibiting."

Moorman is convinced. On a tight schedule, she is able to incorporate writing only three days a week. On those three days, she has noticed, the disruptive children behave better than they do on other days. She now tries to make sure that the children who are most disruptive during the first days of school are among the first to publish their writing for the whole class. Since she has changed her approach to teaching writing during the last few years, she has seen a dramatic drop in the number of children she must refer to guidance for behavior problems. The year I visited her class, she hadn't had to refer one child. A guidance counselor in another inner-city school has noticed the same phenomenon in classrooms where writing instruction has changed recently. "That's my guidance counselor down there," he says, pointing to a classroom where students and teachers write and discuss their writing.

CHAPTEr 6
A Writing Apprenticeship

A student teacher, struggling to do some writing for a college course, confided to a veteran teacher that she felt guilty about teaching writing when clearly she had such difficulty in doing it herself. The older teacher was reassuring: "Oh, don't worry about that!" she said. "I teach creative writing all the time, and I've never done it myself."

Writing is a craft. Beginners learn the craft in a kind of apprenticeship, practicing it under the guidance of an experienced writer. Unfortunately, most teachers are not experienced writers.

The veteran teacher's attitude seems bizarre on the surface. Imagine saying, "Oh, don't worry. I teach piano lessons all the time, and I've never played myself." But the veteran teacher, no doubt, never had reason to believe that *her* teachers had been writers either. Her attitude makes sense in the context of some of society's attitudes about writing. For writing is seen less as a craft than as a set of facts to be learned: correct spellings, rules for punctuating sentences, vocabulary words, grammatical terms, and even formulas for constructing essays, like the "five-paragraph theme" held up as a model in many junior- and senior-high classes.

The veteran teacher who taught writing but did not write had on her classroom wall a large poster with this message in big black letters: A PARAGRAPH SHOULD LOOK LIKE THIS. The diagram below outlined the prescribed formula: generalization, specific, specific, specific, specific, generalization. Although this poster implies that all good paragraphs are alike, a quick look at any published writing will reveal the fallacy of such an idea. Professional writers do not consistently construct their paragraphs in one way; nor do they think of paragraphs in terms of a formula. The case of the paragraph formula is just one example of the discrepancy between what good writers do and what schools teach children to do when they write. That gap can and should be closed.

On their own level, children can do many of the things that professional writers do. On the other hand, professional writers couldn't even accomplish many of the things our schools have asked children to do for years. When children feel secure in their own knowledge and in their classroom routines, they are ready to be challenged. But those challenges must be reasonable and worthwhile. Teachers who understand how successful writers work are better equipped to challenge children in appropriate ways. As a result children write better, learn more, and feel less anxious about writing.

The Conflict of Creativity

Poet Maxine Kumin's study is narrow, plain, and businesslike. She points out that there's not much of a view from the one window and that it's probably a good thing there isn't. Her portable electric typewriter, the kind many college students use, faces the wall anyway. But then Kumin opens a door across from the desk and reveals a secret room. The room is all eaves and carpet. North light from the window silhouettes a day bed. It is the perfect place to lie with one of the books lined up on shelves in the other room, a place in which to let the imagination wander. In a way, those two rooms represent two forces at work in Kumin's method-of writing: discipline and creativity.

When Kumin gets an idea she heads for her typewriter. Soon the page becomes crowded with words—no capital letters, no punctuation, and no spaces between the lines. "I just follow every digressive thought," she says. "Get it all down, no matter how bizarre it may seem: fragments, complete sentences, ideas, images, even rhyming sounds. I might do that at two or three different sittings before I begin to see the shape of the poem."

These early sessions provide Kumin with her raw material. "It's hard to explain what happens, but I just don't want it to sound mystical at all," she says. "It isn't mystical in my understanding of it. You suspend judgment. You try not to censor what you're doing until you have enough material in front of you so that you have something to work with." Even then, much of the material gets thrown away. It goes into "a big, manila folder that's all dog-eared and yellow and ancient, and there it lies."

Time helps Kumin see her work anew. "It's cooled down to room temperature," she says, and she can decide what to retrieve from the folder. "Then a structure organically begins to work. Maybe you begin to see a stanzaic pattern, and once you've got a stanzaic pattern you can impose that rule on the rest of the poem. That's often an enabling agent that makes it possible to force the rest of the poem."

Depending on how elusive a particular poem is, Kumin goes through a series of drafts, looking for the insight hidden there. The insight often stems from a connection between seemingly dissimilar things, such as the King Tut exhibit at a museum and Pearl Harbor Day. Kumin calls that connection the *fulcrum* of the poem, "the point of the poem where it becomes intellectually exciting." Once she has reached that point, she begins to refine her wording.

Years of trial and error have led Kumin to the process that she now goes through when she writes. She summarizes the order in which she tackles the various elements of writing: "Content and organization certainly come first and then some of the refinements of the stanza pattern. I'm constantly tinkering with line breaks, and if it's a poem with a rhyme scheme, I'm constantly tinkering with that. In the final draft, I begin to focus on punctuation."

The process that Kumin has developed shows a natural balance between the two forces that drive and control intellectual activity. Like her study and her secret room, the two forces are different, yet connected. In *Mind and Nature,* Gregory Bateson speaks of rigor and imagination as "the two great contraries of mental process, either of which by itself is lethal. Rigor alone is paralytic death, but imagination alone is insanity."

For years our school systems have killed writing and the desire to write by applying rigor and imagination separately. When rigor is overemphasized, anxious teachers pump students full of rules and forewarnings in an effort to prevent errors. These teachers use formulas as a kind of insurance policy against incoherence. All that insurance makes students nervous—or overly confident. Some, convinced that they could never avoid all the possible pitfalls, give up. Others master the rules and formulas and are convinced that they now know how to write. In neither case have the students had the experience of finding their own meaning in raw material and figuring out the form that best fits that meaning, which, as Kumin puts it, "organically begins to work." Because they have never been encouraged to try it, many students would never dream of putting down uncensored thoughts in search of meaning, surprises, self-discoveries, or their own voices. They're so busy looking over their shoulders at one reader, the teacher, that they can't see where they're going.

Other educators err in the other direction. Anxious to encourage creativity, they ask students to let themselves go when they write. But these teachers fail to balance imagination with the discipline of revising for accuracy, correctness, and coherence. Concern for readers is considered a hindrance. One such teacher wrote in an educational journal: "Children should not be held back by pressure to spell and punctuate correctly or to rewrite several times before submitting their writings for appraisal. I believe this traditional 'polish' technique is obsolescent and debilitating." But students who do not learn to rewrite and polish their work on final drafts experience only the first half of the process that Maxine Kumin goes through. Instead of writing for an audience of one hawk-eyed proofreader, these students are writing for no one. Writing becomes a one-way street, with no turning back even to glance at the reader.

In some classrooms, the two polar approaches exist simultaneously. These teachers have a double standard when it comes to writing. They believe that rigor is necessary only in certain "objective" types of writing, such as reports, whereas imagination is required only in the realm of "creative writing." This distinction is a false one. Contrary to what many people believe, all writing is creative. Whether producing a technical procedures manual or a novel, a writer brings forth words where there were none before.

The raw material is different, but the process remains the same in a number of ways. Technical writers, like poets, set up problems and solve them, entertain ideas and choose from among them. As Maxine Kumin collects all the images and details she can from her memory or a dream, a technical writer collects facts and instructions from an interview with an expert or from a highly technical document. Both writers maintain a visual image in mind as they work, although one may envision a dream while the other pictures a computer screen. Both poet and technical writer eliminate unnecessary material and choose the most appropriate form of presentation. As the poet tries to determine where one line ends and another begins in a stanza, the technical writer struggles to decide where one step ends and another begins in a set of directions.

In recent years, a growing number of educators have been questioning the prevailing methods of teaching writing. One of these challengers is Donald M. Murray. A Pulitzer Prize–winning author, Murray began teaching writing in the early 1960s. After reflecting on his own experience as a student, he realized that formal writing instruction had not helped him very much. His best memories were of the times when he and the assistant city editor at the *Boston Herald* worked "one on one with a bottle of whiskey."

When Murray considered the approaches to teaching writing in use at the time when he began to teach, he concluded that "no one was looking at writing from a writer's point of view." In 1968, Murray's book *A Writer Teaches Writing* presented high-school teachers with a new approach. Drawing on his own experience and the comments of many other professional writers, he offers teachers a model of a process that writing students can try for themselves. Murray's book became part of a movement to change writing instruction, ultimately at all grade levels. The new focus on writing as a process makes sense in the context of a broader view of education.

> *Leading psychologists and educators in a number of fields— including math, science, social studies, and, to some degree, reading—agree that it is particularly important for children to learn how to learn. The knowledge explosion makes it virtually impossible for people to keep up with any given field. Instead of cramming children with facts they may not need, the schools must help children learn to learn, to find the information they need and to apply it.*

When children become conscious of the process by which they write, they begin to notice how they learned to do something. But the focus on process is also practical. It only makes sense to look at writing from a writer's point of view. Once teachers and children pay attention to the steps they go through, they discover there is no one set procedure that works for every person or every piece of writing. The process varies widely even for the individual writer. Although Maxine Kumin is able to give a general outline of her work habits, every poem is different. Perhaps six of the hundreds of poems she has written in her lifetime have come to her virtually intact in one draft. They were published unchanged. The vast majority of her poems have gone through a number of revisions, however, and the most obstinate have required as many as thirty drafts. The length of time that lapses from conception to completion of a single poem varies from several years to a few moments.

Over the years, Donald Murray has collected twenty-four

three-inch-thick, loose-leaf notebooks full of some eight thousand quotations in which writers talk about their craft. The notebooks show how much the writing process varies from writer to writer. Some recommend writing in the morning, even, according to poet W. H. Auden, "before washing"; others, like Jerzy Kosinski, choose to write anytime and any place that the urge strikes, in an airplane or on a train. More striking than the differences among the writers, however, are the similarities. A vast majority speak of a process of gathering material, planning, writing, revising, and editing.

For years our schoolchildren have relied on one draft or, if required, produced a second draft purely for cosmetic reasons. At the very least, Murray's notebooks reveal that this technique is highly atypical among expert writers. The few professional writers who do claim to be able to write with virtually no revision suggest that this state of grace is reached only after years of experience in writing. Over and over again, the writers in Murray's notebooks stress that quantity yields quality. Like Kumin, they need to produce a volume of material from which to select the good stuff. In his book *Night Hurdling,* poet and novelist James Dickey reports, "For every word I keep, I throw away one hundred. . . . I work like a gold-miner refining low-grade ore: a lot of muck and dirt with a very little gold in it. . . ."

Compelled to complete a piece of writing in one draft and urged to avoid errors at all stages, students often try to compose and edit simultaneously, a highly inefficient way to write. Many waste their time polishing sentences and paragraphs that are later revised or deleted. And when writers worry about grammar while they're still finding words for their thoughts, both the thoughts and the grammar may suffer. Professional writers often speak of the different states of mind required by these two different stages of the process, which represent the opposing forces of imagination and rigor, of writer and inner reader. In *Zen and the Art of Writing,* Ray Bradbury writes, "The history of each story should read almost like a weather report: hot today, cool tomorrow. This afternoon, burn down the house. Tomorrow, pour cold, critical water on the coals." As many students have found, it is difficult to burn and douse at the same time.

The creative process remains remarkably similar not just

among writers, from poet to technical writer, but also across disciplines, from poet to painter to chemist. Medical researcher Leland C. Clark, Jr., is well known for his discoveries and inventions, which have included the artificial heart-lung machine and artificial blood. Clark estimates that 98 percent of his research leads turn out to be dead ends. But, like writers, he courts surprises. Doing research, he says, "is like drilling for oil without a very good map. But you usually find other things along the way. You may not find oil, but you find that it's a good place to grow soybeans."

Everyone's an Author

Teachers can help children discover some of the universal elements of the creative process so that they, too, can find oil as well as places to grow soybeans. In fact, a behind-the-scenes look at the things professionals do when they write helps children as much as it helps teachers. The idea that small children can learn from exposure to a professional model, however, is foreign to many adults, even researchers.

> *At Atkinson we weren't expecting children to parallel professionals in the way they went about writing. The melding came about at the point when the children really began to revise. I wasn't looking for that at the outset. "Writing is writing," I say now. In the biological sciences, by looking at simple forms of life such as the amoeba, you get an idea of what life is like in more complex forms. Thus, by listening to six-year-olds who externalize so much of the writing process, you can hear the basic building blocks of composing that later become the substance of inner language and thought.*

When they see the natural parallels between their own work and that of professionals and teachers, children realize that they can learn from adult writers. Cassie explains how the connections are made in her Australian classroom: "We treat everyone as an author in our room. Children are authors, Miss Parry is an author, other kids are authors, and other people are authors. So what we do is study how all these authors write. Sometimes we put a person's draft on a piece of paper. Sometimes Miss Parry writes a draft. We all help to make it better. . . . Or sometimes we actually ask an author to come for an interview. Ted Greenwood came and Michael Dugin and Lorraine Wilson. We could talk to them, author to author. It's good. I remember lots of things they said because I did the same things in my drafts."

An eighth-grade teacher chooses to write with her class because "they watch you struggle with it. They watch you cut your paper up. They watch you cross out. They see me make mistakes. They see me go to the dictionary. If you don't write, you don't do those things." Any adult who writes can demonstrate the same process. A fourth-grade teacher happened to go into her principal's office when he was working on a management plan for the school district. When she found him cutting up paper and taping it back together again, she promptly invited him into her classroom to show the children his work. They immediately responded with questions. "How did you start?" they asked. "What was your focus?"

Teachers write in class not to impress children with their superior skills, but to show that even adults often have better ideas the second time around. Realistic models of the creative process do much to relieve the anxiety many children feel when they write. If Dr. Seuss writes one thousand pages to produce a sixty-page book, then surely it's all right if a rank beginner in the first grade has to scratch something out. If Ray Bradbury can't write and edit simultaneously, then surely we need not expect fourth-graders to do so, either. And if Pulitzer Prize-winning authors put off concern with punctuation until the final draft, then surely a first-grader who has to labor over the formation of each letter can add information first and put in periods later. That chance to reflect and reconsider, after all, is one of the main advantages of writing.

As much as professional examples help, however, the very best way for children to learn about the creative process is by trying it themselves. Children learn to write as they would learn any craft, by practicing, making decisions, and receiving timely and appropriate criticism.

Time to Practice

The simple act of allowing children to write every day for a good block of time tells them a lot about their teacher's attitude toward writing. It says that writing is something important that takes time to learn. It says that people learn to write by writing, rather than by doing exercises. And it says that if practice doesn't make perfect, it at least makes progress.

> *Children, like writers of any age, need to write daily so they can experience writing when they are not writing. One Monday morning John came running into his first-grade class saying, "My dad and I found a bat in the attic on Saturday, and I couldn't wait to get to school to write about it." John was showing that he wrote on the weekend even though he didn't put a pencil to paper. He could do so because he knew that on Monday he would write and that he could choose to write about that bat if he wanted to. This is an elemental example of writing when not writing. A more sophisticated example occurs when children entertain options for revision outside of school.*

A fourth-grader named Amy told one of the Atkinson researchers how she came up with a new opening for her report on the red fox. "I was lying in bed and I couldn't think of another draft," she said. "So I just lay in bed, and it was late at night. My sister came home, and her door doesn't have a knob. The light shone through the crack. So I thought of it—the idea—and I kept it in my head, and when I came to school, I wrote it. It was perfect, because in bed I thought how to put it together. I'd thought that the fox opens his eyes just a slit because when Linda opened her bedroom door, my cat opened her eyes just a slit." Amy translated her idea into these opening lines: "A beam of light shown through the crack in the fox's den. The red fox opened his eyes just a slit and looked around his den. . . ."

> *Children need to write daily in order to keep in touch with the pieces they are already writing, as well as to gain experience*

in retrieving what they know. If children write daily, they also have more time to discuss their work with the teacher. A teacher who teaches writing twice a week instead of every day has 60 percent less time to listen to individual children in the midst of their drafts.

At minimum, children should probably have the chance to write four days a week. When a group that has been writing for a long time misses a couple of days, it's not a major problem. They're thinking about their work anyway. They'll probably write at home or at lunch, even if the teacher doesn't provide time. You simply can't stop them. Children who write regularly often complain when their teacher misses one day. On the other hand, children who write only once a week will always complain about the one day. They simply aren't in shape for writing.

Freedom to Choose

Teachers make another powerful statement about their attitudes toward writing and learning when they give children control of their own work. These teachers believe that writing involves a series of decisions and that children are capable of making those decisions. Sometimes their decisions are good, and sometimes they're bad; sometimes the children need advice, and sometimes they don't. But they have the chance to learn from every decision they make.

Allowing children to choose their own topics not only implies that every child is an expert; it also produces good topics. In most classrooms where children are given free choice, they are allowed to choose 80 to 90 percent of their own topics. The topics they choose to write on are as diverse as the children themselves. In place of contrived topics like "Our Trip to the Apple Orchard," they write about their own experiences with pet pigs, weddings, divorces, deaths, and births. In place of artificial fantasies— "Imagine you are an armchair"—they write their own, about a mouse named Suzy who traveled with Ronald Reagan, a bunch of furry little elves called "snoozles," or the laziest man in the world. Or they catalogue all they know, or can find out, about glaciers, chemicals, beavers, machines, or "things that lay eggs." In short, they often choose better topics than teachers assign.

At the same time, children begin to discover what makes a good topic, from their own point of view, as well as from their readers'. Both teachers and children soon discover that writers write best on topics they really care about. Thus, free topics allow children to do their best work. Among the many topics a child chooses during a year, a few are special. These are topics that, for one reason or another, really excite the writer. An excited writer is not only motivated, but also receptive to new ideas and techniques. The Atkinson data showed that children working on topics of special interest often acquired several new concepts in one burst. Those topics offer teachers a rare opportunity to broaden children's knowledge, develop their skills, and expand their repertoire of forms and techniques.

A child writing on a hot topic is open to trying new genres because the voice is naturally strong. Having written a good narrative, writers are ready to try a piece of exposition based on the same story. If I've just written what happened to my next-door neighbor's food budget because of the new costs of electricity on completion of a nuclear power plant, and someone asks me, "What do you think about that?" I can let fly with some good exposition on what I think needs to be done to correct the problem. It would be much easier to teach exposition, or even poetry, that way.

These topics are hard to come by. Donald Graves estimates that at any given time, only about one out of five children is likely to be on such a topic in a classroom where children have free choice. In a room where everyone writes on the same assignment, the odds are slim indeed. It's difficult to find such a topic for someone else, let alone a whole room full of someone elses. An occasional assigned topic, like a blind date, is bound to be a new experience and a challenge. A steady stream of assigned topics, however, is more like an arranged marriage.

Susan Stires, a special-education teacher in Boothbay Harbor, discovered how difficult it would be to guess at the best topics for her students. "One of my favorite ones was written by a boy who was really excited about his sister's pregnancy," she recalls. "He just had so many thoughts about it. . . . Now who would ever have assigned him 'Your Sister's Pregnancy'?" Stires has also found that some of the children's own topics are more demanding than the standard assignment. Another one of her students found a topic when he happened to read his mother's resume. He wrote down a series of questions an employer who had received the resume might ask in an interview. The boy's mother responded in writing. "I was what I considered to be imaginative in my more traditional writing-teacher role," Stires says. "But never in my wildest dreams would I have been clever enough to think of a topic like that."

After selecting a topic and writing a draft, children continue to make their own decisions on revision, editing, and publishing, with guidance from both the teacher and classmates. Thus, they experience the essence of the creative process. Some teachers believe they are giving students this experience when they require revision on a set schedule: Tuesday, write a first draft; Wednesday, revise; Thursday, submit the final draft. But in reality, the students in these classrooms miss out on the important process of making decisions. And their writing invariably suffers. Some papers may need no revisions, and others may need several. It is just as hard to apply one timetable to twenty-five papers as it is to fit one assignment to twenty-five hearts and minds.

Appropriate Responses

Through the timing, content, and tone of their responses to children's writing, teachers have a profound effect on their students' concepts of good writing and the process that produces it. If a teacher addresses all issues from content to commas in one draft, children may feel overwhelmed. Every piece of writing is different, of course, but a teacher with a clear set of priorities in mind can help students sort out the different tasks they face.

*The teachers' first priority is helping the writers to teach
them about the subject. Thus children may hear their own
voices and become acquainted with what they know and how
they know it. Until there is information, there is nothing to
write about. That's the beginning. In the first response to a
draft, therefore, a teacher draws out what the writer knows,
often orally, so the writer can fill in any missing information
on the page. When there's a fair amount of information to
work with, the teacher can consider focus, helping the writer
to discover the one thing that the piece is about. Then unnecessary material can be deleted. Finally, the writer can do
the fine tuning, adding a few more facts or sharpening the
wording. When the information is right, the thoughts are laid
logically end to end, and the language is precise, it is time to
double-check punctuation, spelling, and grammar.*

Some teachers formalize this process by making distinctions
between different types of conferences. Each piece goes through
a content conference, an organization conference, and an editing
conference prior to publication. Whether they do it formally or
informally, teachers who focus first on the larger questions of
content and organization give children the message that it doesn't
make sense to worry about commas until the content is solid. The
children, in turn, learn to attend to the different aspects of a piece
of writing in an appropriate order. When a fifth-grader took home
a rough draft to share with her parents, she found that her
mother's only concern was the misspelled words. But the little
girl defended her writing methods. "Well, Mother," she said in a
firm voice, verging on testiness, "don't worry about the spelling.
I'll take care of that later!"

While providing a model for writing procedures, both the
timing and content of a teacher's comments also reveal a set of
standards for judging writing. When teachers make mechanics
their sole concern or give content and mechanics the same
weight, their students adopt a warped set of standards. Right
before the teachers at Boothbay Harbor changed their approach
to writing instruction, a survey of their students revealed the
standards their students had absorbed as if by osmosis. One of

the questions in the survey was "How does your teacher know which pieces of writing are the good ones?" The students said things like "She looks at margins." "He has a book with the right answers in it." "She looks at your spelling." "If your cursive is good, she loves it." "If it's neat, it's good."

Something has gone awry when children list margins, penmanship, and spelling as the prime criteria by which to judge a piece of writing. Writers observe the conventions of grammar, punctuation, and spelling in order to make their meaning clear, whether the subject is a fictitious character or a species of amoeba. Ambiguities and inaccurate wording can change a writer's meaning. Misspellings, grammatical errors, and punctuation problems can distract readers and, in extreme cases, may keep an otherwise strong piece of writing from being read at all. Nevertheless, the purpose of writing is always to convey information to someone, and the quality of that message is naturally a writer's first—not only, but first—concern. Even perfect mechanics can do little for a pointless piece of writing. As one junior-high teacher reminds her students, "If you polish garbage, it's still garbage."

As the teachers at Boothbay wrote, read, and talked together, their own standards changed. Their responses to students' work naturally reflected that change. At the end of a year, the teachers surveyed their students a second time. "How does your teacher know which pieces of writing are the good ones?" they asked again. This time the answers were different. The students said things like "I can tell if she laughs." "I can tell if he looks interested." "She doesn't decide—I do." "She looks for how much time I've put in." "She looks for information." "She looks for if it's clear." "She looks at your style." "She looks at your leads and conclusions."

Even without surveys, children reveal their own grasp of writing standards and concepts whenever they question each other about their work. For example, first-graders in many classrooms show that they understand the concept of focus in writing better than a large number of entering college freshmen. "What is the one thing it's about?" a child will ask after reading a piece that seems to have strayed in different directions "Well, you told us your story was about your grandmother and grandfather," one first-grader reminded another, "but the title just has grandmother."

Taking Charge

More than anything else, it is the tone of a teacher's response that bolsters or deflates students' opinions of their own abilities as writers. By pointing out errors too soon, too often, and with too much moral fervor, teachers convince many students they'll never be able to write or do anything right. A self-confident student, on the other hand, is not only ready to write but ready to be challenged. Teachers who understand the creative process accept mistakes as a natural part of learning and as a guide to what a child knows and needs to learn. They respond with tact, keeping errors in perspective and handling them at an appropriate time.

On the first day of school, a Manchester, New Hampshire, teacher named Kathy Diers asked her pre-first-grade transition students to write down the sounds they heard in the word *teakettle*. The responses ranged from D to TKL. As the children started to write from that day on, inventing their own spelling as best they could, Diers would underline every letter in the child's word that matched the conventional spelling. She wrote the conventional-spelling translation in small letters at the bottom of the page, mainly for her own information. Without being told that they were wrong at any point, the children steadily progressed toward conventional spelling. By the end of the year, the child who had written *tkl,* was spelling most words accurately, including *Christina, butterfly,* and *dancing.* Even children who had heard only a *d* or *c* on the first day were highly amused when they looked back through their folders at the end of the year, for they, too, were getting more and more of the letters right in the words they wrote.

Instead of urging her students to eliminate the things they did wrong, Diers had focused on encouraging them to expand on the things they did right. She underlined the right letters where others would have underlined the wrong ones. In turn, the children had a sense of constantly learning, rather than constantly failing. When children like those have positive attitudes toward their own abilities and have a lot invested in work that they have chosen to do, they are ready to be challenged.

If a child knows a lot about a subject and cares about it, I can raise my expectations. If a child knows nothing about the subject and wants to abandon the piece of writing, it is harder to raise standards.

Teachers can provide a model through their own high expectations of themselves, both in their teaching and their writing. When sharing their own work, teachers can respond to new information or ideas by saying: "I didn't know that. I'll have to go to work on that again, won't I?" And they can raise similar questions with their students' work: "There must be another way to look at this. Think for a minute and then we'll talk about other ways to work with that problem." Such a stance encourages experimentation and risk taking but, above all, rethinking. Essential to a sense of high standards is the desire to resee, rethink, rework.

Finally, teachers turn over some responsibility for setting standards to the children themselves. Higher standards are also connected with the careful development of the child's ability to accept and exercise responsibility. Teachers shift responsibility to the child by asking, "How can you solve that problem?" or "Is this your best work?" Then children live up to their own standards as much as the teacher's.

Encouraged to pursue their own interests and free to make their own decisions, children often become active students, willing to take responsibility for their own work and, in part, their own education. At Atkinson, the children's willingness to take this responsibility became apparent when they began to rewrite until they themselves, not just the teacher, were satisfied. When an Australian researcher visited a fourth-grade classroom at Atkinson, she discovered just how vigorous the children's participation in their own education could be. She had walked into the room, when a little girl named Debbie strode purposefully toward her. As the visitor recalls, "She was the first kid who attacked me.

I walked into the room, and she ran over to me and said, 'We're having trouble! We're having trouble! We're having an argument, and we can't decide. Will you give me a conference?' I was so embarrassed. I thought, 'I don't know how to have a conference with her.' But I smiled and went over to the rug with her. Thank God, she talked all the time. I just sat there and nodded. And then she said, 'Oh, thank you, thank you, now I know what I'm going to do.' And she left, and I thought, 'Phew! I made it.' "

At that point, Debbie knew that she needed to talk more than she needed to hear advice, and she knew that she had ultimate control over her work. Soft-spoken and self-possessed in an interview with researcher Lucy Calkins at the end of the year, Debbie explained what that control meant to her. Writing was fun, she said, "because you can write on whatever you want." Then she pulled down the corners of her mouth and spoke in a tone as flat as the voice found in papers on insipid assigned topics. "It's not like you write on 'The Day I Came to School'—you have to write about that."

Then Debbie's voice grew gentle, as if she were counseling the researcher. "Whatever you *want* to write about, you can write about. It's up to you. If you like the way it is, then you leave it, and nobody else can tell you to change it. Like, your mother can go, 'Go up to bed right now!' " Debbie returned to her soothing tone. "But you don't have to change that story right this minute. And if you don't want to, you don't have to." She paused. "It's like you're the mother of the story."

Many other children have grown to treat their work as a kind of offspring, worthy of devotion and demanding attention. Halfway around the world in an Australian classroom, a little boy expressed the same sentiment in different words when he said, "In writing, you're the boss of the piece." Even children who have been labeled failures by the school system no longer behave like failures when they start to feel capable and as committed to their work as a parent or a boss. In 1981, several students in Susan Stires's resource room for learning-disabled children at Boothbay Harbor came up with the idea of starting a school newspaper. They solicited submissions, made selections, arranged for publication, and proofread the articles. Now the paper is an institution at the school. It still comes out every quarter and publishes work written by students and teachers in all grades from kindergarten through junior high.

Teachers from schools around the globe can cite similar examples. And yet, perhaps the best examples come from parents who have seen their children's willingness to take charge of their own work, their own education, outside of school. Transition teacher Kathy Diers had already been impressed with her students' progress, when she burned the cauliflower watching her son decide it was time he started reading. It was not so much his ability to start reading that had thrilled her as his faith in his own ability to attempt it, a faith she believed would carry him through many other challenges beyond learning to read.

CHAPTEr 7
The Rewards
of Writing

One night, Maxine Kumin had a dream about her father, who had been dead for fourteen years. He was coming out of a basement necktie shop, wearing a wild tie with blue lightning bolts outlined in yellow. Like most dreams, it was mysterious, even bizarre. Yet, it was hardly more bizarre than the penchant her father had had for crazy ties when he was alive.

The dream fascinated Kumin, and because she is a poet, she is in the habit of dwelling on things that fascinate her. She does most of her dwelling at the typewriter. As usual, this time she began by pouring out every image, idea, and snippet that came to mind on the subject—or even off the subject. After several sittings, a poem began to take shape. There was something there to be discovered, but she didn't know quite what. She described the dream in the poem and then began to ask herself questions: Why this dream? Why now?

Then it came to her. Her father had been a man who "hid out in the foreign bargain basements of his feelings." That one line seemed to make sense of the dream. It brought everything together—the dream neckties, the real-life neckties, and the significance of both. The neckties said something about her father's relationship with his family, with his own feelings. Once Kumin had that line, the rest quickly fell into place. The poem, which follows, was published in a collection of her work called *Our Ground Time Here Will Be Brief.*

My Father's Neckties

Last night my color-blind chainsmoking father
who has been dead for fourteen years
stepped out of a basement tie shop
downtown and did not recognize me.

The number he was wearing was as terrible
as any from my childhood, a time of
ugly ties and acrimony: six or seven
blue lightning bolts outlined in yellow.

Although this was my home town it was tacky
and unfamiliar, it was Rabat or Gibraltar
Daddy smoking his habitual
square-in-the-mouth cigarette and coughing
ashes down the lightning jags. He was
my age exactly, it was wordless, a window
opening on an interior we both knew
where we had loved each other, keeping it quiet.

Why do I wait years and years to dream this outcome?
My brothers, in whose dreams he must as surely
turn up wearing rep ties or polka dots clumsily
knotted, do not speak of their encounters.

When we die, all four of us, in
whatever sequence, the designs
will fall off like face masks
and the rayon ravel from this hazy version
of a man who wore hard colors recklessly
and hid out in the foreign
bargain basements of his feelings.

The poem embodies many of the things good writing can do for writers and readers of all ages. The thought of a man hiding out in the bargain basement of his feelings startles her readers as much as it did Kumin when she wrote it. She surprises herself, finds out something she didn't know she knew, in every poem she writes. She looks for "the image that is startling and yet apt. It should surprise because it is appropriate," she says. Anyone who has read good literature knows the sensation: "Of course, I've always known that, and yet I wasn't quite consciously aware of it." The source of the sensation may be a minute yet precise detail, or, like the bargain-basement metaphor, it may contain in one kernel the meaning of a whole piece of writing. It is that moment of simultaneous surprise and recognition that gratifies both writer and reader. Kumin's revelation applies first of all to her own father, but it can also illuminate other relationships for her readers.

Kumin's voice adds to the appeal of the poem. Although the topic is personal and emotional, the poem speaks in a voice that is honest, tough, and tinged with humor. As always, the voice is reflected in the writer's choice of words. For example, Kumin calls a necktie a "number," a bargain-basement word with both humor and a hard edge to it.

In this poem, like most of her work, writing has been a way of thinking and listening to her own voice. In the process, she also listens to the responses of a few respected readers. Ultimately, she gains recognition and responses from a wider audience through publication.

Many parents approve of a renewed emphasis on writing in school for practical reasons. They know that basic writing skills will be needed for success in college and on the job. Because they have not seen what children—and writing—can do, however, parents may be unaware that their children can, like Maxine Kumin, find many deeper rewards in writing.

Even for six-year-olds, writing also has its rewards for today. First, the marks on the paper establish their being. The marks say, "I am." Children also use the writing to relive things that are important to them, like going on a trip, or bringing home a new puppy, or getting a cut and going to the doctor's. They may use the writing to come to terms with something that hurts—a father's absence or a grand-mother's death. In the "All About" books, children attempt to show all they know about a particular subject, such as weapons, prehistoric animals, Star Wars, *or fish. Readers reaffirm the writer's experiences, knowledge, and thoughts. But that's just the beginning.*

Finding a Voice

If a piece of paper with writing on it is found on the floor in Judi Hilliker's kindergarten classroom, the children can usually identify it immediately. In her room, where children write freely, each child's work is distinctive. The drawings, the scribbles, the letters, and the words all announce who the author is. When Hilliker visits the first grade, she can still identify her students by the titles of their published books. Even on a printed cover, the children's choice of topic or words is often as distinctive as their handwriting.

The students in Hilliker's room and similar classrooms have each found a voice, in more ways than one. As they listen to one another's stories throughout the year, each child has a special place in the group. Both through their writing and their classroom responsibilities, they all have a voice in the room and the way it works. It is their room as much as the teacher's. But these children are also starting to exercise their own voices as writers.

In another school, the children frequently practice copying sentences from a workbook. While every child in the first grade wrote "People are fun" several times, children in Hilliker's kindergarten were all writing, in their own words, on different topics. "Daniel be's bad n tezs me (Daniel be's bad and teases me)," wrote one child at the start of a classic younger brother's lament. Another five-year-old opened a four-page piece on her grandmother's funeral this way: "I love you nanny, even tho you DID (I love you Nanny, even though you DIED)."

Young children often try to translate speech directly into writing with underlinings, interjections, and words written two lines high. These writers don't yet trust their own voices to show through, so they try to put them in with voice marks. A third-grader at Atkinson, for example, wrote a piece called "I HATE MAKING MY BED!" Her first two lines went like this: "I just hate it. I JUST HATE IT!"

"Daniel be's bad n tezs me" is less grammatically correct than "People are fun." "I love you nanny, even tho you DID" isn't spelled just right. "I HATE MAKING MY BED!" is about a mundane topic. Yet which of these four lines would make you want to keep reading?

It is the voice in each of the children's original opening lines that reaches out and speaks to us, drawing us in. The voices sound honest and heartfelt. The kindergartners promise to speak on real issues of life and death, and they seem to have something to say. The third-grader promises to make even a household chore interesting. In place of genuine feelings, the workbook has children spouting empty sentiments.

The children in Judi Hilliker's class sound like themselves. They haven't yet been trained not to. Hilliker wants her students to write in their own voices, to say what they want to say in the way that they want to say it. Thus, she allows them to write for their own reasons and to choose their own topics. Most important, they choose their own words.

Debbie, the little girl who feels like the mother of her stories, told an Atkinson researcher: "If you go and let somebody else take over your story, it won't be yours. It'll be somebody else's own words and everything. If they want to write about it, they can go write about it in their own words, not go and put it in my story."

For small children, the freedom to choose their own words means the freedom to use invented spelling. In Hilliker's room, children are encouraged to spell as best they can. They choose their own words and make valiant attempts at spelling them. As a result, one little boy was able to label his picture of the "HIEEDLBrG KASL" (Heidelberg Castle). A kindergartner named Sam at another school wrote this sentence: "The daune wadpkr eats upsad dawn." (The downy woodpecker eats upside down.) If he had been restricted to using words he could spell correctly, he could not have said what he wanted to say at all. Even an older child might have had to replace *downy woodpecker* with the safe and spellable word *bird,* and the sentence would not have said the same thing. Thus the acceptance of invented spelling not only let the kindergartner speak in his own voice; it allowed him to be true to his meaning and precise in his language.

> *Writers sometimes hear their own voices best when they talk. Teachers can help small children develop their voices by allowing them to talk a lot. They tell each other stories and share their experiences with other children.*

First-grade teacher Ellen Blackburn believes that children develop their writing voices by talking about their drafts. In her class, listeners are allowed to tell their own related stories after a young author has just read a piece of writing aloud. The very idea of giving children such free rein in a discussion would be anathema to most teachers. But Blackburn has found that the process of comparing experiences to find likes and differences spurs a child to search harder for the exact words that will convey the uniqueness of his or her own experience.

When a little boy named Parks wrote about his grandfather's death, he included a line about the tears shed in his household: "My father was crying a lot, so was my mother." After he read his story to a small group of classmates, each child seemed to have a story to tell about seeing people cry. Only then did Parks become more graphic in his description. He said to the group, "My father had a big tear in his eye and it fell out on the woodstove and bursted out like a frying pan." Blackburn immediately called attention to his figure of speech and suggested that he add the line to his book. In trying to convey his own experience, Parks had hit upon an original metaphor unique to his own way of thinking and speaking. Like Maxine Kumin's bargain-basement image, the figure of speech also distilled the essence of his experience into one line, capturing the grief that had enveloped his whole household. Here is the published version of his book about his grandfather's death.

My Papa Is Dead

My Papa died last night 8:00 'cause his heart stopped beating. He was sick with cancer for a long time. The funeral is Saturday. My father was crying a lot, so was my mother. I was, too. My father had a big tear in his eye. It fell onto the woodstove and bursted out like a frying pan. And I was very, very, very, very sad. I miss him.

Amy, another child in Blackburn's class, wrote about playing with her little brother. After discussing a draft with several classmates and her teacher, she, too, made some additions, including the last line. In this light-hearted tale, her voice and tone are quite different from Parks's. Here is the story as it appeared in published form, a story that sounds just like Amy.

Me and David Have Make-Up

I have make-up. I put my eye-shadow on and my lipstick on and my crown I got when I was 3. My eye-shadow is green with sparkles. I was the queen of the world.

My brother puts my lipstick on. He gets it on his nose, on his cheeks, too. He makes a mess. He gets in trouble. When he gets in trouble, sometimes Mom and Dad laugh at him. He really looks funny.

We play dress up sometimes. I dress up like Snow White. My brother dresses up like a dwarf. We try to dress up like a character. When we put the make-up on, the longer we keep it on, the harder it is to take off. We use hot water sometimes.

When we take off the make-up, I am not the queen of the world anymore. Me and David are plain old Amy and David.

Even with free choice of topic, form, and words, children still may not exercise their own voices if they are working hard to write what the teacher wants. Intellectual ventriloquism begins at an early age—by second or third grade—when the child starts writing with the teacher's voice. But teachers who write with their classes, who know what it is to write, are much more sensitive to children's voices.

Joan Tornow, the mother of two young writers, found a teacher who showed respect for each child's voice and point of view. Because Tornow does some writing herself and is interested in the teaching of writing, she has spent a lot of time volunteering and observing in elementary classrooms. She and her husband also held a series of informal gatherings for a group of parents who met to talk about ways of sharing stories and writing with children. At one of these meetings, she described a scene that had impressed her in Jan Roberts's third-grade classroom in Lee, New Hampshire.

Although the children usually chose their own topics, Roberts had asked them all to write about their class trip on a lobster boat. According to Tornow, "One little kid said, 'Is it all right to write an interview with a lobster and pretend I'm a lobster being interviewed?' And the teacher said, 'Oh, what a wonderful original idea!' And some other kid said, 'I really don't want to write about the lobster boat. I just want to write about the dead seal we found on the beach.' And she said, 'That's good.' And everybody wrote a different story. And she went out of her way to say, 'Isn't it wonderful that from the same trip, we have so many different things that people noticed and chose to write about?' "

One piece in particular struck Tornow. It made her realize how far writing instruction had come since her own schooldays. "Stephen wrote about the lobster trip," she recalled, "and he wrote, 'I sat in the seat where Matthew Wilson threw up.' And probably that was something they all feared because as they got on the boat, they heard that this other kid had gotten seasick." The parents gathered in the Tornow living room tittered. "When I was in school," she continued, "if I had to sit in the seat where somebody had thrown up in the last hour, it might have been something that was very interesting to me. But I doubt that I would have written it down because I wouldn't have thought that was what the teacher wanted. You'd say, 'We had a nice time on our trip.' " The parents nodded and laughed aloud, recognizing the familiar sound of an attempt to please the teacher.

Making Discoveries

When children write and talk about their writing, they gain new insights into their own experiences and behavior. Ellen Blackburn reports that her first-graders often learn more about their experiences when classmates question them about their writing. "When you went to camp," one child will ask another, "did you sit around the fire and tell stories? We did."

> *If I describe the world around me and what happens to me, I understand more clearly where the world ends and I begin. In short, I define myself when I try to define the world.*

An Atkinson fourth-grader named Birger discovered that the rest of the world—even the weather—could be insensitive to the individual's feelings of grief. Birger had written a draft of a piece about his cat, Romeo, who had been hit by a car. He was talking about his plans for revision when he said, "I'm trying to make it longer. I think the most will be when I'm walking across the driveway. And I heard sounds—like the vet with the siren—and then I smelled the air. And I remember thinking it wasn't bad air. It was just hard to think that a part of me had just died. The air was so clear and nice."

A very few children as young as the first grade are capable of the kind of sophisticated thinking required to generalize from a particular experience or example. As children get older, they develop the ability to think in the abstract. The ability to revise, in situations where it is allowed or encouraged, is one of the first signs of this maturation. By the third or fourth grade, a number of children are able to draw conclusions from specific incidents when they write.

A little girl named Susie, one of the better writers in a third-grade class at Atkinson learned more about her trip to Canada after she got home. One day as she went through her list of ten potential writing topics, she chose "Camping (Canada and what I saw)." By the time she discussed her ideas with researcher Lucy Calkins, Susie was already narrowing her focus. She asked whether she should talk about wildlife in general or just "deers." Calkins said that was up to her, and Susie began trying out differ-

ent openings for the piece. Each had a different angle. The first
was about Canadian wildlife in general, the second one focused
on the drive to Canada, the third one was about the bears she saw,
and the fourth one began at the moment her father spotted a deer
on the road. At that stage, she hardly knew what her story was
about, let alone what conclusion she might draw from it. But she
chose her fourth opening, and three drafts later she had the following piece:

A Surprise in Canada

My father jammed on the brakes for there at the edge of the
road was a young doe! I could not believe it was really there.
It was eating the tall weeds and bushes. It did not seem
scared at all and went right on eating. And then it started to
walk across the road. It seemed to be walking on air and had
big brown velvety eyes. Then it ate some more weeds and
disappeared into the trees. We just stared and finally drove
off but my father turned around to see if it came back. It
didn't so we headed home. In the front seat I saw the camera
and we didn't even take a picture of it. But I don't think it
was all our fault because I don't see how anybody could
think of anything else.

At the age of eight, Susie was able to choose her own topic,
narrow it down to one important experience, and then find the
significance in it, three processes many college freshman find
difficult. At the end of the piece, she is on the verge of an insight
into picture taking that many adults have missed.

Susie probably would have found no insight at all without the
chance to select her own topic, the freedom to try out different
approaches and drafts, and the opportunity to talk over her work
with an adult willing to listen yet shy about telling her what to do.
Given those opportunities, many children can find the
significance in an event and, like Maxine Kumin, surprise themselves.

When seventh-grade teacher Karen Weinhold was asked
whether she could think of any examples of students who had

learned about themselves or surprised themselves in the process of writing, she replied, "I can't think of any that didn't." At that level, she is able to address the question of meaning directly. By the time they reach the upper grades, most children should be able to generalize from particular experiences. Her writers are old enough to ask, and be asked, "So what? What's the point?" Soon, they start to ask themselves the same questions. When one former student came back to see her recently, he said he wanted to read her a paper he was working on. "I've got a whole page of 'so what's,' " he explained.

Eighth-grade teacher Nancie Atwell has seen the same kind of growth in her students, particularly when they write about personal experiences. "Everybody talks about writing as a mode of learning," she says, "and this may be the most important mode—that self-discovery. It's not 'touch me, and feel me'; it's 'This is how I connect with the world. This is how I connect with this person and this family and this town.' "

Atwell has seen papers in which students become aware of their own mortality, realize the importance of certain relationships, and make many other discoveries. "The boys wrote lots of pieces about so-called bravery—things they had done that were scary," she recalls of one class. "And they were bragging about things like swinging out on a rope over Barrett's Cove, way out over a brick wall. There's only about five feet of water there. If you fall, you'll kill yourself. And these pieces aren't about bravery; they're about fear. What they discover is how scared they were and how they were doing things they were scared to do because they cared so much about what other people thought."

When children write, they not only draw conclusions from their own experiences; they also gain a new perspective on themselves as writers, thinkers, and people. Many of these discoveries are likely to come together when a child is working on a topic of special interest.

The Atkinson fourth-grader named Debbie learned a lot about herself in the process of writing about a tree in her backyard. At the end of the year, she chose that piece as her best. Soft-spoken and self-assured, she explained her feelings about the tree in her year-end interview with researcher Lucy Calkins:

"You know how sometimes dogs are like your best friend? You can go and talk your matters out with them?" Calkins nodded. "Well, that tree was sort of like my dog. If I got really angry at my mother or something—or scared—I'd just run out to the backyard and maybe hug the tree, if I could get my arms around it." Debbie laughed and made a circle she couldn't quite cinch with her arms. "And talk the matters out with that. You know, sit under it.

"And we used to play London Bridge because it went over like this. And the kids would go around it like this." She made a leaning tree with one arm and the children going around it with the other, becoming animated as she recalled the game.

Debbie paused and then winced. "It was cut down, though," she said softly. She nodded, still wincing, as if she could not bear the picture in her mind. And here she lost her usual fluency for a moment as she tried to come back to talking about her paper. "And it was sort of about what—it was written about—it didn't start out to be what it ended up to be." She swallowed hard, still moved by the emotions that had led her to change her topic. "It started out for a different story—my apple tree now that's supposed to be in place of it. But nothing will ever take the place of Old Birch." Debbie shook her head. Here is the story she had to write, a story that surprised her parents as much as it surprised her by insisting on being written:

I Miss You Old Birch

Oh boy, this is fun! London Bridge is bent over. It's fun to go round and under Old Birch. "Daddy, Daddy, why did you do that?" I wondered. Thump, thump, thump went my feet on the stairs. Ka-boom went my bed. My bed was almost a lake of tears. "Debbie, can I come in?" my mom asked. "No! No! No!" I yelled. "Debbie, you know that tree was dead." "IT WAS NOT!" I yelled louder than before. By that time I was really having a temper-tantrum, yelling, crying. It lasted a week or two. You can tell I was very upset. One way or another I got over it. My choice was to almost forget about it or to make everyone miserable. I didn't forget about it completely because I'm still very close to Old Birch. Sometimes my thoughts about Old Birch make me cry myself to sleep. "I miss you, Old Birch!"

Debbie realized what putting all those thumps, ka-booms, tears, and exclamation points down on paper was doing for her. She told the researcher that writing is important because "you learn about yourself" and because "you can take out your feelings on it. If you're really mad, you can dig a pencil into the paper"—she jabbed at an imaginary piece of paper—"instead of breaking a lunch box or something. You can get all your anger out on paper instead of out on somebody." Debbie smiled, as self-possessed as ever, looking like the last person on earth who would purposely damage a lunch box.

"Maybe you've had a really tough day," she went on, "and nothing seems to be going right. And you think, 'Well, I can't do *anything.*' You know, nothing's *mine.* Well, your writing is, you know. It's up to you whether you want to do it or not."

Because writing preserves an author's knowledge, skills, and thought processes, it gives children a new perspective on themselves as time passes. At the end of the year, they are often amused to look back at their more primitive efforts and proud to see how far they have come. In one class that combined first grade and kindergarten, some of the first-graders were convinced on first glance that some of the kindergartners' work must have been put into their writing folders. They themselves could never have produced such a silly-looking jumble of letters.

When you write, you transcend yourself. You leave yourself and circle, looking at your own thinking from many vantage points. You circle not only what you know but who you are. Writing transforms the self from a one-dimensional personality to a multidimensional personality. It's like drawing the same person from four different points of view. Each drawing would be of the same person, but each perspective would reveal more of that person.

Questions posed by teachers and classmates stimulate this transformation. Perceptive as usual, the Australian fourth-grader named Cassie explains how she gets a new perspective on her own writing, and thus herself, just by anticipating her teacher's response before a writing conference. "You read it first out loud just before you go to conference," she says. "When you're reading it out, you put your mind as the listener and it makes you the audience. So you can be the judge if you can understand it or if something doesn't sound right."

If certain parts don't make sense or "sound right," Cassie has no qualms about making changes. As an experienced writer, she doesn't expect herself to always get it right on the first try. Like Debbie, she knows that she can surprise herself, that a second thought may be better than a first one.

> *If writers get to the point where they realize that first perceptions are not necessarily right ones and that there is a need to revise for clarity, then the dimensions of the self increase. But even children who never really make that larger breakthrough to the flexible view of information can still increase the dimensions of self. When they write about their own experiences, they come to realize that valuable things have happened to them and that they can share those things with others.*

Thinking Writers

Children want to make sense of the world. Take a little boy named Nathaniel, for example. In the first grade, Nathaniel didn't do much writing in school, but he did plenty at home. When he wrote, he often posed questions and tried to answer them. One day he started a piece of writing called "wiy chilgrin Like Thar MoM Betr hen DaD" (Why Children Like Their Mom Better than Their Dad). But he couldn't find an answer to his question, and he stopped writing soon after he began, at the end of three pages. Later, he wrote a second draft that went like this (translated into conventional spelling):

Why Children Like Their Mom
Better than Their Dad

My father is nice. I wonder why people like their mothers better than their fathers. That is a question the genius of geniuses could not answer. Well, maybe!

Why They Do

They like their mom better because they were born by their mothers.

Nathaniel's piece was complete with drawings of a mother and father, the genius of geniuses, and a pregnant woman whose infant was knocking on the womb ("Baing, Baing"), ready to be born.

Nathaniel's ten-year-old sister, Meg, also has an inquiring mind. Since second grade, she, too, has been in classrooms where writing receives little emphasis. But she likes to write at home. Recently, she decided to write a paper about colonial education. After doing some research, she concluded that in some ways things haven't changed quite as much as people might think. In colonial days, she discovered, well-to-do children went to private school, middle-class children went to public school, and poorer children left school to become apprentices. Meg decided that children often fall into similar slots today. Even though they don't write much at school, both Nathaniel and Meg have learned to use writing as a tool for thought.

The act of writing calls into play many different kinds of thinking: classification, synthesis, analysis, transformation, and organization, to name just a few. There is hardly any aspect of human thought that isn't part of the composing process. Many school systems have started instituting special programs in "thinking" but the exercises they contain often have no. context. They are disconnected from the child's life and other schoolwork. These programs have come about because children aren't really being challenged in many classrooms. If they are regularly writing and discussing their work in science, math, and social studies, as well as language arts, I see no reason at all to have extra think-sessions.

A scene in Jan Roberts's third-grade classroom illustrated a number of the types of thinking involved in producing one piece of writing. When Roberts called her class to the rug at the front of the room, the class suddenly resembled a model of molecules in motion. It was the week before school let out, after all, and sunshine and warm air were pouring in through the windows. But before long the children had arranged themselves in a loose circle on the rug and grew still, expectant. Glen and Brandon had been working on their report on Einstein for more than six weeks, and the children had been hounding the pair for at least two weeks. "When are you going to read it to us?" was the refrain. "When are you going to read it to us?"

First the children heard about Einstein's life. They learned that his fascination with a compass at the age of five foreshadowed his career as a scientist. They heard about his two marriages and his final days in the United States. But Glen and Brandon's report also told about Einstein's work. The boys explained his theory of relativity in the context in which it was conceived, on one of Einstein's many train trips in Switzerland. A sequence of imaginary events—a passenger looking at a mirror while traveling at different speeds—grounded the theory in the real world that the children knew. The nine-year-old co-authors used another sequence of events—the burning of a piece of wood—to try to explain Einstein's equation $E = MC^2$.

The children listened to Brandon and Glen intently. After they had finished reading, the group applauded. Then hands went up all around the circle. Roberts had her hand up, too, and Glen called on her first. "Where did you get all your information?" she asked.

"We got our information from the encyclopedia and from a physics professor we interviewed from the university," Glen said.

"How'd you get your topic?" another child wanted to know. The answer came from Brandon, a chubby redhead with freckles, a husky voice, and a shirt that seemed to defy all efforts at tucking in. "We thought it up," he said. "We just brainstormed and brainstormed and . . ." He paused, and then his face seemed to light up like an idea lightbulb in a cartoon. "Ohh. Ding, ding, ding, ding, ding!" The children giggled.

Someone else wanted to know how long it had taken to write the whole piece. Glen thought back for a moment. "It took us a month and a half," he said.

"We were going to do a series of books on scientists," explained Brandon.

"We *thought* we were," Glen said. The group laughed, conscious that the close of school was near and that a series of such scholarly works would require much time and effort.

"What was the hardest part?"

Brandon reflected. "All this stuff about atoms clashing—we had to translate it simpler."

Roberts had another question. "Do you think this was a good way to learn?"

Glen answered first. "Yeah, because we can keep it and we don't have to look it up in the library."

"It's better to find information yourself in a book than have someone else find it for you," Brandon said. "You can find anything you want."

This particular piece of writing gave the two boys practice in researching, synthesizing, collaborating, and simplifying complex material. But they had also used skills that would apply to any piece of writing: brainstorming, gathering, selecting, organizing, and revising. When children are taught to write by using rules and formulas, they become well acquainted with those formulas. Junior-high students, for example, may learn to produce a five-paragraph theme on command. They write an introductory paragraph listing three main points. Three paragraphs follow, each covering one of the points. Then the summarizing paragraph goes over, yet again, the three main points. The paper itself is a poor model of writing. But worse, the student has learned to produce only that model, one found nowhere in the real world.

When children can practice finding appropriate meanings and forms for different subjects, however, they have a way to go about writing anything, even a five-paragraph theme, if they have the misfortune of being assigned one. In fact, experience with this kind of process serves children well not only when they write, but also when they try any other intellectual activity. They are used to planning—coming up with ideas and evaluating them. It is this ability teachers most often cite when asked how writing affects their students' thinking.

A first-grader in Ellen Blackburn's classroom revealed his understanding of the creative process when he wrote a book called *Designs*. After demonstrating how to make designs with geometric shapes, he gave an example of a design and offered a conjecture as to how it might have been produced. "I bet a man or a woman was drawing shapes and he or she messed up. He made the shapes together. He said, 'I might call it a design. Yeah!' "

Teachers from first grade to eighth grade have seen their students transfer questions and approaches from writing to other subjects. One teacher reports that students working on math problems used to ask each other, "Did you get it wrong?" Now she hears them asking questions like "How did you figure out how to do that?" or "What will you do next?"

When it came time for the annual science fair at Boothbay Harbor, fifth-grade teacher Connie Bataller noticed that since she had changed her approach to writing her students had changed more than just their writing habits. A seventeen-year veteran of the classroom, she had struggled for years to find a way to help them carry out independent projects such as science exhibits. Experience with writing, she discovered, gave her students a way to solve other problems. They began work on their science projects by "drafting an initial plan and then sharing it with somebody else." They asked themselves and their classmates questions: "How do I approach this?" "What do I like best here?" "How am I going to get people into this project so when they come to the science fair, they'll really want to look at it?" In turn, classmates asked, "How's it coming?" "What do you plan to do next?" After talking them over, many children revised their plans.

Reading Writers

As children become better writers, they also improve their reading skills. At the end of the year in one kindergarten where children were allowed to write instead of filling in worksheets, every single student in the class tested in the seventh stanine or higher on a reading-readiness test. In a Florida county school system, researchers made a study of five hundred first-graders and kindergartners. Nearly half the children were black, and nearly half came from households with incomes below the poverty line. When the children were allowed to write before they could read, their median reading scores rose twenty-five percentile points above those of previous years. And not one child in the writing group was judged to be dyslexic. Older students who write fare just as well. Since the writing project started at Boothbay Harbor in 1980, median reading scores for grade eight have jumped from the fiftieth to the seventy-second percentile.

Many of the teachers I talked with at all grade levels have found that their children's test scores run higher than those of students in other classrooms. These teachers do not claim to have scientific, statistical proof that specific teaching methods have caused the higher scores. But it seems safe to say that children who read and write regularly under the guidance of a well-trained teacher can safely skip many standard exercises without hurting their standardized test scores.

When we write, we construct reading. Thus, as I write, I try to match the words with my meaning. I constantly reread to see whether the parts I put down match the whole of my overall intentions. But then I can also reread from the vantage point of other readers, matching what I have written with what others might need to understand. Ultimately, if I construct reading through my own writing, I can take apart other people's writing when I read.

All writers frequently reread their own words as they write. Thus young writers improve their reading skills through sheer practice. Very young children learning to write before they even know how to read go over and over each word (sometimes a single letter) in a process that may seem painful to observing adults. Yet the children perform the exercise willingly because they want to express themselves. In a sense, they have assigned themselves much of the grinding repetition that characterizes worksheets. Often, these children are surprised one day when a teacher points out that since they can decipher what they have written, they can obviously read now. Older children also get plenty of reading practice when they write.

Rising self-confidence can also lead to rising reading scores. One mother came to Boothbay special-education teacher Susan Stires and told her about the progress she'd noticed in her fifth-grade daughter's reading. "She's reading the commercials on television!" the mother said. "And she's reading the newspaper, and she asks me what all these words mean!" By springtime, the child had leaped two grades in her reading level in one year, according to one test.

As a writing student with Stires the year before, the little girl had been very dramatic in the way she went about writing, spreading things out on the floor in one corner of the room, cutting up pages, and taping them back together. She loved to show her work to visiting teachers. The following year, she was referred to Stires, not for writing, but for reading. "I think her success just came from her feeling that she could do this reading," says Stires, "as much as she could do the writing."

Of course, the little girl's mother was thrilled not by test scores or even the skills they represented, but by her daughter's eagerness, her desire to read the things around her. Enthusiasm is just one of the many qualities that cannot be measured by standardized tests, which generally assess a child's mastery of component skills, rather than the ability to make use of those skills or to engage in higher level thinking tasks such as analysis and synthesis. Tests also fail to reflect children's attitudes toward literature, for example, or toward learning in general.

The little girl's enthusiasm for reading had been kindled in part by the opportunity to read books of her own choice. She loved mysteries, so she read mysteries. In Ellen Blackburn's first-grade classroom in a New Hampshire mill town, every child may choose to read any of several hundred available books ranging from popular and classic children's literature to standard basal readers and the children's own original books. Although some of the children have had little experience with books and reading at home, they soon grow to love books and often use their snack time at school to read and discuss what they have read.

After Blackburn read E. B. White's *Charlotte's Web* to the

class, a number of children were so eager to get their hands on the book that tears were shed over the one copy available at the school library. One child, who had missed several chapters during a bout with the chicken pox, chose to read the book from cover to cover on her own, a challenging task for even the brightest first-grader. A visitor in the classroom was amazed at the sight of six-year-olds toting around a thick volume of E. B. White's letters. Asked why the book interested them, they pointed out letters in which White referred to his work on *Charlotte's Web.* There were also photographs of him with his own piglets, models for the main character, Wilbur.

Older students, too, can take more pleasure in reading if they write, choose their own books, and share what they've learned and enjoyed with others. Nancie Atwell's junior-high English classroom is lined with several hundred paperbacks. Every day her students read from books they've selected or she has suggested. They reflect on the things they've read in one series of letters to Atwell and another to their friends. On average, each student reads about thirty-five books during the course of the school year. One girl read more than two hundred. And when Atwell sees or hears from a former student during the summer, the conversation inevitably turns to the latest books each has read.

Of course, enthusiasm by itself does not guarantee that students will read perceptively. But discrimination is more likely to develop if children write regularly and their teacher points out the connection between their own endeavors and those of published authors. Because they are used to judging their own and others' writing, the children soon view published works with a critical eye.

Just as children who grow up on a farm know where milk comes from, children who write know where writing comes from. And children who rewrite know that any draft is a malleable thing, subject to scrutiny and possible improvement. One fourth-grader told a researcher: "I read a lot of books where the first four chapters are lead-ins. And you wonder why they don't just get to the exciting part so it'll catch your eye."

As children develop their ability to change roles between writer and reader when they write, they can also take up different points of view when they read. The same fourth-grader explained: "Sometimes when I read a book, I think about *how* they wrote it. If I like it, I might try it out in my own story."

> *Just as writing makes me a better reader, reading makes me a better writer. I need material for my writing. I need new vocabulary, ways of organizing things, and other ideas. I suspect that most of the influence of reading comes on an unconscious level. When I read a novel, only occasionally am I consciously reading as a writer. Most of the time, I'm reading just for myself, reading for enjoyment, picking up things for life.*

Many children find that they can learn from professional writers by borrowing techniques. One third-grader was obviously influenced by books she had read when she wrote about herself in the third person, with an omniscient narrator, no less. The following year, a third-grader in the same classroom read the little girl's book and realized that she, too, could write in the third person.

Even very young children can pick up writing techniques from published authors. In Ellen Blackburn's first grade, one little boy wrote a series of books about a character named John. He had the idea of doing his own series after he had read some of the *Little Bear Books.* Children in her class have also tried parodies or imitations. When the class read *Miss Nelson Is Missing,* one child wrote his own version, called *Miss Blackburn Is Missing.*

A first-grader at another school imitated some of her favorite writers, such as children's authors Russell and Lillian Hoban. "Much as children try on other people's clothes or shoes," says her teacher, "Kasey would try other people's styles." Children like Kasey and Blackburn's students are playing with language, seeing just what their own voices can encompass. They imitate what they admire.

Although Kasey's extensive imitations are relatively unusual, many young children will often borrow a title or a phrase or an idea for an ending from published authors. One little boy, for example, wrote a book about the class fish and named it after Leo

Lionni's book *Fish Is Fish*. This kind of borrowing is quite different from the incipient plagiarism found in many grade-school reports or the assignments in which children are forced to copy someone else's words. Like professional authors who use phrases from Shakespeare as titles for their own books, the children who borrow phrases do not try to pass them off as their own. They proudly announce the source because other children in the classroom have often read it, too. They're showing their love of literature, their sensitivity to language, and their willingness to experiment. Children who plagiarize, consciously or not, do so out of desperation. They feel unable to find their own words because, as one child put it, "the encyclopedia took all the good ones."

The Whole Child

Craig was a problem child. His sleepy manner hid an inner tension that would sometimes burst into violence—like a Marlon Brando character, one of his teachers thought. He often beat up other children on the playground, and he was a poor student. Then the researchers came to his third-grade class in Atkinson.

At first, Craig wrote like this: "Iwasserwolanoloasantocarscrashingon." As he wrote more and more, he soon began to crack the code of written English, but much of his work was disturbing. His fantasies were violent. In one, Goofy the Cowboy "killed a few people, but he didn't care a bit. He was having fun." Even Craig's real-life tales had a mean-spirited tone. "Going Home is a Pain" opened with "I get home. My brother kicks me and I chase him. Cut it out Mike or I'll kill you."

By the fourth grade, Craig had changed. No longer a bully, he now wrote about dolphins, Harriet Tubman, Christmas, and playing with his friends. He gave a copy of his favorite piece to his parents as a gift. At the end of the year, he was so interested in his report about white-tailed deer that he worked on it in bed at night. The final draft displayed an appreciation of life and language that belies the tone of "Goofy the Cowboy" and "Going Home." The report begins:

The baby fawn is awakened by a twig snap. He looks around.
He sees a bear coming toward him. He doesn't move a whis-
ker or even an eye. The bear sniffs the fawn. The bear leaves
because it thinks the fawn is dead, but really the fawn fools
the bear. After the enemy leaves, the fawn feels safe. . . .

Children like Craig seem to make progress on many fronts at
once, intellectually as well as socially and emotionally. Although
the human mind and psyche are far too complex to reduce to
simple cause-and-effect relationships, the researchers and
teachers who worked with Craig had little doubt that his intellectual development was interrelated with his emotional and social
growth, and that all three were tied to the way in which reading
and writing were handled in the classroom.

Many parents, as well as teachers, have seen children use
writing as an outlet for strong emotions. When Linette Moorman's son was young, she would find scraps of paper on which he
had written things like: "I think tunafish stinks." Children who
use invented spelling may start writing their feelings on paper
much sooner than their parents expect. In a fit of pique, one
kindergartner wrote down every dirty word in his growing vocabulary. Despite his unique brand of spelling, his parents and
older brother were able to decipher the words and had to go into
another room to stop laughing before going to tell the child that if
it wasn't OK to say a word, it wasn't OK to write it, either.

All children go through traumatic experiences of one sort or
another, and many write about them. Sharing those experiences
through writing not only allows the author to air troubling emotions, but it also allows classmates to tell about their own similar
experiences. First-grade and transition teacher Susan Porter recorded in her journal the discussions spawned by one little boy's
story about his late pet piglet.

The children had been writing as best they could for several
weeks. For some the best was, like Robbie's work, quite close to
words. Others represented each word with one letter, and many
were still at the scribbling stage. All began their "writing" with a
drawing. On this particular day, Robbie had drawn a picture of a
pet piglet that had died shortly after birth. When Porter came by

to see his work, Robbie told her that he had cried all day when the piglet died. That was what he was going to write.

Soon, other children in the classroom were talking about the same subject. Amy brought up her cat. Three weeks before, she had written:

MY CAT	My cat
Goe KoTi	got caught
EYn The	in the
Belt	belt
I MY MOM	in my mom's
KIr	car.

She had read her piece to the class at the time and received a very compassionate response. Now when she brought it up again, the children around her all remembered the story and began to ask her more questions about the mishap.

Meanwhile, Ericka signaled that she was ready to discuss her work with Porter. Ericka had just finished a piece on a pet black sheep, but now she planned to write about her white sheep. "Her name is 10," she said. "It's really Bo Derek but we call her 10. She's real old and is going to die soon. We are going to keep her until she dies. I want to remember her."

The topic of dying pets had become an epidemic. "Ms. Porter," Chris announced, "I felt so bad about my little dog dying, I just had to draw a picture of her in my book."

In the meantime, Porter overheard a conversation between Mike and Jeff. "Everything dies, you know," Jeff said.

"Yeah," Mike countered, "but *some* things don't."

"I know that," said Jeff, "but most everything does."

"Yup," Mike answered philosophically. "Doesn't it make you sad?"

Of course, not all students use writing as an emotional outlet. When Nancie Atwell asked her eighth-graders what they saw as the benefits of writing, one-third of the group included the expression of emotions among their answers. And to suggest that a classroom or an activity helps children handle emotional problems is not to suggest that the teacher in that classroom is counseling students. Allowing children to express themselves and receive a sympathetic response is often enough in itself. After her cat was injured, one little girl posted daily medical bulletins on the board that served as a kind of newspaper for the class. Eventually, the cat died. But the child's teacher noticed that the little girl wasn't especially eager to talk about the subject; writing it down seemed to be enough.

When students share their writing in an atmosphere of tolerance and cooperation, some use their work as a tool for gaining social acceptance. One fifth-grade teacher reports: "When a kid would share his piece, there would be five or six comments on what the others liked about it. And nobody had to tell him: 'Gee, you're a great kid,' because he was getting that feedback from his classmates. They might get mad at him on the playground because he teases too much, but he sure wrote a neat piece about his trip to Windsor Fair, and the kids can appreciate that."

There may be no time in life when people are more conscious of their social standing than in junior high. One junior-high English teacher tells about a girl who was "socially ostracized. She looked like a boy. But she started writing mystery stories, cliff hangers, in installments. And the kids turned right around. She was accepted—I would like to say overnight, but it was almost that sudden." Although it was hard to get the student to venture away from the genre that had won her friends, she did. And she continued to write when her audience of peers was gone: she called during the summer to ask her teacher to read a piece of nonfiction she had written.

> *Some people believe that teachers should limit their domain to intellectual development and ignore social and emotional development. But all of the language arts involve social and emotional acts requiring social and emotional risks. I want children to be able to listen, read, speak, and write so that they may understand and influence others.*

At the same time, emotional and social factors can have a profound effect on intellectual progress. Teacher after teacher has stories to tell about individual children who make strides in many facets of their life at once. The stories are most dramatic when they are about children who are at a disadvantage in some way—physically, emotionally, socially, or intellectually. In fact, when asked to talk about their students, most teachers do not begin with their star pupils. Instead, they tell about a child like Aerica. Linette Moorman apologized before she told me a story that sounds almost too magical to be true. But her observations have been corroborated by the other adults who worked with the child.

Aerica was a black girl from a family her teacher describes as "very, very poor." She was held back in the second grade, and when she started second grade for the second time, she missed the first couple of days of school. On the day she did arrive, she came in at ten, dragging her shoulder along the wall as if her own two feet were not enough to hold her up. That first day, Aerica would not look Moorman in the eye, and everything she said came out in a mumble. "And that was the end of Aerica for two weeks," Moorman says. "She came irregularly, and she came late, and she came dirty."

When she did come, Aerica was sent out of the room for remedial reading work. But she did write with the other children, and in October, she finished a book modeled on the plot of Maurice Sendak's *Where the Wild Things Are,* which her teacher had read to the class. In Aerica's version, the characters and details were different, but she, like the little boy in the original story, put on a magic suit and went on a fantastic trip. She was too shy to read her story aloud to the class, but she did consent to read it into a tape recorder out in the hall. When it was time for sharing books, her teacher played the tape for the class, and the class was delighted. They applauded and Aerica beamed. The next day she went up to Moorman and said, "I have another story to write." And she began to write pieces about her family and her experiences.

"Aerica started arriving at school on time," Moorman recalls. "She was on the line in the gym with the other children. She was cleaner. She just looked completely different because, for one thing, I think she wanted to come to school." At the beginning of the year, she had been reading way below grade level, but now the remedial-reading teacher reported that Aerica no longer needed help. By the end of the year, she was reading above grade level.

On the last day of school, Aerica's class had a "read-around" in which every child read one thing he or she had written that year. Aerica chose to write a new story for the occasion. This is what she wrote:

The Little Girl Who Was Ugly

Once there was a little girl who thought no one liked her. They said she was ugly. One day she was in her room crying. Suddenly a bright light appeared. There was a beautiful lady. She said, "You may have one wish." I wish I was beautiful like you. She waved her magic wand. And the little girl was beautiful. No one believed it was her. No one ever teased the little girl again. As for the little girl, she writes stories and lived happily ever after.

But the true happy ending didn't come for Linette Moorman until two years later, when the assistant principal called her into the office. "Your Aerica," the administrator said, "is going to the class for intellectually gifted children. Her reading score, her math score, and all her performance this year have been so outstanding that the fourth-grade teacher has recommended her for IGC."

CHAPTEr 8
Learning Together

Language has been described by educator James Britton as "the exposed edge of thought."* Children who write every day expose and record a lot more of their thoughts than those who write infrequently or copy what they do write, exposing only the thoughts of the teacher or original author. When children talk about their writing, they give a teacher further evidence of their knowledge and thinking abilities. Teachers can use this evidence of what's going on in a child's mind to continually readjust the curriculum to fit the individual. But they must know how to gather that evidence and what to make of it.

If children learn in part by teaching others, then teachers must teach in part by listening and observing, two activities usu-

*Quoted in "Let Me See You Learn" by Bryant Fillion, *Language Arts,* September 1983.

ally associated with the student's role. Many teachers find their preparation has been lacking in these skills. All of the teachers interviewed for this book have supplemented their initial training with some combination of courses and workshops in teaching writing. But they have found that the extra effort has not only helped them respond better to individual children, but has also given them a broader understanding of how people learn.

> *Our whole educational system ignores the teacher's need to keep learning. The idea receives much lip service through in-service education, but because of the way most sessions are conducted, the teachers don't leave with a sense of having learned. Worse, the format of the workshop suggests that the leader knows everything and the teachers don't. That is bad medicine even if the workshop leaders are right, and of course they aren't.*
>
> *If anything, the revolution in teaching writing has taken off because teachers are finding something in it for themselves. Their writing changes, their reading changes, and, above all, when they listen, the children demonstrate all the ways in which they learn. Thus, teachers become acquainted with a broad repertoire of techniques that can help them, as well as the children, learn.*

Learning to Listen

> *The hardest thing for teachers, and administrators, to realize is the importance of listening to children. When the teacher listens, the children are finding out what they know, learning how to say it, and discovering that another human being really wants to hear it.*

An understanding of the importance of listening in itself, however, may not be enough, no matter how many courses a teacher takes. Richard Sterling, codirector of the New York City Writing Project, tells about a teacher who thought she was doing a lot of listening—until she taped her class and found she was

doing about 80 percent of the talking in the room. A number of
teachers have been able to monitor their own progress under the
guidance of another teacher with more experience in listening to
children.

> *Teachers become good listeners by practicing. They practice*
> *because they've made a conscious commitment to spending*
> *more time doing it. In one sense, listening never exists in a*
> *pure state: it is like the rests in a piece of music. A rest means*
> *something only in light of the music that surrounds it. Most*
> *textbooks, articles, and curriculum guides emphasize good*
> *questions for teachers to ask. But questions are only as good*
> *as the listening that precedes them. Anyone can ask a good*
> *first question, but the real learning takes place with ques-*
> *tions two and three, which are based on the child's re-*
> *sponses.*
>
> > *For example, a child says, "I'm stuck."*
> > *His teacher says, "Where are you stuck, John?"*
> > *"I just don't know what to say next."*
> > *"When you first chose this topic," the teacher asks.*
> *"what did you want it to be about?"*
> > *"I wanted it to be about how my dog had puppies. You*
> *know how dogs sometimes get all nervous when they don't*
> *know where to have their puppies, and Rags was running up*
> *and down stairs. She even pulled my shirt, my old soft shirt,*
> *from underneath my bed and she was trying to pull it to the*
> *other end of my closet." He pauses. "I don't know. I just*
> *wanted to write about how my dog Rags had puppies."*
> > *The teacher looks at what the child has written and com-*
> *ments, "I notice that you didn't tell about how your dog*
> *pulled your shirt to the other end of the closet. Do you think*
> *that is important? Will the other children ask you about that*
> *when you share it?"*
> > *In this instance, the teacher helps the child to overcome*
> *a writing block. She has done enough writing herself to know*
> *that when a writer is blocked, it is often time to go back to*
> *other times when the writing went well, in order to move*
> *ahead again. So she asks a question that will take the child*
> *back to better writing days, when he first chose the topic.*

After careful listening, she then switches to a new set of questions to help him decide whether the new information about the dog is important. But the teacher couldn't have asked the second question first because it was based on new facts.

Since teachers have long been considered to have all the answers, it is often hard for them to wait for a child's answer. More than one study has found that teachers often wait only one or two seconds before providing their own answer, changing the question, or asking another child. Kindergarten teacher Judi Hilliker says, "I always have to bite my tongue, and I often don't bite it soon enough."

When teachers hold their tongues and children speak up, the classroom structure may appear topsy-turvy to many. If the old way was to pour out information into child receptacles, this method may look like drawing out information from child oracles. But it's not that simple. As New York City Writing Project codirector Sondra Perl points out, "teachers will always be powerful" in the classroom, no matter what role they take. But they can learn to use their power more skillfully, collaborating with children rather than intimidating them or catering to them. A good teacher wants to help children accomplish their own objectives and then go one step further: to help them broaden their knowledge, try a new form, learn a new skill.

So teachers must take on a variety of roles. As versatile in their repertoire as the children are, they listen and observe in order to respond as needed, now waiting, now challenging, now asserting. They even give brief lectures when the majority of a class seems ready to learn a new skill. Australian researcher Marilyn Woolley made a list of some of the lessons Jo Parry taught her mixed class of fourth-, fifth-, and sixth-graders as she wrote in front of the class or discussed published books with them. The list of thirty-five examples included topics such as brainstorming, consulting resources, paragraphing, cutting and pasting, deciding on main ideas, and writing lead sentences.

There's one person I go to first when I'm having a problem with writing. He has a gift of knowing when to shut up, when

to insult you, when to hit you over the head with a brick,
when to say the most flattering thing you've ever heard in
your whole life. Anyone can do those things; the gift is in
knowing when. Every once in a while he'll say, "Would you
like me to edit this as if I were the editor of Time *magazine?"*
Then he'll cut the piece to the bare bones. Of course, that's
an example of an adult talking with an adult, but teachers
can be equally versatile.

Nancie Atwell describes the different roles she and her colleagues have played as their teaching has changed: "I was very
directive," she recalls. "All of the teachers were. Then everyone
climbed in the backseat to watch the children. And now we have
come full circle and everyone's directive—the kids, too." A
teacher like Ellen Blackburn is constantly challenging and testing
her first-graders. As a child in her class prepares to read a piece to
a small group, Blackburn asks her a routine question: "What do
you want to get from us?"

"I want to know if it's good and if I should add anything,"
Sarah responds, in a routine answer.

"You just want us to say, 'It's good'?" Blackburn asks.
"What if we don't like it? Should we say, 'It's bad'?"

Patterns of Learning

Teachers can further hone their ability to listen and observe by
keeping journals or performing research, usually case studies, in
their own classrooms. Just the act of recording observations gives
teachers a new perspective. Nancie Atwell led a group of
teachers at Boothbay Harbor in a year-long research project. "It
was every day that something exciting was happening for them,"
she says, "because suddenly there were so many ways they had
of looking. We didn't have those ways of looking before. Joyce
Parent's second-grade students were taking clipboards out on the
playground with them so they could continue their writing at
recess. And because she's a teacher-researcher, she's got her log.

So she's looking for stuff to put in it, and she sees that, and all of a sudden it makes her day."

Once they start recording their observations, teachers begin to make sense of them, drawing conclusions about individual children, children in general, and the politics of education. The teachers at Boothbay Harbor decided to use a case-study approach in observing their own classrooms. Each teacher chose one child who interested her for some reason. The teachers kept logs on these and other children for one year and, as Atwell puts it, "tried, like ethnographers, to record what they saw happening in their classrooms." They also wrote about their cases, continued to read literature on language development and instruction, and met regularly to discuss both their writing and their reading.

One case, a fifth-grader named Marcy, showed Connie Bataller a lot about the balance of power that normally exists in the classroom and how it can be redistributed. Bataller had been unaware of the degree of power she herself wielded as a teacher. "At the beginning of the year," she says, "I was talking with Marcy about a piece she had written. And one of the questions we were asking kids was 'Would you be willing to leave out this sentence?' " Hoping that the children were beginning to develop their own standards and powers of evaluation, the teachers picked particularly good sentences and expected a negative response followed by an explanation.

Marcy's response was a disappointment, but a revealing one. "When I asked Marcy that question, she read into it right away 'Oh, Mrs. Bataller doesn't like that sentence. If she's asking me why it's in there, then it must not be any good.' And so she immediately capitulated: 'Oh, it's really not very good. I'm going to leave it out.' " Bataller was "just floored."

By the end of a year, however, Bataller's research showed her how much Marcy had changed in a classroom where her teacher took pains to draw children out and respect their ideas. Conferring with Marcy on an early draft, Bataller commented in passing on one section. "Oh, gee, Marcy, I really liked that part. That's really good," Bataller remembers saying. "And then later when she turned in her final copy, it was gone. It just wasn't there." Bataller smiles. "She had just changed 180 degrees. At first, she was a little kid who was supersensitive to what the teacher likes. Now, here's this teacher telling her 'I really like this,' and Marcy says, 'I don't!' " Bataller shrugs. "And she left it out."

Bataller noticed that Marcy had also become more confident in her approach to the things she read. One day "we had read Armstrong Sperry's *Call It Courage,* and I said, 'What do you think about the book?' After some cursory comments, Marcy chimes in, 'You know, he really should have added more stuff there when he was on the island. He could have found a cave to live in.' And she went on and on about how Armstrong Sperry could have improved the book!" Bataller laughs in delight as she tells the story; that sort of self-confident and critical reading was new to her classroom that first year.

Teachers can come to a new understanding of learning through an analysis of their own experiences, as well as their students'. In fact, if French teachers must speak French, pottery teachers must make pottery, swimming teachers must swim, and so on, then it's probably true that any teacher must continue to learn. Some teachers find that taking up something new—drawing or piano lessons or even writing—for the first time can give them more empathy for the child for whom schoolwork doesn't come easily. But often their own experience with trying to improve their teaching parallels their students' experience in the classroom.

First-grade and transition teacher Susan Porter recorded both her own and her students' progress in the journal she kept for her course in teaching writing. At the end of a semester's worth of entries, she noticed a pattern in her own struggle to change her teaching methods. "I find my journal filled with two-steps-forward, one-step-backwards kinds of entries," she wrote, "feeling great and then feeling like I've blown it, or was a failure. Closer examination reveals an approach to learning—setting up problems and overcoming them."

Some of her students seemed to be doing a similar rhumba with their writing. Toward the middle of November, she was disturbed by the first outbreak of Garfield, Smurfs, and Pac-Man in the children's writing. She had heard from a colleague that children will sometimes extend and elaborate on the video version of a character. But hers weren't. They just drew pictures of Pac-Man gobbling ghosts and power pellets. Even her best writers were drawing cartoons or half-heartedly addressing other topics. Mike and Jeff were doing Pac-Man, and Amy was filling book after book with a list of the names of all the children in the class. In a series of three "NAM BOOKS," she varied only the color of the crayon she used. Meanwhile, there was more noise than usual, and a feeling of restlessness pervaded the classroom.

On November 18, Porter wrote: "For almost two weeks now, my best writers have been in limbo . . . in transition—some sort of self-imposed holding pattern. Perhaps these cartoon-character types of writings have emerged mainly to get something down on paper. I don't know." Then she added: "This type of behavior still causes me anxiety, but I guess I'm beginning to see that it usually precedes a period of growth and change in the children. Once through it, they seem to emerge with some new skill, awareness, or motivation."

Sure enough, over the next few days many of the children finished up their cartoon books. The room quieted down again, and several children tried new topics or even new types of writing. One child tried for the first time to extend one topic through the length of an entire six-page book.

Another boy, Jeff, drew an elaborate picture of two boys and then told Porter the book would be about people from different lands. What lands? Exeter (a neighboring town) and "the mountains." In response to further questions, he began to tell a story about one of the boys. For several days, he continued to work on his piece during writing time and his free time, convinced that it was his best work so far. In his tale, a little boy got lost in the mountains, cried, found a path, and followed it home to his mother. This was Jeff's first attempt at fantasy and his first complete narrative. But when it was done, Porter observed that "in attempting all the new stuff with topic and structure, the conventions went down the drain. His spelling vanished, as did his sentence punctuation (capitals and periods) and any spacing between words. The learning process is such a see-saw . . . balance and loss of balance."

When you do research or make systematic observations, you gather information over time. If you gather information over time, you learn how up and down learning is—good days, bad days. It's a gradual upward spiral. An understanding of that spiral helps a teacher to say on bad days, "Well, that's the way teaching is. I've got the records here to show it."

These and other patterns appear often as people learn. Like the researchers at Atkinson, teachers who discover patterns must keep an eye out for ways in which individual children differ. Porter had discovered that children often go through a period of apparent regression before making progress. If left alone, they often find their own way to move ahead. She had seen the principle at work a number of times. Just as she had become frustrated with an epidemic of scribbling at the very beginning of the year, two children began writing words. The others soon began to follow suit. And in Jeff's case, Porter needed only to watch and ask a few questions. He, too, progressed on his own.

But other instances called for a different strategy. For several weeks at the beginning of the year, one little girl had made nothing but "rug books," page after page divided into squares of different colors with fringe on the borders. Porter decided that this child needed an ultimatum: no more rug books. After writing a book or two about her family, the little girl had a brief relapse with a series of birthday-cake books. But then she changed topics on her own. She started writing about a number of things, including chasing her boyfriend on the playground.

The art of teaching for Porter lies in knowing when and how to intervene. She wrote in her journal, "I am continually amazed at how idiosyncratic and unpredictable writing and writing behaviors are for children."

Children Show What They Need

"There's a big push to individualize instruction," says Karen Weinhold, "and it was breaking my back trying to meet the individual needs of every student, using the grammar curriculum, using the poetry, using the drama. It was almost impossible." Now that her junior-high students are writing hundreds of pages a year, however, she feels more relaxed. "The writing curriculum by its nature is individualized," she says. "You don't need to give them a diagnostic test to ask, 'Do you know how to capitalize? Do you know how to punctuate?' Because it's there in their writing. And if it's a class problem, you do a lesson or two or three, and you use examples from their writing and say 'These are the problems we're having. What can we do?' "

Transition teacher Kathy Matthews agrees that her students' writing reveals more than tests. "The very best thing about writing is how visible it makes children's minds to me," she says. "On paper they're showing me all the language skills they have. Syntax, vocabulary, grammatical structure, phonics—it's all there. Using tests, I can see if children recognize the letter *v*, but if they're using it in their invented spelling, I consider it mastered." The distinction between recognition and mastery is an important one that component testing often ignores. The ability to identify any tool—an oil-filter wrench, a scalpel, or a floppy disk—is quite a separate matter from the ability to use it.

Matthews learns about her children's abilities in a much broader way, as well. "I also find out what they know about the world," she says. "I get a sense of where they are in terms of their thinking abilities. I can see who can think more abstractly."

Children who sit in rows quietly filling in blanks do not leave any clues as to how they have arrived at their answers. Children who are encouraged to talk and write in school give the teacher a lot more to go on. They not only show what they can do; they leave substantial evidence pointing to what they don't understand. In fact, a teacher can use the things children already know to teach them what they need to learn. If, in answer to questions, children show that they already have a sense of where one thought ends and another begins in a piece of writing, for example, their teacher can use that knowledge to teach them how to use periods.

Fortunately for all involved, what the children need is often the same thing that teachers and parents want them to know, but the timing is crucial. Students who care about their writing need to learn how to improve it through revision when necessary. Yet their teacher need not assign revisions or deliver lectures on the virtues of rewriting. Only when a first-grader named Bobby discovered that he had left Elliott out of his E. T. book did Susan Porter help him find a way to insert new information.

Textbooks and teacher's manuals cannot substitute for this kind of individual attention. If the needed skills are in the book, the material has little chance of appearing at the time when it is needed by, or meaningful to, the majority of the class, let alone individual children. And textbooks cannot make use of a child's strengths as a teacher can.

Linette Moorman is one teacher who tends not to go by the books; she relies on her second-graders to show her what they need and when they need it. Like all young children, the students in her Brooklyn classroom need to expand their vocabularies. If she gave them lists of words to memorize for a test, some would pass the test and others wouldn't, but the chances of long-term retention would be slim. When a little girl named Jeanette wrote a piece about a movie she had seen, however, she needed new words to help her say what she wanted to say. She smiled as she read the piece to Moorman, hitting every word and extending it. She had written that she did not like a scene in which the characters "had worms coming out of their mouths." Together, she and Moorman discussed words that would describe her reaction more precisely than the phrase *did not like.* They talked about *disgusting* and *sickening.* After Jeanette chose *sickening,* she returned to her seat to write a new line and paste it onto the old draft.

This kind of approach makes teaching more difficult. Moorman admits, "It's harder for me to write my lesson plans because some of my planning now comes from what I see; it doesn't come from 'I covered page 42; next week it's 43 to 47.'" Instead, her reasoning goes like this: "When we wrote, they didn't understand the concepts of 'before' and 'after,' and the manual doesn't tell me to teach that, so the manual goes out the door. And I'm sitting there for a much longer period of time, not saying 'page 44 of the manual,' but saying, 'What do they need? What do they not know? And how am I going to help them?'"

There are compensations for the hard work, the extra intellectual effort required to follow the children rather than follow the teacher's guide. When Moorman's colleague Lila Edelkind teaches, she often digresses from her lesson plan in order to explore the children's responses to what she's said. The discussions that follow not only satisfy the children's curiosity, she says, but "very often the tangents are far more interesting than what I actually had planned."

Karen Weinhold agrees that allowing her students to learn by pursuing their own interests has kept up her enthusiasm for teaching. "If twenty kids do a grammar drill," she explains, "then they're going to have the same thing. And if you have three sections of twenty kids doing the same grammar drill, then it's pretty hard to become enthusiastic by the third time around. But if you have sixty kids writing, nobody's writing the same thing."

Children Show Who They Are

Mary Anne Byrne and her fellow teachers "always used to laugh about how kids see you in the supermarket and, oh, my gosh! they're so surprised." Now that her students are writing, she has a new perspective on both students and teachers. "It's no different for teachers looking at children," she says. "There's a whole life that you have to consider when you're working with them. I see them as human beings now. It's not that they were inhuman before, but now they're three dimensional instead of two dimensional. They walk and talk outside of my classroom. They have a life beyond."

That life beyond comes into the classroom with children, whether teachers are prepared to acknowledge it or not. Anyone who has taken a standardized test, like the Scholastic Aptitude Test, knows that a whole welter of emotional and physical factors may refuse to be dismissed during the ordeal. A recent death in the family, a previous history of difficulty with tests, a nervous stomach, a cough, even someone else's cough—any of these or hundreds of other factors can affect a test taker's performance. Children's daily scholastic performance is equally subject to such influences, which are more likely to be revealed to a teacher when children write and talk freely in class. So teachers can add an awareness of that life beyond to their insights into the patterns of intellectual growth in their effort to work more effectively with students.

Because she teaches children designated "learning disabled," Mary Anne Byrne often works with the same child over a period of years. But when her students began writing, she discovered things she had never known about children she'd already been working with for three or four years. Now Byrne has started to use some of her writing-conference questioning techniques when she first evaluates and tests children who have just been referred to her for their learning problems. "They'll start talking about something," she says, "and I'll just keep asking questions to get a really good picture of what they're dealing with in their total life, rather than just in the classroom." Transition teacher Kathy Matthews notes that through their writing, her students "expose a lot of themselves, their inner selves. So I can work more efficiently, knowing what will work best with each one."

What sorts of things do children expose? Things that are important to them, for whatever reason; things that influence their performance and behavior in school. When teachers discover these influences, they may be able to remedy a bad situation or capitalize on a good one.

Sometimes the outside influences are purely physical. One child who had been coming to school in an angry mood revealed in his journal that a mismatch between his mother's work schedule and child-care arrangements was causing him to miss breakfast on some days. Another wrote about an eye infection that was giving him difficulty in the classroom. A note sent home by the school nurse alerted his parents to the problem.

Other influences, both positive and negative, affect a child's emotions. Children sometimes write about a relationship with a sibling, a divorce or separation in the family, a squabble, or the death of a pet. Whether a teacher responds differently to children who have revealed difficulties or just takes the knowledge into account in an attempt to understand their behavior, the children usually benefit.

One junior-high English teacher had a student who was exhibiting "bizarre" behavior in the classroom. The girl's teachers were baffled. In her journal, she disclosed that she felt caught in the middle between her real parent and a stepparent. This knowledge allowed the English teacher to respond to her more intelligently. "I'm not saying that we can be social workers," the teacher cautions, "not that you have to say, 'Come put your head on my shoulders and cry.' But if you've got a child who's going through some terrible trauma, then that is going to affect who that person is in front of you. You're really going to deal differently with a child who is having that kind of emotional upset."

Sometimes children inadvertently give a teacher hints as to the best way to approach them intellectually. Some of Mary Anne Byrne's students, for example, have written about their learning disabilities and ways of compensating for them. Other students have also written about the teachers who have been able to help them most.

Most common, and perhaps most valuable to teachers, all children will reveal their special interests when they are allowed to select their own topics for writing. Everyone in Susan Porter's transition and first-grade classroom knew about Robbie's love of pigs and questioned him when he changed to a new subject. Older students sometimes learn things about their classmates of many years. One junior-high student had been collecting toy soldiers since he was two, unbeknownst to his classmates and teachers until he got a chance to write about his hobby in Karen Weinhold's class. Teachers who start sharing writing with their colleagues discover that people of all ages will often write about things they don't normally talk about. The revelation of hobbies, interests, and idiosyncrasies can round out the personalities of even the shyest members of a group. Those revelations also give teachers a fertile area in which to encourage children to try new things.

> *Teachers need to know about a child's life outside of school because that's most of the child's life. The world-knowledge that a child brings to reading and writing comes from what happens outside school. Most classroom lessons are abstract, with concrete counterparts in the child's experience outside school. The more I know about the children's outside world and the more the children are aware of what they know of that outside world, the more I can demand of them.*

Equipped with a knowledge of every child's interests, a teacher knows when to push. "I've got kids that I'm nudging into trying research," says eighth-grade teacher Nancie Atwell. "I'll say, 'You've been interested in astronomy all year. You've talked about it. What can you do to learn about astronomy in this class? You know that's OK. What kind of writing could you do that would help you know more about astronomy?' " Atwell's students write on "all free topics," she explains, smiling, "but I nudge like crazy."

CHAPTEr 9
The Teacher's Voice

The principal left the school several years ago, but in one teacher's words, "old habits die hard." This principal had very definite ideas about how her teachers should conduct themselves and decorate their rooms. "A teacher should never be sitting" was one of her mottoes. When she walked by the classroom doors, teachers would gasp and virtually stand at attention. The largest bulletin board in the back of each classroom "had to have social studies" on it, the teacher explains. She then goes around her room, giving a tour of the prescribed subjects: "The one over there had to have library arts. The one by the sink had to be art. This one had to be routines. And these on the side would be math and penmanship."

Only last year, however, things changed in some of the class-rooms. "Last year was the first year we started to go crazy. I tore off my bulletin board," the teacher says and then lists the other teachers who joined her. "It was like a mutiny! A little revolution." She and the other rebels were all teachers who have changed their approach to teaching writing. In many cases, the big back bulletin board now features writing "because that is the most important subject in the classroom," she says. "Social studies was not the most important subject. It wasn't being given the most time. If a teacher does a lot with math, and that is her strength, math shouldn't be relegated to one bulletin board. It should be reflected throughout the room."

Although the control of a bulletin board may seem like a trivial matter, it reflects the atmosphere within a school and the attitude the system takes toward the people in it. School systems often treat teachers the same way teachers treat children. In many communities, administrators, school boards, and textbook publishers all try to tell teachers exactly what to teach and when to teach it. Curriculums may be minutely detailed and rigidly structured. As one teacher puts it, "The school system doesn't trust the teacher as capable of doing the best for the children in the classroom." It is natural in such circumstances for teachers, like children who are always told what to do, to doubt their own abilities.

To draw parallels between the progress made by teachers and children neither degrades teachers nor elevates children. It simply points out the basic human need we all have, to be able to set our own goals and find our own ways of reaching them. When children write on an assigned topic and get their papers back covered with red ink, their writing doesn't even seem to belong to them. They don't care to improve it. When teachers follow step-by-step curriculums and the administration controls their bulletin boards or their plan books, teachers may also feel a lack of commitment to improvement. When children are allowed to make choices in their writing, they demonstrate their ability to choose and to learn from their choices, good or bad. They can find their own topics and make their own revisions. Likewise, teachers who are given, or take, the freedom to make decisions show their ability to go beyond textbooks and canned curriculums.

For both teachers and children, the freedom to make choices stimulates motivation and self-confidence. When children are taken seriously, they extend their intellectual efforts outside school. They write letters to newspapers and authors and members of Congress. Teachers who are taken seriously extend themselves in parallel ways. They publish articles, speak at conferences, present workshops for other teachers, and even go back to graduate school to learn more. Confident in what they do, yet ever on the lookout for better ways to do it, these teachers make better models for a child to look up to. They also make better teachers.

A Chain of Disrespect

In an article called "The Politics of Respect," Donald M. Murray argues that freshman composition programs suffer from a pervasive lack of respect—between instructor and student, administrator and instructor, community and university. A close examination of our public school systems reveals a similar chain of disrespect stretching from the man or woman on the street to school committees and administrators all the way to the last link—our children. Next to last, however, are teachers. The problem begins outside the school system, where complaints and negative reports chisel away at teachers' reputation, status, and self-confidence. The message is always the same: there is something wrong here. The commissions and complainers seldom point to schools where things are going right.

Louder and louder calls for "accountability" put more pressure on teachers. When the pressure takes the form of tests, teachers must adapt their instruction accordingly. Administrators check up on teachers in other, often trivial, ways. Many principals require teachers to submit their daily lesson plans for review one or two weeks in advance. In some cases, the plans must be written in ink. Teachers cannot be trusted, these rules imply, and teaching consists of carrying out a preconceived plan, rather than responding to children's needs. The conduct of classroom visitors reveals more of administrators' and society's attitudes toward teachers. Even in schools where they do decide how to decorate their rooms, teachers do not control their own work space in other ways.

We show an enormous disrespect for a teacher by making it possible for anyone to enter the room and interrupt instruction at any time. It would be unheard of for a teacher to walk unannounced into a principal's, or even a reading supervisor's, office. But the classroom seems to be a place that anyone can violate. Teachers never know who will walk in next: an administrator, custodian, parent, aide, or some kind of specialist, to name a few examples.

The pattern is the same in businesses and other organizations. Anthropologists point out that the power people possess is reflected in their ability to control their own space and time—that is, who can enter that space and when they can enter it. Teachers have control over neither of these, which shows just how low an estate they have. Yet they have more responsibility than anyone else in the building.

In short, teachers may feel assaulted on the front lines in the classroom and on the flanks by administrators and testing procedures. They are attacked from the rear by angry parents and a society that is critical and disrespectful of its teachers. No wonder an air of defeatism pervades the teachers' room, and the tales swapped during time-out resemble war stories. Off-duty teachers tend to focus on the negative aspects of their jobs and their students, talking about bad actors, pranks, and problem children of all kinds. When asked about the teachers'-room tales she used to tell before she changed her teaching methods, one junior-high teacher recalls, "I didn't have stories before. I had complaints."

In turn, completing the chain of disrespect, children tell each other delightful stories about harassing or being harassed by, their teacher. Worst of all, they lose respect for their own abilities. Fortunately, that chain can be reversed, so that each link respects the others. But in many cases, teachers themselves have to take the first step.

Self-Respect Comes First

Many teachers lump writing and teaching writing together into one category surrounded by anxiety. "I never felt comfortable with writing at all—teaching it or doing it," confesses a third-grade teacher. "Last year my total writing program consisted of haiku. We did one. We did start other things, but they were so horrible, I'd just drop it." The anxiety that inexperienced writers feel when they try to teach writing is as natural as the anxiety of a nonswimmer trying to teach swimming. If teachers are to feel good about themselves and their work, they must feel confident in their ability to do the very things they teach others to do.

> *What most parents don't know is that teachers have not been prepared to teach writing, either in school or in teacher-training programs. That's why most of us don't particularly care to write today. We may bear scars and injuries from two kinds of teachers—those who thought they didn't know how to teach writing but felt they had to and those who thought they did know how to teach writing but didn't.*
>
> *Writing is a craft. Because it is a craft, it involves an apprenticeship, working with an experienced practitioner. Asking inexperienced writers to teach writing is the same as passing out scalpels to medical students who have never put one foot into the operating room and asking them to perform surgery. It's tough on the surgeon and its tough on the patient. No wonder students and teachers are nervous about writing.*

The scars left by bad teaching may persist for years. When Maxine Kumin was a college freshman, she took a poetry-writing course. Six weeks after she submitted her sheaf of poems to the instructor, she got them back with one comment: "Say it with flowers, but whatever you do, don't try to write poems." For seven years she heeded that instructor's advice. Then she did try again, with so much success that she eventually won the Pulitzer Prize. Kumin was lucky. Few adults have the drive to keep writing in the shadow of English teachers past and to overcome memories of painful experiences as she did.

Teachers have suffered along with everyone else. When they think back on their own experiences with writing in school, they often find they have no memories or bad memories. One teacher remembers being praised for a poem she had written, but then she was required to copy it over so many times that she concluded she wouldn't try that again. Another teacher can't recall any writing in school, only worksheets and blanks to fill. "I never considered myself a writer," she says. "I was not a member of that club. So as a result, all my adult life I avoided situations that would require writing."

Whether future teachers develop a distaste for writing or not, most of their experiences with writing in school reflect the distorted priorities prevalent in classrooms everywhere. "My own memory of writing in school is penmanship," says a third-grade teacher, "ovals and up-downs."

Unfortunately, teachers' attitudes toward writing—their insecurities and their misconceptions—follow them into the classroom. University education programs have done little to remedy the problem. Teachers, even English teachers, have a weak spot in their training when it comes to writing. As part of a study he did for the Ford Foundation in 1978, Donald Graves took a look at the status of courses in writing instruction in teacher-training programs. In a random survey of the offerings in education departments at thirty-six universities, he found 169 courses in reading, 30 courses in children's literature, 21 courses in "language arts," and 2 courses in teaching writing. There has been little improvement in the situation since then, as enrollments have dropped and funds have declined in university education departments.

Of course, many teachers, including famous writers, teach by drawing on their experience rather than education courses. But most teachers have not written much. As college students they have seldom taken any writing courses beyond Freshman English, and many have been exempted from that. Outside college, they have often written even less. When one group of teachers took stock of their writing habits, they realized that they did little or no writing other than lists and thank-you notes. With neither experience nor training to guide them, the majority of teachers naturally rely on their own experiences with writing in school, paltry or unpleasant as those may have been. Thus, old teaching methods are perpetuated.

Many teachers first start writing in earnest at summer institutes and in-service workshops offered by organizations like the

New Hampshire Writing Program, affiliated with the University of New Hampshire, or the New York City Writing Project, located at Herbert Lehman College in the Bronx and affiliated with the National Writing Project, an organization that has given thousands of teachers a chance to write. These summer programs are usually intensive sessions lasting two or three weeks. Often the teachers spend the mornings writing and talking about their writing. Afternoon sessions focus on teaching skills. The courses are taught by professors and experienced writing teachers.

At the outset, a large percentage of teachers regard their writing courses as they would a dose of bitter-tasting medicine. Two days before one summer program began, a teacher called up to express her fears. "I hate writing," she confided. "How can I possibly learn how to teach it?" Every director of a summer writing institute for teachers has similar stories.

But the teachers come to the institutes and take their medicine, and many discover that they can, indeed, write. That is not to say that writing necessarily becomes easy or, in all cases, enjoyable. "I hated writing," says transition teacher Kathy Matthews, who attended a summer program called Project Write. "I had a real phobia about it. I assumed I was supposed to get it right the first time." Asked when she stopped hating writing, Matthews answered, "I still do! I hate that it doesn't come easily. But I stopped hating myself because I couldn't write easily. My perception of myself as a writer changed."

While Matthews, like hundreds of other teachers at summer writing institutes, discovered that she could write, she also came to see writers and writing in a new light. "Now I see it more as a process," she says. "I don't see it as an ability people are magically born with. There are some people who are gifted with an innate talent for writing. But they're going through the same process as I am. That's comforting. When I was involved in Project Write and saw these intelligent, talented, capable people [project leaders] going through the same thing I was, it started to dawn on me. It has also helped me to see that there are lots of different kinds of writers. Prize-winning novelists are not the only type. I'm a writer with a little *w,* as opposed to a big *W.*"

While gaining confidence, the teachers improve their own writing skills—skills they can pass on to their students at an appropriate level. A teacher who participated in the Boothbay Harbor Writing Project recalls, "It was doing my own writing that made me understand writing as a process. We talked about revision, and it was six months until I understood what revision was. I had been refining, not revising. I would go back and fix up one or two words."

Ultimately, these teachers make some of the same discoveries that they can now expect their students to make. Whether the writing is personal or professional, the teachers surprise themselves with what they didn't know they knew. A Vermont teacher named Dale Paul wrote an essay about her reaction to the news that she would never be able to have children. The piece went through three drafts, but the ending eluded her. After a while, she stopped writing and just thought about a resolution for the essay. It was during that time that an insight finally came to her. As she later described it, "I didn't write anything for the paper that week, but I did think about how to write a conclusion for a paper in which the issue was unresolved, and there sat the ending. This wasn't an issue to be resolved. It was a fact to be accepted. I wrote the last three paragraphs in a half-hour." Paul's essay, "Without Child," along with her comments on how she wrote it, has been published in *What Makes Writing Good: A Multiperspective,* edited by William E. Coles, Jr., and James Vopat. The ending she finally arrived at reveals a new perspective on her situation:

> . . . I told myself to examine the options rationally.
>
> That's what women in my generation do—select from limitless options. The first of the post-war baby-boom babies, we expected to have it all. We wanted the world to be fair and just, the air and water to be clean. We planned productive, fulfilling careers, we discussed the many options in our futures: children, husbands, careers, travel, politics. All the time we were picking and choosing among the options, doors were quietly closing around us.
>
> This time, a door slammed for me. I will not have a child of my own, will never experience pregnancy, will never give birth. That is a loss which needs to be mourned. I don't need to examine the options rationally. I need to feel angry and sad, to grieve. The women of my generation have not yet learned to mourn.

Packing away the Christmas decorations this year, I wondered what will become of them when my husband and I die. We have been collectors, makers of tradition. Of what use is the tradition if there is no generation to inherit it? I am learning to mourn.

Teachers, like children, may also begin to hear their own voices for the first time when they are encouraged to write freely. As with students, it is often the teachers who have written successfully in school who need more than anyone else to hear the sound of their own voices. When Nancie Atwell recalls her own experience with writing in school, she says, "I never, never thought of myself as a writer. I thought of myself as somebody who did assignments, and I'm sure that's the way my kids thought of themselves in my classes for a long time."

When she took a writing course, Atwell says she "discovered how badly I wrote, and that was important for me because I'd always thought of myself as a good writer. I found out I was pretentious—polysyllabic for no reason—just because I thought that was good writing. My papers sounded as if God had written them. I never used personal pronouns. There's some omniscient being who says, 'It seems . . . One would guess . . . One would surmise. . . .'" Even as she utters these phrases, Atwell's tone of voice changes. "I found a voice," she says, "and that happened partly through writing letters and finding that I liked letters better than anything else and then going back and thinking about how they were different from the other writing I was doing."

As teachers develop their own standards for judging writing, they also become more critical readers. "I just assumed if it was in print, it was great," says Kathy Matthews. "I like *Sophie's Choice,* but at times I got bogged down in Styron's style and irritated with him because of that. I realized I don't enjoy reading Taylor Caldwell because of her style. Before, I would have just read a book and assumed that it was good because the author could write and I couldn't."

When teachers become sure of their own ability to write, they have taken an important step. They think of themselves as experienced writers who have something to teach beginners. But this newfound self-assurance by itself may not be enough to carry them through a drastic change in teaching methods.

Independence—Not Isolation

Isolation is a word that often comes up in conversations with teachers. Like homemakers and babysitters, teachers spend hours at a time in the company of children alone. At the end of the day, many have their own children to contend with. An outsider might expect teachers to turn to each other for support, ideas, and the pleasure of adult conversation. Unfortunately, the negative air that prevails in many teachers' rooms is more conducive to griping than sharing ideas and solving problems.

Of course, there are organizations, such as the National Council of Teachers of English, in which educators can exchange new ideas and techniques. But the vast majority of teachers do not belong to professional organizations (outside of unions) because many teachers do not feel a part of that world of theories, abstract research, dry journals, and professionalism. For one thing, teachers often aren't treated as professionals. The lack of respect they are shown reveals administrators' low expectations of their staff. When administrators assume teachers are incapable of making their own decisions, teachers are likely to question their own abilities. The sheer number of directives coming down from on high worsens the problem, giving teachers a sense of inadequacy.

> *In one year, the school board and the administrators might decree that all teachers in a building shall give greater emphasis to writing, use new computers in the classroom, administer a new test, and teach from a new textbook series. So much comes at teachers that they are constantly torn between administrative or school-system demands and the children's needs. When they don't feel up to the task they face, they become isolated. Teachers who feel good about themselves are more likely to search out other teachers. Those who feel inferior keep the doors shut. Administrators may even stand in the way of collaboration among teachers who share special interests. If four second-grade teachers get excited about a new science program, for example, the administration may feel threatened.*

Without respect, support, and the freedom to make their own choices, few teachers are likely to risk trying new approaches in the classroom. They, like children, need to take an active role in their own learning. When they help themselves and each other, they learn more and enjoy teaching more. Ultimately, their students benefit.

Teachers immediately recognize the respect implicit in any system that grants them autonomy. The principal of Boothbay Region Elementary School (BRES) supported the writing project started by Nancie Atwell but did not require anyone to attend. The teachers who were interested got together in August of 1980 and began writing, reading extensively, and discussing what they read and wrote. One participant later declared: "We got together and spent a week just talking. And I'd never seen anybody have the guts to get a bunch of teachers together for a whole week and the agenda was just talk."

Reading, writing, and talking provided the Boothbay teachers with new ideas and new perspectives on their classroom experiences. But it was Writing Project director Atwell and the BRES administration who made the teachers feel free to try new approaches, make their own decisions, and even perform their own research. The teachers believe they learned more than they would have if they had been told what to do.

Susan Stires says she ultimately adopted a new approach to teaching writing in her special-education resource room "because I saw what worked. I was sitting there taking notes all the time and writing a log and observing and reporting and keeping track of everything. I was able to see patterns develop. Surely, it would have been nice for me to read a book or have consultants come to us and say, 'This is the way.' I could have adopted their theory and gone and done it. And maybe it would have been successful. But I don't think I'd be as convinced that the information can come from the kids themselves if I hadn't already done it through our own Writing Project."

Writing institutes and projects show respect for teachers in two ways. They offer workshops and presentations led by skilled teachers. Just as important, institute leaders encourage teachers to learn from their own experiences and trust their own perceptions.

Atkinson teacher Judy Egan later became an instructor in the Project Write summer institute for teachers. Many who attended wound up questioning not only their handling of reading and writing, but also their approach to other subjects. "You want to tell them that in the beginning," explains Egan. "You want to throw it all at them. And you know you can't. It's just like dealing with the children. They need to discover it on their own and at their own rate of learning. Eventually it comes around to, 'Gee, the way I'm doing other things during the day just isn't right. I should be doing it the way I'm doing writing. I should be asking the children questions. The learning should be coming from the kids.' "

Educators like Judy Egan treat teachers the same way they expect teachers to treat students. Ideally, school administrators should accord teachers the same respect and freedom—not only freedom to make choices, but freedom to make mistakes. "When you try something new, you must be allowed to fail," says Richard Sterling, codirector of the New York City Writing Project. "Otherwise, you're not going to change."

Sometimes the freedom to fail is granted by unexpected circumstances. At Linette Moorman's school, P.S. 152 in the Flatbush section of Brooklyn, teachers and administrators began their search for new ideas out of desperation. Over a period of years, the reading scores at their school had steadily dropped. Since *The New York Times* publishes the reading scores at New York City schools in rank order every spring, the decline at P.S. 152 was no secret. That fact alone exerted pressure on the teachers at the school.

The makeup of P.S. 152 had changed over the years as the neighborhoods feeding into it changed and some parents moved their children into private schools as a result. White middle- and upper-middle-class children have been replaced by poorer minority children. Ninety percent of the children now at the school are from minorities, mostly black, and twelve hundred out of fifteen hundred students are eligible for the federal free lunch program. A number of students, children of immigrants, come to the school unable to speak English. At the same time, the school has become increasingly overcrowded. Lunch, for example, has to be eaten in four shifts.

"Our reading scores had just gotten lower and lower and lower," the assistant principal reports. "And we tried patching it up with different test-taking techniques and stressed skills in the upper grades. But we finally said, 'Stop! It's no good. It's ridiculous. We're starting in the wrong place. Maybe working backward would help.' "

Meanwhile, Linette Moorman and her colleague Lila Edelkind started thinking about making some changes in their second- and first-grade classrooms. "One of the things that convinced all of us and gave us confidence," says Moorman, "was that we had nothing to lose. These children were not performing well. Their reading scores were well below what they should have been, and they had very poor writing skills: spelling, organization, and the sequencing of ideas. It was very important to say, 'Well, they're not doing so great with whatever we've been doing. And we don't think they're going to do that much worse.' "

During the course of several years, Moorman and Edelkind, along with another teacher and a professor from a nearby university, tried a number of alternatives to their old ways of teaching children language skills. First, they tried manufacturing experiences for their students, taking them on a trip to a botanical garden, for instance. The result: "We went to the garden." "We saw tulips." Flat, skimpy, predictable writing. The children seemed unable to write, and yet clearly they were capable of talking.

So the teachers gathered a menagerie of pets in the classroom and tried tape-recording what the children said in hopes of translating that fluency onto paper. Again, the result was a big disappointment. The writing was, according to Edelkind, "very flat, very—I don't even know the words to use for it. There was no voice. There was no life in it. It became very much a sterile report. 'Mrs. Moorman brought in animals and I touched this and this one touched this.' There was no excitement. The excitement that was in their voices on tape wasn't on paper."

Next, the teachers tried taking dictation, a favorite method in the early 1970s for capturing "all that rich language that they use." But soon the teachers realized that even in their trial runs with a small group of children, there simply wasn't enough time for the teacher to go around spelling every word for every child. Worse, "we discovered that by writing for them, we were making them dependent on us," Moorman reports, "and they were afraid of taking the risk of putting anything on paper." Reading, listening to speeches, and attending the New York City Writing Project Summer Institute brought Moorman and Edelkind to their final solution—allowing children to write on their own topics and with their own spelling.

Moorman and Edelkind ultimately succeeded in part because their administration supported them in their efforts to find their own solutions to classroom problems. If the administrators had required the teachers to do the same thing—letting children choose their own words and topics—the effect wouldn't have been the same. The directors of writing institutes do not recommend mandating new teaching approaches of any type.

Jean Robbins was the elementary-school principal at Atkinson during the time when Donald Graves conducted his study there, and she has since directed Project Write. When the results of the study became known, an Atkinson school-board member approached her and asked, "Why can't we mandate this for every teacher in the district?" Robbins replied, "We speak of readiness for children. There's also the idea of readiness for teachers." In other words, teachers need respect in the form of freedom to choose their own actions, and that includes the freedom not to change.

> *Mandates don't work. A mandate says, "We know, but you don't. We, the board of education, the superintendent, the principals, and supervisors, believe that writing is important. And it doesn't matter what you think. So we will all move out and do writing."*

Once introduced, new ideas often spread of their own accord anyway. In schools where one or two teachers have attended writing institutes, other teachers soon become interested in finding out about new methods. Participation in the writing project at Boothbay Harbor was entirely voluntary, but after two years three-quarters of the teachers at Boothbay Region Elementary School had chosen to change their approach to teaching writing. In the Shoreham–Wading River School District on Long Island, 75 percent of all elementary teachers and 75 percent of all English teachers have attended the Shoreham–Wading River Writing Project, an offshoot of the New York City Writing Project. Even teachers from other fields, including physical education and art, as well as several administrators, have chosen to attend writing-project sessions. All together, nearly half the teachers in the district have had training in the teaching of writing, and every one took that training voluntarily. In fact, Shoreham–Wading River teachers participate in developing curriculums and programs such as the writing project. Before selecting writing consultants to work in their system, administrators sent several highly respected teachers to a number of workshops and conferences in search of the educators and methods that would be most helpful.

At Reservoir East Primary School, in Reservoir, Australia, where Jo Parry teaches, task forces of teachers work with the local university to investigate possible curriculum changes. One group of five teachers went to work on writing instruction. Within a year, the results were similar to those at Boothbay and Shoreham–Wading River—twelve out of seventeen teachers had voluntarily changed their methods.

In addition to autonomy and respect, teachers need support, ties with other colleagues who are going through the same experience or who have been through it before. University courses, summer institutes, and in-service workshops provide a way for teachers to break out of the isolation in the classroom and make connections with colleagues. Since the teachers in these courses begin writing immediately, the first connection they make is usually that of writer to reader or reader to writer as they listen to one another's work. And often that link is made on a personal level before it's made on a professional level because many teachers begin by writing from their own experiences.

Junior-high teacher Karen Weinhold had been writing for years before she attended her first summer institute at the New Hampshire Writing Program. Her writing, however, had never received a response because she stuffed it all into her bureau drawers. At the writing program, she found an audience for the first time. Her first piece was about her experience as a young mother in the mid-1960s. She wrote about what she called "the myth of motherhood," the idea that a mother automatically feels an instant bond with a newborn baby. "I thought there was something wrong with me for months," she explains, "and I certainly didn't tell anyone that I was not feeling this bond. Well, I've come to realize that at least for me . . . until you get to know something you can't love it or hate it. You've got to know it first and that only comes with time." The reaction to Weinhold's piece in her writing group was mixed. But one woman confided that she had had a similar experience. "That made me feel that at least one other person had felt that way," Weinhold says.

In daily discussions during the program, Weinhold discovered that she shared many of the feelings expressed by other teachers. Their lives had run parallel to one another in many ways. She felt able to identify with her classmates "as a woman, as a mother, and as a teacher." The writing and talking in the summer program allowed those parallel lines to intersect, intellectually and emotionally, and it was that intersection that Weinhold missed the following fall when she went back to her classroom. "After it was over, for months I felt left out again," she says, "back into isolation. I really felt bereft."

That sense of isolation can inhibit teachers from making changes. According to Richard Sterling, "You need a support system if you're going to fail—not just administrators who will get off your back, but also some you can call and say, 'I tried this great idea, but it doesn't work!'" Some teachers find it easy to adopt new ideas back in the classroom. But many find the going rough, especially at the beginning and especially if they have always been anxious about writing.

Teachers worry about their own performance. They worry about how parents and administrators will react to changes. They also have many practical obstacles to surmount, for they must develop and maintain the infrastructure that allows a classroom to run smoothly. According to Linette Moorman, "You really have to have groups like the [New York City] Writing Project and small groups of people in your own school who speak the same language, someone you can go to and say, 'I'm really having a hard time organizing myself with this writing business. All the folders! They're getting pieces lost.' It's important to know that you're not going to be judged negatively, that you're going to be given some help or even just be heard, so you can talk it out. And by talking, you can often solve your own problem. You see it for yourself when you hear it."

Many of the writing institutes and projects try to help teachers develop stronger ties with colleagues. The New Hampshire Writing Program provides consultants who make visits to participants' classrooms throughout the year. The New York City Writing Project has regular monthly meetings for its permanent members, as well as occasional weekend retreats. And Project Write refused to accept teachers who could not bring at least one partner from the same building. Some teachers find their own ways to strengthen ties with colleagues. Karen Weinhold dispelled her own sense of isolation by starting a writing group among interested teachers in her own school and returning to the New Hampshire Writing Program the following summer for more advanced work.

With renewed self-confidence and the support of their colleagues and supervisors, some teachers are able to go beyond the training they receive in writing institutes and courses. These teachers begin to question their methods in every subject. Third-grade teacher Jan Roberts has changed her methods of teaching social studies, science, and spelling. She's as likely to involve students in setting as in solving problems. Her students now write some of their own math problems, for example; then the whole class works through and discusses each one. Next year, she wants to teach geology differently.

First-grade teacher Ellen Blackburn changed her methods of teaching reading as well as writing. She had always believed in learning by doing. Her students acquired math concepts by counting and sorting objects; they studied science in part by working with live animals and plants. Language instruction had always bothered her, however, because the prevailing "philosophy toward reading and writing was that you had to know how to do it before you can do it." She smiles at the paradox. There was no apparent way to have the children learn to read and write by reading and writing. As a teacher, Blackburn felt "like Jekyll and Hyde."

After taking a summer program at the New Hampshire Writing Program, she felt at last that she'd found a way to teach writing by allowing the children to write, from the very first day of school. But she was still in a quandary about reading. Drilling splintered skills and having the children read from sterile readers didn't feel right to her. She was given a second boost when Donald Graves and his colleague Jane Hansen selected her classroom as the site of a study on the relationship between reading and writing. More than other teachers or books, the research team offered Blackburn the emotional support and intellectual springboard she needed to develop new methods.

During the course of the first year of the study, she developed a way of teaching reading that satisfied her. "I just figured it out," she says. "I said to myself, 'Look, this is how you teach writing. If you're going to make your teaching of reading consistent, what are the main elements you have to preserve?'" For example, "They should choose topics in writing, and they should choose books in reading. If I have writing conferences where we ask questions and talk, then we should do the same thing with reading. If we do revision, then I should allow and encourage reading and rereading. I shouldn't always expect them to read something new. And if kids read to the class, then they shouldn't always feel they have to read something the class hasn't heard. If we were going to publish in writing, then it was important to have a corresponding activity in reading, which is what having the kids read to the class is." The result was an innovative and effective way of teaching reading that even the researchers had never observed before.

Reversing the Chain

Feeling confident in their work and looking for new challenges, many teachers begin to reach out beyond the classroom through both writing and teaching. Karen Weinhold, for instance, had her piece about the myth of motherhood published in a parents' magazine in a deliberate effort to help other mothers. "Since men have been the predominant writers," she says, "I suspect there are lots and lots of things that women experience in isolation because they haven't been written about. And I suspect that they have felt like I did—that they were weird. They were abnormal. There was something wrong with them because they weren't following the norm."

But Weinhold, like other teachers, has also come to feel much more a part of her own profession. Before her participation in a writing program, she used to think, "What do I need researchers for? It seemed as though people did research because they didn't have anything else to do. If anybody had told me that I would be reading education journals on my own free time, I would have told them they were *crazy*. And yet, now I can't get hold of them fast enough because I want to know what people are saying. It's like I'm a sponge and I can't absorb it fast enough."

Most of the teachers who have published their work write for professional magazines and journals. They have enlarged their audience to include their colleagues across the country and even around the world. One special-education teacher reports that she enjoys getting notes from Ireland and England asking for reprints of her article. Even the teacher who considered herself "not a member of that club" when it came to writing had an article accepted for publication in a book about teachers' research in the classroom.

Many teachers also reach out to others by conducting workshops in their own buildings or at other schools and by giving presentations to professional organizations—organizations that, in many cases, they hardly knew existed before. An assistant principal in the Shoreham–Wading River school district estimates that of the seventy to eighty teachers who have been trained in writing instruction, twenty-five to thirty genuinely feel that they are "part of the writing field." Ten to fifteen write for publication and give presentations at professional conferences such as those held by the National Council of Teachers of English and various New York state education organizations. According to the administrator, "They've really been professionalized."

A few teachers, like former Atkinson teacher Mary Ellen Giacobbe, have returned to higher education and even taken doctorates in order to devote full time to working with other teachers. In a time when morale is low within the profession, many have been revitalized by their new attitudes toward themselves and children. Richard Sterling has seen twenty- and thirty-year veterans of the classroom change their whole attitude toward teaching. In more than one case, he recalls, "they were about to retire and they'd had it with the system. They were fed up." After attending the New York City Writing Project summer institute, however, "they got a new lease." These teachers chose to put off retirement for another year or two because they were fascinated by what was happening for the first time in their own classrooms.

Whether or not they publish their writing or do consulting work in other school districts, all teachers talk about their work. And when schools run on mutual respect instead of disrespect, teachers start telling a different kind of story in the teachers' room. Before her students wrote regularly, Karen Weinhold used to devote a lot of time to grammar exercises, and her students sometimes devoted themselves to other activities. There would be "airplanes shooting, and the floor would be littered with bits and pieces of paper," she recalls. "What stood out in my mind at the end of the day was the kids I had trouble with, and that is no longer the case because I rarely have trouble with anyone now." A fifth-grade teacher says she now tells stories about the times when she gets goosebumps in the classroom.

If children are encouraged to tell and write about what they know, their teachers soon have new stories to tell—positive stories about the things children say, write, and do. A first-grade teacher tells about the day when a boy who had struggled and struggled suddenly realized, as he went over his own book, that he could indeed read. Another teacher describes how delighted she was when a first-grader who had written a lot the previous year came into class the first day and, without being told, immediately sat down and started writing about a caterpillar the teacher had put into a butterfly cage.

Many of the stories teachers tell revolve around the process children go through when they write. Learning-disabilities specialist Susan Stires enjoys telling the history of a piece of writing—how it was conceived or how it was chopped up and then taped back together again. "I am so interested in not just what I can show somebody," she says, "but all of what I know went into a particular line or story."

> *Most research, because of the way it's written, doesn't give teachers much to talk about among themselves. In our research, we were always trying to show the classroom so that teachers could picture the child. That's why we always gave each child a name instead of "the subject."*
>
> *Our study brought out another type of story teachers could tell one another. They could tell stories about children's topics, drafts, and conferences. Thus teachers found a new framework for telling stories about children.*

Administrators who listen to the teachers and children in their building have their own positive stories to tell. One Canadian principal likes to take visitors down the corridors, pointing out drawings and pieces of writing, telling about the children and teachers behind them. Ultimately, the stories spread outside the school through local papers and by word of mouth. Many newspapers publish children's writings regularly. In areas where children in a number of classrooms start writing, newspapers often print feature articles reporting on the phenomenon of young children who produce hundreds of pages of writing.

But perhaps the best publicity comes from proud parents. Linette Moorman loves to tell about the father who took one of his son's published books and pinned it up on a bulletin board in his office at the World Trade Center for all the world to see.

CHAPTEr 10
But Will They Be Able to Spell?

When Ed and Heather McGarrigle's daughter Kasey started school in a pre-first-grade transition class, her teacher explained her method of writing instruction in a meeting with parents. But just how different this method was didn't really hit the McGarrigles until later: "And then things would come home, funny looking," according to Heather. At first she was skeptical. Then she noticed that Kasey was very excited about writing. She would write at home, and she took to carrying a little notebook around with her. When her friend had a birthday, she chose to write her own card rather than buy one. Meanwhile, her writing was looking less and less "funny." By the end of the second year in this type of classroom, Kasey had written many little books, including her own version of the "Nutcracker Suite," more than four hundred words and forty pages long. And her parents had been impressed by what they had learned about this method of instruction, from Kasey's teacher, professors at the local university, and Kasey herself.

Many parents have questions about new teaching methods that diverge from their own experiences, as well as the experiences of the majority of children in schools today. Parents are surprised to find teachers allowing children to produce "funny-looking" writing not only in their early stages of development as writers but even in later years on early drafts. The news that writing now takes up time formerly committed to basic exercises in grammar and reading dismays many parents. So they naturally want to know how children in these classrooms will fare compared to those in standard classrooms where workbooks prevail.

How Will They Learn to Spell?

One Australian mother was clearly upset about invented spelling. Whenever her six-year-old daughter brought home schoolwork, it would come back to school the next day, covered with circled spelling errors. Finally, the first-grade teacher, who had been pleased with the little girl's writing, found a solution. She collected everything the child had written and classified every word by grade level. As it turned out, 80 percent of the misspelled words were considered to be on the sixth-grade level or higher. The teacher needed to say no more.

Australian parents are not alone in their spelling worries. The American misspelling phobia approaches the national obsession with reading problems. One survey of parents found that spelling was third on their list of concerns, two places below reading and, like handwriting, far above composition. Parents who worry about a very young child's ability to spell, however, have inappropriate expectations.

If adults doubt that a kindergartner has something to say and the will to put it onto paper, they underestimate the child. But parents who expect perfect handwriting, spelling, and punctuation from the same child are asking too much. Children that young have neither the coordination, the skill, nor the experience to deliver perfectly formed prose without copying and tracing. Although children will respond to challenges, unrealistic demands can cause problems. And many well-meaning adults make unrealistic demands. One woman wrote to Donald Graves to complain that her next-door neighbor's three-year-old was writing thank-you notes with atrocious printing and spelling.

Parental fears also stem from deeply rooted misconceptions. Research has repeatedly shown that there is little connection between spelling ability and intelligence. Many highly intelligent and successful people, like John F. Kennedy, for example, are poor spellers. Even some brilliant writers cannot spell. Few American novels have been held in higher regard than *The Great Gatsby;* yet Fitzgerald's handwritten manuscript for the classic reportedly contained no fewer than fifty-five hundred spelling errors.

Whether they should or not, however, many people judge others by their spelling. Misspellings are as much of an affront to the natural speller's eye as sour notes to the trained musician's ear. Given society's attitude toward spelling, misconceptions and all, it is only fair to ask whether a new method that helps children write better will also help them spell better or, at the very least, leave them spelling no worse than they would have been under other methods.

Most spelling books are based on a "structural analysis" of words. Children study suffixes, prefixes, syllabification, silent letters, double letters, and more. In 1976, a study of current spelling books showed that nearly 50 percent of the exercises were devoted to structural analysis of words. Another 34 percent was taken up by a whole host of exercises that have nothing to do with spelling: handwriting, alphabetizing, and identifying homonyms, synonyms, and antonyms, among others. Only 18 percent of the exercises asked children to use spelling in context.

At least as early as 1929, researchers were questioning the wisdom of having children manipulate bits of spelling words. Then in 1969 a study showed that children spell better when asked to focus their attention on the meaning, rather than the structure of words. High achievers and low achievers, good spellers and poor spellers alike did best when they used their spelling words in sentences. Nevertheless, spelling books continue to put students through the paces of structural analysis.

Just as conventional exercises may actually weaken spelling ability, conventional responses to spelling errors in written work may ultimately encourage a number of students to play it safe when they write. They write very little, or not at all, simply because they might make a mistake. These students and their teachers have lost sight of the reason why spelling exists: so that people may write.

In classrooms and homes where invented spelling is allowed, young children use spelling for its intended purpose from the start. And as they do, their spelling gradually improves. In *GNYS AT WRK,* educator Glenda Bissex chronicles the steps her son went through as he evolved from an inventive speller to a conventional speller between the ages of five and nine. Many teachers and parents have witnessed the same evolution.

Although every child takes a different path in learning to spell, there are a number of mileposts that most children pass. Unaware of the match that writers make between sound and symbol, many children begin writing with long unintelligible strings of letters. When asked what they have written, they often say something like, "You tell me. You read it to me." As they begin to understand the concept of sounding out words, children often represent each word with a single letter, the initial consonant. Before long, they'll use two consonants, representing the first and last sounds, and next they may include consonants in the middle. Eventually, beginning writers tackle the vowels between consonants.

If they are aware that conventionally spelled words have more letters than theirs, children sometimes fill in the extra space with nonsense letters, as in *SGHYR,* Emily's version of *sir.* During this period, children often write with capital letters only, or mix capitals and small letters together, more or less at random. They may run all their words together and line up letters from the top of the page to the bottom, Chinese style, or in some original configuration—wrapped around a drawing, for example.

At first, inventive spellers rely on the sounds they hear when they say a word, as well as the position of the tongue when they articulate it. They may match a letter with its phonetic sound or with the sound of its name. Thus children may spell *cat* with a *k* or *with* with a *y (yith)*. As they are exposed to published books and conventional translations of their own writing, children develop their ability to remember how words look. Conversations with the teacher and other children also nudge them toward conventional spelling and punctuation.

If there is one rule that applies to every child, it is that progress is always uneven. Children never follow any series of stages exactly and sometimes appear to be regressing in one area as they advance in another. A few selections from one child's daily writing illustrate this principle.

When Bobby came to Susan Porter's split transition and first-grade class, he knew only a handful of the letters of the alphabet. In October, the class began "writing" every day. All the children drew pictures, and some added scribbles or letters. Two children wrote decipherable words from the first day. Bobby just drew pictures for a while, although he copied the alphabet one day and counted by tens on another. On a different occasion, a more advanced friend help him write words. But soon Bobby was making his own attempts. Like most children, he began by labeling pictures, sometimes with a single word, other times with a caption. One booklet began with a drawing of a car, labeled *CAR* (a word a friend had taught him to spell); the next page showed another vehicle and the "word" *BHNOU,* meant to represent the sound of an engine ("vrrroom").

On November 1, Bobby seemed to retreat from writing words when he made a book full of drawings and added only *DE* (The End) on the last page. In another book of labeled pictures later in the month, he drew a picture of a spaceship and wrote, *DE.ET SP EB* (The E.T. Spaceship). Every letter in this caption approximated a sound in the words he spoke, and every word was set off by a dot or a space.

At the end of December, he tackled a far more advanced form than labels—a narrative based on "A Visit from St. Nicholas." These more difficult sentences looked like strings of nonsense letters at first glance but, on closer examination, revealed a match between some of the sounds of the words he told his teacher and the limited number of letters at his command. But he seemed to be making an attempt to separate words with dots, his own device. By now, Bobby was beginning to use lowercase letters, although these seemed to be distributed at random. The first line of his Christmas book looked like this: *WePethm.nee.msh.WH"* (Once upon a time not even a mouse was heard).

Three weeks later, Bobby was back to labeling pictures. But his spelling seemed to show the influence of the printed word and a somewhat better grasp on the letters of the alphabet when he added *-ing* to a word in the phrase *a car jeping* (a car jumping). He was also setting off each word with appropriate spaces. In early February, a line in one of his books revealed four out of seven words spelled conventionally in a complete sentence. But he had gone back to his dot system for separating words. He wrote, "the.car.iz.goi.tothe.iPot" (the car is going to the airport).

In mid-March, Bobby wrote a book that showed just how far he had come in less than six months. It also showed how children sway back and forth as they try to master the balancing act of writing. The book itself, for example, was a kind of hybrid between a complete narrative and a series of labeled pictures that told a story. One sentence in the book was spelled, punctuated, and capitalized to perfection. On another page, he spelled *operation* correctly. Elsewhere his application of capital letters and periods was uneven. But overall his writing revealed his growing knowledge of conventional English spelling. He now knew all his letters and was able to fill out his words with vowels. His use of a silent *e* and a double consonant, *ll,* showed that he was beginning to remember how some conventional spellings looked. This is what he wrote:

A Slit Misteke	A Slight Mistake
A car is goring	A car is going
up on A hil.	up on a hill.
The car is on	The car is on
the hill.	the hill.
the uvu car went	The other car went
the won wa	the wrong way.

it gut demig	It got damaged.
hee gut Bad wie	He got badly
hot	hurt.
A hstbol	A hospital.
A operation	An operation.
hee is ok	He is OK.

As is the case with all inventive spellers, some of Bobby's errors, like the omission of spaces between words, disappeared without any comment from his teacher. Other skills, such as the use of capitals and periods, were introduced by her. Still others came from his peers. Porter attributes his swift and complete mastery of the whole alphabet in the middle of the year to the influence of his friends. Their words simply looked more like words in published books.

Because she was trained to work with invented spelling in a university course, Bobby's teacher recognized even his early work as just the beginning of a whole process of development. To the untrained eye, however, such primitive attempts still look like garbled spelling. Some parents fear that children will memorize their unconventional versions of words. Evidence shows, however, that those fears are unfounded.

Glenda Bissex of Norwich University, Carol Chomsky of Harvard University, and other researchers concur that inventive spellers do not see a word as a fixed entity that can only be spelled in one way. In fact, young children often spell one word in several different ways in the same piece of writing. A first-grader at Atkinson, for example, wrote the word *flowers* in two different ways on the same day:*FLLAOWZ* and *FLLAWRZ*. (In earlier times, this practice was accepted among adults. Shakespeare, for example, never seemed to decide how to spell his own name.) Over a period of weeks and months, inventive spellers continue to spell the same word in numerous ways, but the approximations gradually make uneven progress toward accuracy. The following chart shows all the different ways Bobby spelled *The End* over the course of his year in first grade.

October 28	DED
November 12	DE

November 10   DAF
November 18   DF
November 21   DtHe eND
December 6   DND
December 19   DETD
January 5   DED
April 20   Ve End
May 23   End

Eager to reassure concerned parents, some teachers administer standard spelling tests in addition to their usual writing program. The teachers I talked with believe that their students are spelling at least as well as students in other classrooms or in standard spelling programs. More important than the ability to pass spelling tests, however, is the ability to spell in a piece of writing.

> *Spelling is usually taught and tested in isolated lists. Unfortunately, a child can get 95 percent correct on a list and then misspell the same words in a composition. Spelling is only one of about twenty operations that make up the act of writing. The spelling often gets sacrificed for handwriting, punctuation, or focus on a difficult subject.*
>
> *But spelling suffers for other reasons, as well. Many people spell poorly because they simply don't care about what they're writing. The piece belongs to someone else. It belongs to the teacher who assigned the topic and wrote corrections all over the page. The writers feel like tenants, and tenants seldom do their own repairs or yard work.*

If children care about their work and understand the importance of appearance from a reader's point of view, they will care about spelling. Older children who take charge of their own work can learn to find and correct many of their errors when they edit their own writing. That ability will serve them well outside school, when teachers no longer hover nearby, red pencils poised for action. When teachers collaborate with children instead of punishing them, even poor spellers can develop strategies for finding their own mistakes. In the meantime, these children can enjoy writing as much as their classmates do and need not feel ashamed or hindered by their difficulties with spelling.

Jo Parry encourages her Australian fourth-, fifth-, and sixth-graders to focus on questions of content and organization in their early drafts. Thus, the children spell difficult words as best they can until they are ready to prepare their work for publication within the class. In her report on Parry's classroom, researcher Marilyn Woolley noted the strategies the children used in their pursuit of correct spelling when it came time to edit. First, the writers themselves identified any spellings that they had had to approximate. Other children also read the drafts and underlined any words they considered misspelled. The writers then used their knowledge of spelling patterns and variations to check each approximation. Finally, they drew on a whole series of other sources, including dictionaries, books, telephone directories, classmates' published work, and classroom maps, charts, and lists. Once a correct spelling was found, it was entered into the child's own "word book." Working in pairs, the children practiced spelling the new words until they could write them correctly without assistance. At that point, each mastered word was entered into the child's personal dictionary.

"In *A Day to Remember,*" a fourth-grader told Woolley, "I learnt *direction, barbed wire, billiards, waterproof,* and *signaled.* They're all pretty hard words, I reckon, and now I can spell them." More important, he had learned how to learn new words.

Fourth-grader Cassie has not only mastered words like *embarrassed* and *commiserate,* she has appreciated the opportunity to develop a quality she values highly: self-reliance. When Jo Parry was away, Cassie went to another classroom, where she met with a different method of teaching writing. She didn't like what she saw: "You do one draft, and then you go to conference, and they do your spelling for you. It gave me the irrits. I don't like it. . . . It's no good. You don't get to take away or add more. I haven't changed anything from my first draft, and I'm sure I could have made it twice as good. I didn't do any work on information. I just had to go straight into spelling, and then it wasn't me doing the work. It was other people doing it for me. Instead of them circling or underlining the words, they just crossed them out and wrote them for me, so my brain wasn't doing the work."

Don't Grammar Count?

In recent years, a new breed of columnist has developed. These writers have taken upon themselves the duty of chivalrously defending the English language from what one has called "assaults" from two directions: the ignorant and the pretentious. In their attempts to ward off both assaults, these knights shield themselves with shining armor made of grammatical rules, finely burnished sensibilities, and reverence for antiquity. *Saturday Review*'s knight recently wrote an essay called "Don't Grammar Count?" which appeared in *Literacy as a Human Problem,* edited by James C. Raymond. Like many of the other columnists, Thomas H. Middleton had always considered himself an ally of English teachers, assuming that their main goal "was to make their students more or less comfortable with what educated users of the language had thought of as its rules." His illusions were shattered, however, when he attended a national convention of English teachers, where he "learned that, for the past twenty years or more, hardly anyone had taught grammar rules. I also learned, to my extreme dismay, that those many teachers who continued to feel that rules were important and that they were not impossible to master had often been forbidden to teach them."

Perhaps more shocked than Middleton to hear of what he had learned, I made a quick survey of one freshman English class at a public university. The class consisted of twenty students from six different states. All twenty reported that they had done many punctuation exercises throughout their school years. Nineteen had had extensive training in grammar in elementary school, as well as junior and senior high school. A full three-quarters of the students had been required to diagram sentences. If this group of students, products of our schools during the 1970s, had difficulties with grammar, it was certainly not for lack of formal instruction. Their instructor considered the group about average in their command of grammar and punctuation.

Of course, such an impromptu poll is hardly scientific. But with thirty-four years of experience in elementary-school and college classrooms between us, neither Donald Graves nor I have seen any evidence that contradicts its results. In addition, Donald Graves has twice analyzed the contents of elementary language texts published by leading textbook companies. When he examined eight fifth-grade texts in 1976, for example, he found that a full 40 percent of the exercises focused on the mechanics of language, and 76 percent of those exercises were devoted to grammar and punctuation. A second study in 1983 yielded similar results.

How influential are these texts? One study conducted by a nonprofit consumer organization found that approximately 95 percent of all classroom activities stem from textbooks and other classroom materials. If that figure comes close to reality, textbooks are very influential indeed. As for teachers who are forbidden to teach grammar—many find themselves in quite the opposite situation. In one school, for example, eighth- and ninth-grade English teachers are required to devote the equivalent of seventy out of one hundred eighty school days to grammar and punctuation lessons. The equivalent of nineteen days is reserved for writing.

So grammar does still count. But research suggests it often isn't taught effectively. The course of educational research has not always run smoothly. New studies overturn the findings of old ones; new analyses find fault with earlier methods. There is one finding, however, that has been repeated again and again: traditional grammar training does not deliver the things its proponents promise. Since 1906, study after study has shown that knowledge of grammar fails to correlate with the ability to interpret literature, the ability to learn a foreign language, or, most important, the ability to write or speak well. One study showed that knowledge of grammar was more highly correlated with mathematical than verbal abilities.

Unaware of the research, or perhaps in spite of it, many parents share Thomas Middleton's suspicions and dismay. They are convinced that grammar lessons made them better writers. In a survey of 150 educated adults, for example, the majority of the subjects said they believed that the ability to diagram a sentence was an important skill. Fifty-seven of the adults claimed that they visualized words as if in a diagram as they wrote. When put to the test, however, only two of the fifty-seven, and four of the other respondents, were actually able to diagram a sentence.

Although the formal study of grammar may have intrinsic value, it should not be confused with writing instruction or allowed to usurp writing time for years on end. Traditional exercises often fail to enhance students' ability to write or even to understand grammar, for several reasons. To begin with, time-consuming drills prevent students from getting needed practice in writing. And, like structural analysis of spelling words, most grammar exercises remove words from the contexts that make them meaningful and interesting, a surefire way to weaken motivation. Isolated drills also divorce instruction from the largely intuitive but substantial knowledge of grammar that all competent speakers possess.

> *I find that parts of speech can be useful if I point to what the writer already has. "Oh, you used a good adjective there." "Now there's a verb that is much more precise." In this way, students will understand that the names of the parts of speech exist to refer to the power of language as opposed to the curious art of identifying words for no apparent purpose at all. Unless parts of speech and punctuation are used to enhance the intentions of a writer, they become empty drills for a game that will never be played.*

If grammar yanked out of context tends to confuse and bore students, even worse things happen with grammar in context. Too many teachers treat usage as a moral issue—a question of right or wrong, rather than clear or not clear, appropriate or inappropriate in a given context. As a result, students have no sense of learning something they need. Instead, they feel, as one mother recalls from her own experience in school, "like a puppy who's made a mistake and then had his nose rubbed in it."

Students do need to understand grammar and punctuation.

They need to avoid dangling modifiers, not for goodness' sake, but for the sake of clarity and grace. The misplacement of one comma can confound a reader, cost a government money, or change a political party's statement of philosophy. Students need to understand how to use language that's appropriate for an intended effect or audience. *Ain't* is neither bad nor wrong, just inappropriate in certain situations; it can be appropriate, even powerful, in others.

Of course, some ways of speaking and writing are more socially prestigious than others. If children who speak nonstandard dialects are to become upwardly mobile, they must learn the more prestigious dialect. But they need not be taught that the language they use at home is inferior. Linguists have found nonstandard dialects, such as urban black English, to be just as clear, consistent, and systematic as the kind of English spoken on the evening news.

Whether it leaves them feeling like bad puppies or inferior humans, overzealous correction undermines students' self-confidence. At the same time, it leaves teachers with a sense of having done their duty. Thus, simple correction too often takes the place of genuine instruction in the context of a piece of writing.

> *Telling writers they've made a mistake is not teaching. If the child can already do what I've corrected, then correcting is only reminding. And reminding is not teaching. If the child doesn't understand the error, then correcting it isn't enough. Many errors have to be ignored simply because children can only take in so much at one time. When I choose one type of error to work on, then I use what the child already knows to help him or her learn the new skill.*
>
> *Suppose a little boy has used dialogue without quotation marks in his piece of writing. The first thing I have to find out is whether he knows what conversation is. I'll ask him to read the piece to find out where someone starts talking. Then I ask him to tell me where the speaker finishes talking. If the child can do that, then he has shown that he knows what conversation is and how to find it. Now he is ready for the symbol that stands for something he already knows.*

But my job isn't done yet. I still need to point out how the quotation marks help me, as a reader, to better understand the child's meaning. I might exaggerate a little and say, "Oh, now I know that Frankie's talking. It's important for me to know that because Frankie was saying, 'I think I just broke my leg,' and, if I didn't know that, I might miss out on why they went to the doctor and why he had to stay out of school for two weeks. That was a close call. And now you know how to show that someone's talking."

Thoughtful and judicious instruction in the context of their own writing equips students to seek out and correct their own mistakes. Concern for their own work and their own readers motivates children to do so. Junior-high teacher Karen Weinhold reports that her students voluntarily use grammar books and other references in the room to check their own grammar and punctuation. "Now they need to find out because they want it to be the best it can be," she says, "because they want to share it. And that's a lot different from making it right so you don't get a red mark on your paper. They're all dying to get something published for the class or for the school, outside on the bulletin board."

What About Handwriting?

Handwriting has suffered the same fate as spelling and grammar. In most classrooms, penmanship has been severed from its reason for being. Teacher Kathy Diers saw the results of two years of penmanship instruction when she asked her new class of third-graders to copy a Shel Silverstein poem as a handwriting exercise. Since the poem was humorous, she awaited their reaction with anticipation. But not one student chuckled or even cracked a smile. Finally, she couldn't take it any longer. "What's wrong?" she asked. "Didn't you think it was funny?" After a long pause, a little boy raised his hand. "Mrs. Diers," he asked, "were we supposed to *read* the poem?"

The children can hardly be blamed. Most of their handwriting exercises in the past were probably not worth reading. To many children, "handwriting" means empty sentences of the "People are fun" variety, copied over and over. Or it may mean all writing, a far worse misconception. Writers can hardly produce good first drafts if their thoughts are consumed with concerns about ovals and up-downs and strokes and counts.

Concern with penmanship does have its place. As usual, Cassie has an opinion on the matter. She explains the difference between practicing handwriting for its own sake and using good handwriting in books that will be published in the classroom. "You get to make your own stories and you become proud of your work," she says. "Instead of just looking in your handwriting book for neat handwriting, you write neat for others to read. With handwriting lessons, you get sick of just having to write neat. In our drafts, we don't have to write neat. You can just do a blob of words or pictures and that could be your first draft. In your second draft you look for information. And then prepublishing— that's when you worry about handwriting and spelling. It seems long, but it isn't if you get interested in it."

Once again, whether children "get interested in it" makes all the difference as to whether they care about how it looks. When one little girl with cerebral palsy started kindergarten, she had difficulty forming her letters. Nevertheless, she soon became very interested in writing about her family and her experiences. Whenever she had a choice of what to do, she chose to write. At the end of the year, she went to the local public school for a pre-first-grade screening. There, the first-grade teacher remarked on the little girl's handwriting. Despite her disability, she was producing better-looking penmanship than most entering first-graders.

How Do We Know Our Children Are Learning?

Many school boards, administrators, teachers, and parents have come to look at test scores as the "bottom line" in their children's education. The use of the business metaphor is no coincidence. Some parents want to see a direct link between rising budgets and rising scores. "I'm not happy with the school system," an engineer told a researcher. "It's not producing the product in terms of dollars and cents. If we spend three times as much money, I expect the product to be three times better." Numerical scores on worksheets and tests seem to suggest a businesslike objectivity and efficiency. At the same time, these scores provide a neatly packaged "product" for parents. Yet many educators warn that standardized tests tend to have a negative influence on teaching and that the scores are not the best reflection of the product parents pay for in school taxes.

> *Teachers teach the things they know their students will be tested on. We have produced a different kind of teacher because of the way in which we test. Instead of teachers who are excited about the discovery of learning, we have teachers who are knocking their heads off on component skills. The situation reminds me of Picasso's comment on "the academic teaching about beauty." He said, "When one loves a woman one doesn't take instruments and measure her, one loves her with desire. . . ."*

Since achievement tests measure knowledge and skills in terms of component parts, teachers feel compelled to teach components. Competency tests, instituted or under consideration in many states, often have the same effect. A U.S. circuit court of appeals heightened that effect by upholding a Florida court's ruling that schools administering these tests must prepare children to take them.

Even when they don't emphasize components, competency tests can have negative effects on teaching. On the surface, these tests appear innocuous, if not beneficial. The bottom line of bottom lines, they seek only to ensure that children meet a minimum standard before moving on within the system. Theoretically, the tests should stimulate less able students to meet the minimum and should not hurt better students, who would meet and surpass it anyway. In practice, however, testing for a minimum encourages teachers to teach to a minimum.

In one school where seventh-graders had to take a statewide competency test, for example, a teacher had been working on persuasive essays with her class. She talked about "psyching out the person you're arguing with and conceding certain points to strengthen your argument." Her students wrote to *The New York Times,* trying to convince the editors to change their policy barring publication of student work. But then they came to the competency test, which was aiming at a lower common denominator, a minimum. The graders weren't looking for concessions, the teacher says; "they were simply looking for two good reasons to support an argument. So I felt that the students were becoming confused because the grader would read their papers and see these concessions and say, 'Oh, they don't know how to develop their own reasons.' And it would take their points down. So I really simplify when teaching them persuasive essays now because I don't want them to suffer on the test."

Some teachers, confident in their ability to teach skills in the context of reading and writing, are able to withstand the pressure exerted by competency and component testing. But even they insist that "objective" tests cannot measure many important skills and attitudes. The tests ask children to recall facts, identify components, circle letters, and fill in blanks, rather than using facts and skills to analyze, synthesize, or evaluate material. Nor can the tests cannot assess a child's attitude toward reading, writing, and learning in general.

> *Teachers must help students to think, to integrate the information they've been reading, talking, or writing about with knowledge they already possess. Children need to get information in an action state. They need to be challenged to use what they've got. To me, the important question is "How can we help children to have that self-driving force, the insatiable will to learn?"*
>
> *To encourage these activities and attitudes, teachers need better ways of evaluating students' work. Teachers who want to keep track of their students' progress in writing, reading, and thinking, for example, must keep much more complete records than mere columns of checks and numbers. But it's easier for teachers to keep complete records when children are doing most of the talking. As long as the child is talking, the teacher is free to take notes. Teachers keep rec-*

ords on who shares his or her writing and who responds to the writing in group sessions. They keep records of skills taught and skills learned.

Experienced writing teachers are also concerned about the things children say about their own writing. When they talk, children reveal how they approach and solve problems in their writing. They display their knowledge of the subjects they write about. They also demonstrate their ability to make critical judgments about the quality of a piece of writing.

Children reveal much of this information in response to teachers' questions. Predictable questions not only help children give more carefully thought-out answers, but also show the teacher how a child's understanding of basic concepts changes over time. Atkinson teacher Mary Ellen Giacobbe, for example, made a point of asking her first-graders the same series of questions before and after they wrote on two occasions in December and June. Their answers, which Giacobbe reported in an article for a professional journal, showed how much the children had changed in between. When asked to evaluate a piece of writing in December, for example, Lauren said it was good because "I like it. I really want to publish it because it's the best so far. I like it. It's a good book. It's good because I just thought about it this minute and it's good." In June, she was asked to evaluate another piece of writing, and her answer revealed her developing standards. She now considered her own feelings, mentioned the reactions of readers, and referred to one specific criterion for judging writing. "I like it a lot," she said. "It makes me feel good. That's what makes it a good piece, but it may not be to other people. It is good because it has a lot of information in it. I told a lot about my boat. I think I want to write even more."

Teachers can also enlist the children's aid in keeping records. In many classrooms, children use the covers of their writing folders to record ideas for future topics, as well as lists of skills learned. Sometimes the simple act of recording motivates a child. In a second-grade classroom I was observing, one of the boys seemed to have difficulty in just getting to the writing. As it turns out, the boy is very interested in keeping records on everything. When he was shown how to keep bar graphs on his daily word count, his writing tripled.

Of course, the most important record is the writing portfolio. Looking at the whole folder, teachers can evaluate writing on many fronts. They evaluate the children's ability to choose topics and to sustain efforts over a period of time. Teachers judge how well the children can take responsibility for their own spelling, handwriting, grammar, and punctuation.

Teachers also evaluate individual pieces of writing, but always in light of the writer's own history. They look at the current piece in relation to the whole folder. That perspective helps teachers focus on the one or two main problems in a piece because it is not the only thing the child will write for the next month. There will be time to work on other problems in subsequent pieces.

Although teachers can immediately recognize the benefits of keeping more complete records and evaluating more complex tasks than worksheets, parents are often initially baffled when all their child brings home is an occasional published piece of writing. In most cases, of course, the child continues to take annual achievement tests. And, as mentioned in previous chapters, there are many indications that children in these classrooms test as well as, or better than, children from component-oriented classrooms. But when the familiar outpouring of worksheets dries up, parents may wonder how they can keep track of their child's progress throughout the year. It is up to teachers to replace the familiar scores with more meaningful information. Different teachers reach that goal in different ways. Some send home regular newsletters explaining different aspects of the children's work. Others rely on occasional but lengthy conferences with parents to interpret the evidence contained in a writing folder. Still others send home at regular intervals a progress report including samples of a child's writing in different subjects as well as examples of both rough and polished drafts.

Perhaps the hardest thing for parents to accept is the idea that nearly all of a child's work must stay in the classroom during the school year. They may resent having to go to school to see daily work. But the various drafts and pieces of writing must be kept together if they are to reveal a child's growth over a period of time. A complete writing folder allows both teachers and parents to monitor a child's progress. Just as important, it helps children do the same.

Atkinson teacher Judy Egan, now director of her own private school, tells about a kindergartner whose parents never really questioned her insistence on keeping the boy's writing during the school year. They went over his folder from time to time in conferences with Egan and took it home at the end of the year. But they didn't quite understand the importance of the folder until the following year, when their son attended first grade in a public school. About a month after school began, he took out his kindergarten writing folder at home one day and began to go through it, piece by piece. As he reread each one, he explained how he had written it. He also evaluated his work, pointing to the ones he liked best and the ones he liked least. When he was finished, he suggested that it might be a good idea to get a new folder for his first-grade schoolwork.

Why Not Give Children "Creative Writing" Assignments?

In many classrooms, students write only one type of composition. Considered incapable of coming up with their own ideas and too young to do serious work, they are asked to exercise their imaginations with infrequent "creative writing" assignments. "Imagine you are a pencil," the teacher says, "and write about how you see the world." At first glance, many parents approve of these assignments. Childhood is a time for giving free play to the imagination, after all. In fact, when children start bringing home papers on dinosaurs and Grandma's funeral, some parents wonder whether an occasional dose of the world view of a pencil might not be a good thing. Those who remember similar assignments from their youth, however, may be less likely to wish the same on their children. One mother recalls her sense of hopelessness as she faced a blank page, straining to think of a way to describe the life of a hypodermic needle. She still blushes at the thought of what she finally came up with.

Aside from the question of enjoyment, however, parents and teachers must ask themselves whether a roomful of thirty children all writing on the same assigned fantasy constitutes creativity. The first time a group of children were asked to pretend they were pencils, creativity was no doubt involved—on the part of the teacher who conceived the idea. But the children were simply carrying out another exercise, taking the teacher's idea and trying to suit her in their execution of it. Of course, it is possible to be creative in carrying out someone else's idea. One of the students, no doubt, came up with the most humorous, the most extreme, the most unexpected perceptions as a pencil. But children can best explore imaginary worlds, and the creative process, by dreaming up, carrying out, and refining their own ideas.

With what one father calls "their crazy minds," even very young children can write imaginatively without the standard creative-writing assignment. Kindergartners and first-graders write their own fantasies about a brontosaurus with chicken pox, a ghost that stepped on Mother's foot, a ride on a tyrannosaurus's head, a hero who put the Ayatollah Khomeini in "a container," or a monster in the closet.

Older children can concoct rather elaborate fantasies; sometimes the whole class joins in. A couple of girls in one third-grade classroom created a character named June. Before long, other girls collaborated on books, June evolved into a cross between Nancy Drew and a soap-opera heroine, and a series was begun. Each story was labeled *A June Series Book.* The titles included *June's First Christmas, June Gets Married, June Gets a Baby, June's Life Lives On, June and the Ton of Curls, June Goes to Spain, June's New Job, June Gets Married Again,* and *June Becomes an Artist.*

By the end of the year, the series contained thirty books written by nine little girls, individually or in collaboration. Then the boys decided to release their own June book: *June Dies* (tragically enough, swept up by an "awesome tornado" created by two mad scientists, then dropped into the ocean and caught in the jaws of a shark). But it turned out that June's original creators had struck a deal with her destroyers. She could be killed only if she would be brought back to life. Hence, in *June's Miracle,* the shark turned out to be, on closer examination, a "Natsi ship." After a heroic escape through a garbage chute, June swam to shore and returned to her second husband, Tony.

Children may surprise teachers not only with their originality or inventive imitations, but also with their striking wording. Sue Clancy, a kindergarten teacher in Wagga Wagga, Australia, reports that her students did little writing in the past, and when they did, "I knew what I wanted, and I tried to get that from them, whereas now I'm more interested in getting from them what they want to say. This is a big change." As it turns out, her students have much to say, and they sometimes say it with surprising grace. Clancy uses Melissa as an example. An only child, Melissa loves books and has a rich imaginary life populated with numerous friends and animals invisible to the adult eye. Although she usually writes about her own experiences, she occasionally creates a fantasy like the one that follows, translated here into conventional spelling.

The Secret Tree

The tree is going to grow a long way away. Mum didn't know. I know about it, but no one else knows about the tree. The tree is going to grow up and up and up and up into the sky. And when the tree is big I will ask my mum if I can climb up the tree. The tree is going to grow up to be a big tree. The tree has lots of water.

"I love the flow of the 'up and up and up' part," Clancy says. "She's just got the flow of language. Once a child would never have dreamt of [writing that way] and probably would have been corrected. You know, 'You don't need to say it that many times!'"

Children who create their own fantasies have a chance to exercise their imaginations while they entertain their readers. At the same time, these young writers may be satisfying inner needs and wishes. Many children, like Melissa, put themselves into their fantasies. Sometimes they use fantasy to include themselves in real-life events they've missed. One little boy wrote all about taking a trip to Bermuda, as if he had gone with his parents. A little girl wrote about her grandfather's funeral, as though she had been there. But children, like adults, also combine fact with fantasy for effect. Instead of just describing her trip to the circus, one of Melissa's classmates wrote about her life as a clown.

Adult writers often grow weary of answering questions about how much of their fiction, or autobiography, is "true." In many pieces of writing, it becomes nearly impossible to draw the line between fact and fiction. Even in autobiography, the memory sometimes needs assistance, and the artistic sense comes into play. If writers were able to record every single detail and happening surrounding an event, the result would be meaningless and too tedious to read. Memories, like documentary films, must be cut and edited. Writers select, arrange, and emphasize certain elements of information to reveal the meaning they have discovered.

The Atkinson fourth-grader named Birger explained how he added a touch to his story about the death of his cat so that his meaning would be clear and his readers would get the full impact of the event. "Sometimes you have to write a little more than what happened," he said. "Like, they just came down and said, 'Romeo got hit.' But I had them say, 'Romeo got hit by a car. Your cat got hit by a car.'" Children who approach their work with such sensitivity to their own meaning, their readers' needs, and even a kind of artistic vision may begin to see the world a little differently.

It is important for children to create personal narratives in which they are the heroes or heroines. Many of these are part fiction even though they are in personal narrative form. But if children can write these pieces regularly, they see themselves and their friends more realistically. They realize that a hero or heroine need not slay dragons, fly to the moon, or drive a truck. Rather, through the testing of their stories, as well as the stories of friends and professional writers, they see that there are heroic events in the context of everyday life at home and at school.

Good writers have always been able to create great characters in the midst of very ordinary events. The setting of the children's book Superfudge *is an everyday, believable school, but the main character is overdrawn to make enjoyable fiction. In a way, we want children—through both literature and their own writing—to see what is ordinary in their eyes as extraordinary. You may walk by a lily of the valley every day and say, "Oh, that's that white thing." But then you reach down and pick it up and look at the intricate design inside the floret, the very delicate pistol and stamen. Suddenly, it's no longer common.*

If a child is able to describe a very common thing, such as an occurrence at the family breakfast table, in enough detail, it will no longer be ordinary. Extraordinary stuff is around us at every turn. By discussing literature and drawing out the significant details in children's own stories, teachers can help children see the everyday in a new light.

A third-grader named Stefanie did write about an ordinary scene at her family's breakfast table. Here's how her piece began:

Monday . . . Monday

It was a cold, rainy Monday morning when Stefanie woke up. She knew it was a wet day right away because the foliage on the trees had a warm faded glow. Stefanie thought, "Today is Monday. The class has art. I wonder what we're going to do." She got up and got dressed.

Stefanie heard her mother and David talking, then she had her breakfast of Nutri-Grain Cereal. Then Stefanie and David had their morning argument.

David said, "You always have cereal now. How come you don't have oatmeal like you used to?"

"Shut up! You should be thankful I'm here. I'm eating all the cereal you and Blake don't like. *Oatmeal can go stale.*"

Blake was standing a little way off listening to the argument. He disliked it when Stefanie and David argued. He argued himself, but not as much as his stepsister and brother. . . .

In just the opening lines of a long piece, Stefanie has demonstrated a keen awareness of the natural world, human behavior, and the conventions of fiction. From her description of wet leaves to her characterization of the "morning argument" and her insight into her stepbrother's thoughts, her writing reveals the beauty and the humor she finds in the everyday life around her. And writing isn't even her favorite subject. She much prefers math.

Will It Be Bad for Children to Go from One of These Classrooms to a More Traditional Classroom or School?

The best preparation for a bad experience is a good experience.

Popular opinion, of course, holds just the opposite. Many adults justify their "if it was tough for me, it should be tough for them" attitude with the idea that unpleasant schooling prepares children for the real world. The common belief is that rigorous, if not brutal, training makes tough soldiers; in education it prepares young warriors for the battle of life.

In the *Dictionary of Misinformation,* a compendium of myths and misconceptions, author Tom Burnham points out that history has shown this common belief to be false. Athens defeated Sparta, he notes; the "soft" democracies defeated Hitler. But as final evidence, he offers the findings of an experiment performed at an academy for new policemen in Los Angeles. On two occasions, an assistant sheriff split his training group into two parts. One half was given the usual tough and humiliating form of training. The other half received more humane treatment. In both cases, the recruits who had had the less stressful training performed better in every aspect of their jobs.

Educational research has shown that one good year can affect students for the rest of their lives. In 1975, *The Harvard Educational Review* reported the results of a study conducted at a school in one of the poorest districts in Montreal. An examination of school records and interviews with graduates showed how different teachers had affected their students over a period of years. The researchers found that the students of one particular first-grade teacher saw significant increases in their IQs in her classroom. More surprising, her students maintained their gains all the way up through the school system. But most astounding of all was the discovery that even after graduation, for years to come, these students were significantly more successful than those who had other first-grade teachers. Some of her alumni went on to become college instructors, teachers, musicians, social workers, nurses, and technicians. (One key to her success: high expectations. She firmly believed that every child could learn to read.)

> *Think of how many teachers you had who actually helped you with your writing. Most people can name one or maybe two. I say to teachers, "Be that one teacher for a child."*

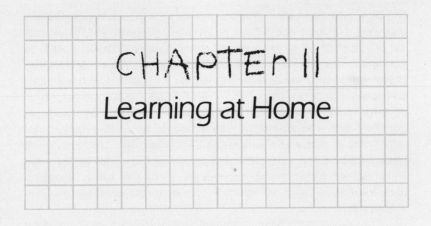

CHAPTEr 11
Learning at Home

Laws mandating school attendance imply that children can learn more in school than they can at home. Most people believe, for example, that teachers are better equipped to teach basic language skills than parents—especially parents in the lower income brackets. Convinced that these parents could not provide what their children needed, the U.S. Congress established the Head-start program in 1965 to give preschool children oral-language "enrichment." The British, who also equated financial with linguistic disadvantages, instituted a similar program.

British researcher Gordon Wells challenges the assumptions underlying such programs. In an ambitious study of language development, he analyzed 1280 recordings of spontaneous conversation in the homes of 128 British preschoolers from all levels of society. Wells and his research team followed thirty-two of the children into the early grades of elementary school, gathering recordings of their conversations in the classroom. He found that the home, more than the school, gives children opportunities to practice talking and to learn from their conversations with adults. In the homes he studied, children spoke more often, started more conversations, drew more responses from adults, asked more questions, and used more complete sentences and complex syntax than they did at school. In an article in *Theory into Practice,* Gordon Wells and Jan Wells conclude that "there were no homes that did not provide richer opportunities than the schools we observed for learning through talk with an adult." And all the children became competent speakers before they reached school age.

Parents seem to have a natural ability to help small children learn how to talk. In fact, when it comes to talking with children, many teachers would do well to take a cue from parents, or even from their own behavior with children at home. In his study, Wells found that differences in parents' conversational styles were highly correlated with the rate of oral-language development in preschool children. He was able to identify the characteristics that mark the kind of interaction that helps children most. Some parents in his study were much more likely than others to pick up on something a child had said and expand on it, affirming the child's meaning and developing it further. But all the parents used this collaborative style more than the teachers he observed. So the difference between home and school is partly a matter of numbers but largely a matter of style.

In his book *Learning through Interaction,* Wells offers a brief conversation between a mother and her two-year-old son Mark as an example of the kind of talk that helps children learn. The child has just drawn his mother's attention to some birds, which he sometimes calls "jubs," outside in the garden.

> "Birds, Mummy," he says.
> His mother responds with "Mm."
> "Jubs," says Mark.
> "What are they doing?" his mother asks.
> "Jubs bread."
> "Oh, look, they're eating the berries, aren't they?"

"Yeah."

"That's their food," the mother adds. "They have berries for dinner."

"Oh."

Wells's example is rudimentary because the child is so young; yet it includes the kernel of a whole attitude toward children and learning. In short, it represents a mother's belief that her child wants to learn. To help him do that, she draws out what he already knows and helps him add to that knowledge.

For better or worse, parents are still the most influential teachers their children will ever have. Too often parents think they must mimic teachers, who work with twenty-six children. Even teachers don't teach with one child as they do with an entire class. But the teaching role at home is different. Parents teach by listening to their children and helping them gain control over what they already know. Parents teach by reading and writing to their children. Children also learn by watching their parents solving problems, writing, and reading.

Children's ability to talk, listen, read, and write will have a lifelong effect on their ability to learn. In turn, parents have a profound influence on the development of those skills during the preschool years and beyond. Parents can develop children's love for reading and writing in concert with, or in spite of, schooling. Expanding on their own natural strength, a knack for conversing with children, parents can help children to use their own knowledge and add to it through reading and writing. And if they don't try to be imitation teachers, parents can have a lot of fun in the process.

Laying the Groundwork

One day my daughter Laura was teaching her three-year-old niece Margaret how to set the table. First, Laura put the

*spoon and knife on the right side and the fork on the left side
of the plate. Then she said to Margaret, "Now, you do the
next one." So Margaret put the fork and the spoon on the
right side with the knife on the left side of the plate. Laura
then said, "Oh, Margaret, I forgot to tell you that the spoon
and the knife are friends. The fork already knows them, but
they're not really very good friends. So the fork stays over
here, but the spoon and knife just love to talk." That was the
end of that episode.*

*The next morning, Margaret set the table again. This
time she put the fork on the left side and the knife and the
spoon on the right, but the handle of the spoon was facing up
toward the blade of the knife. Then Laura said, "You've got it
just right. But they can't talk even though they're right next
to each other. Now, if you turn the spoon around so that his
head is up instead of down by the knife's feet, then they can
talk."*

*Without realizing it, Laura had used a technique psy-
chologist Jerome Bruner calls "scaffolding." The temporary
structures parents use to help a child learn resemble the
scaffolding contractors erect around a building as they follow its growth upward. But often the scaffold has to keep
changing as it adapts to the actual structure that it sur-
rounds. In short, the scaffold exists for the building, not the
building for the scaffold. The child doesn't exist for the parent so the parent can be a teacher. The parent exists for the
child that the child may learn, and if the child learns, then the
parent will.*

*In her lesson on table setting, Laura followed Margaret.
Laura introduced the information, and then when the child
went another way, Laura transformed her language to fit
Margaret's own understanding. She had to adjust twice so
that Margaret, in turn, could come up with her own version,
using the language given to her.*

*The two episodes contained most of the elements of
good teaching. Laura gave a demonstration. She used language that tied her lesson to information the child already
had and simplified her presentation so Margaret could focus
on just the information she needed. Laura also gave Mar-*

*garet a chance to practice and corrected her without making
her feel bad. Most important, it was all done in the spirit of
play. The one missing element was role reversal, in which
Margaret demonstrates something for Laura. But that's
more advanced.*

The same principles underlying Laura's lesson and Mark's
conversation with his mother can be applied to conversations
with children of all ages. With older children, parents can ask
more questions and encourage more role reversals. Like
teachers, parents can help children become more conscious of the
things they do know and of the ways in which they learn. Thus
children become independent—eager and able to learn more on
their own.

*Parents help children learn by showing them how to do
things. When a child does something successfully, the parent
confirms what the child has done. "Oh, I didn't know that you
knew how to take a chain off the bicycle, get it in the right
gear, and then put it back on," a father might say to his
daughter. "How did you learn to do that?" Thus, he has made
it possible for the child to explain how she knows what she
knows. But he is also showing that people can ask other
people how they know how to do things. Before long, the
child reverses the role and asks the father how he has just
managed to do something.*

*Parents also help a child learn through the language
they use. When a mother shows her son how to build a fire in
the woodstove, she uses the appropriate vocabulary: "air
space," "draft," "vent," and "baffle." Thus she has given the
boy the language he needs to talk about stoves and to get
more information about them when she isn't there.*

*When people perceive themselves as knowledgeable,
they want to learn more. People who think they know nothing
often work hard to impress others with their knowledge, as
opposed to listening to what others might have to teach
them. People who are secure in what they know see no need
to compete. They can just plain enjoy learning from other
people.*

It is the parent's role to help children to know what they know, to help them establish their own territory. Someone's territory is the area of knowledge or expertise for which that person becomes known. My own son, Bill, for example, has had a love affair with the Civil War. He became interested in it when he was in first grade and was still pursuing it when he graduated from high school. But he put his own twist on it by becoming a rabid rebel, a disciple of the Southern cause, even though we lived in the North. That established the uniqueness of his territory still more. Not that he was in favor of slavery, but he did admire military prowess.

He studied the battles, knew all of the generals on both sides, and could show the stupidity of politically appointed Northern generals. For him, the Southern cause was ground he knew he could easily defend and win. A child who establishes an area of knowledge like that will continue to read about it, write about it, and teach other people about it.

Some parents help a child establish territory, but for all the wrong reasons. A father may develop his son's interest in fishing in order to create a fishing companion. That's all right, as long as the father seeks to bring out what's unique in the boy's fishing knowledge and experience. But parents sometimes give children knowledge in order to use it against them, by implying that "everything you ever learned came from me and always will." The territory, in that case, has the parents' fingerprints all over it.

At home or in the classroom, I want children to have outright title to the territories that interest them. That's a little hard at first, because buyers never own the land or house right away. The bank does. But over time, through experience and the help of others, people gradually learn what it is to be an owner and, finally, a responsible one.

The Parental Model

At the end of his ten-year study of language development in Bristol, England, Gordon Wells examined the link between preschool experiences and abilities, and later success in primary school. Although oral-language skill proved to be highly correlated with school attainment, he identified an even stronger predictor of success: "knowledge of literacy." (So few of the preschoolers he studied did any writing at home that Wells was unable to draw any correlation there at all.)

In other words, the preschoolers who are most likely to succeed are those who come to first grade equipped with a familiarity with the written word. They know which way to hold a book, for example, and where to find the words. But that's not all they know. It is likely that this acquaintance with the superficial features of the act of reading signifies a much deeper understanding of the purpose of reading. Children who have been read to know that words carry meaning. Children who have not been read to may not be aware that written words are meaningful. And the endless exercises that fill workbooks may reinforce their misunderstanding.

Wells believes that storybooks help preschool children in an even broader way by introducing them to imaginary worlds they wouldn't otherwise encounter. As he puts it, they develop the ability to "disembed" themselves from the specific world of the here and now. That ability, he believes, forms a bridge to the other imaginary or abstract realms found in academic disciplines such as history, science, mathematics, or literature.

Thus, as many parents realize, reading aloud to children can make strong contributions to their future success as students. Reading aloud also makes children want to hear more and, eventually, read more by themselves. Parents may have better luck with motivating young readers than teachers do, simply because bookstores, libraries, and many homes are filled with good children's books that are well written and enjoyable to read. Schools, on the other hand, often limit children to insipid basal readers.

Many parents, nevertheless, fail to instill a love of reading in their children. Despite frequent reading-aloud sessions during their early years, these children often lose interest in books during the middle grades. Given the quality of the reading materials and instruction in many classrooms, this loss of interest should come as no surprise. But most parents make no effort to reverse the process. They stop reading aloud, even though children of all ages, as well as adults, can take pleasure in listening. Parents may also be unaware of the effect their own reading habits have on older children.

Nathan, the son of a farmer, and Sarah, the daughter of a doctor, were fifth-grade classmates. One day, Sarah came home and told her mother, "I can see why Nathan is so smart: because he reads all the time at school. Every spare minute he has, he reads." The next time the two mothers met, Sarah's mother commented on Nathan's interest in reading and added, "I don't understand why our children don't read more. We read quite a lot, and we're interested in books and literature. We have a lot of books around the house."

"Do the children ever see you reading?" Nathan's mother asked.

As she thought about it, Sarah's mother realized that she and her husband did practically all of their reading when the children were out of the house or in bed. In Nathan's family, on the other hand, both parents read off and on throughout the day. Nathan's father came home in midmorning for his second breakfast and at noontime for dinner, and he always had a fat book on the table next to his easy chair. Nathan's parents often discussed things they had read in front of the children. In short, both parents read voraciously, and both children read voraciously.

When it comes to reading, first-grader Kasey McGarrigle has acquired not only her father's appetite but also his tastes. Ed McGarrigle loves fantasy and science fiction. Kasey has often seen both her parents reading. "When she sees that," her father says, "she trusts that we wouldn't be doing it just to waste our time. She realizes there's probably something in there that's treasurelike, whether it's a fantasy or another world or a character she can relate to. She's looking for things in books. And it's funny—I know she's a page-counter like me. She really likes the satisfaction of having read. 'I read twenty pages,' she'll say." When the little girl visits a friend or goes on any overnight trip, she carries her current book in her suitcase.

Parents who want their children to read and write must read and write themselves—and talk about the experience. The principle is so simple that even a six-year-old could understand it. One six-year-old who did was the little boy named Nathaniel, author of "Why Children Like Their Mom Better Than Their Dad." In a piece called "Kids Thd Whit" (Kids Should Write), he speculated on the reason why they don't: "Thy Doont Whit be Cus Thy wont to be liuk Thr MOM and Thr Muthur's Doont Whit." (They don't write because they want to be like their mom and their mothers don't write.) Nathaniel himself doesn't get to write much at school. He does have the occasional assignment, such as "write about your pet" (a difficult one for children who, like Nathaniel, have no pets). But he does most of his writing at home, whenever he feels like it. He often feels like it after his mother or his older sister Meg has written something. He wrote "Kids Thd Whit" shortly after his mother wrote an article. He wanted to write an article, too. Not long after the children's grandfather wrote a letter to the editor of a newspaper, fourth-grader Meg wrote a letter to the state governor, recommending the installation of seat belts in school buses. She also sent copies of the letter to two local newspapers.

Sometimes children inspire their parents to write. In one family, both parents began keeping journals after their son started writing in school. That child was lucky—his experiences at home and school were mutually reinforcing. Other parents often become inspired to write for, or to, their children. A surprise note in the lunchbox is nearly always well received and usually answered. Parents with a stronger interest in writing may enjoy composing their own children's stories or making a gift of a piece of writing.

> *About ten years ago, I wrote a piece for each of my children—as well as for my mother, father, and wife—on their birthdays. I just sat and wrote several pages of vignettes of very special moments between us. I didn't realize it at the time, but I was trying to give them a mirror image of how special they were to me and to the family. Last Christmas, I tried to put together everything I could remember about all the Christmases we had had together from the time when I was first engaged to Betty. Then I wrote a Christmas book full of all those memories.*

Parents who read and write not only demonstrate that those activities are an enjoyable part of life, they also demonstrate the process that they go through when they read and write. Children who hear their parents reading aloud to one another or arguing about the interpretation of a letter from the government see that reading is something to share, interpret, and discuss. A child who sees a parent crossing out lines and crumpling up paper understands that writing is a process that may go through several stages before completion. When Susan Stires took a trip to Indiana, she received a letter from her younger daughter, who had just finished first grade. "She not only sent me the final copy, which was written in Magic Marker and highly decorated on a paper towel in perfect printing," Stires recalls, "but she also sent me her draft—she knows that I'm as interested in her draft as I am in her final copy."

Most parents enjoy work or a hobby that requires a creative approach, whether painting, repairing cars, writing computer programs, playing the guitar, training horses, cooking from scratch, or even shopping for clothes, to name just a few examples. These parents can help their children see the similarities between such activities and the process of writing: the need for cultivating unexpected ideas, entertaining alternatives, accepting failure, and being persistent. Unless parents draw attention to these parallels, however, children may miss them, especially if schooling instills a get-it-right-the-first-time mentality. Joan Tornow, for instance, grew up in a home where she was constantly exposed to the creative process on a high level. Her father, Leland C. Clark, Jr., has invented the artificial heart-lung machine and artificial blood, among other things. Tornow remembers seeing him rush into the kitchen with ten pounds of fresh spinach one day. He chopped it up, boiled it, and then dried it in front of a fan, all in search of an enzyme that would help measure lactic acid in the blood. The enzyme he extracted from the spinach worked, but not well enough. Four years later, he found the enzyme he needed.

The spinach incident was just one of many. Yet despite her father's repeated and graphic demonstrations of the creative process of working by trial and error, Tornow held herself to a different set of standards when she wrote. "I used to think that all my scribbled drafts were something to be ashamed of," she says.

"They were like your slip was showing. It seemed that you should have gotten it right the first time, and I always thought of that as an indication of inferiority." When she took a class on teaching writing, she began to see the connection between her father's process of discovery in medicine and the process of discovery in writing.

As important as the example parents set through their activities is their attitude toward those activities and toward members of the family. Although it is good to read to children, listen to children, and write to children, the energy for doing those things comes from my own view of their importance. I stress importance because there are countless examples of illiterate people who valued literacy, rejoiced in their children and in each other and, in fact, raised children who grew up to be highly literate. On the other hand, I've seen people who religiously read to their children and raised them with a book in hand but failed to laugh and enjoy them.

The important thing is to enjoy your children and, above all, to find things you and your spouse enjoy doing and learning. Parents need to help themselves and each other as much as they help their children. Husbands and wives need to develop their own territories and interests. They must share their own knowledge and experiences with each other because children will be observing that model for a long time. That's the only one they'll have. If between husband and wife, one works hard to show how dumb the other one is, that model also can be infectious to the children. So, any consideration of literacy within the family falls on the backdrop of the enjoyment of people and learning and oneself.

The Opportunity Taken

When Adi Rule was three, her favorite book was *Animal ABC's*. As a result, she became familiar with the letters of the alphabet, and she would often put one letter on each of her pictures, imitating the book and perhaps her mother, Becky, who did a lot of writing. Becky noticed Adi's interest and after a while suggested, as teachers often do, that Adi might label her drawings. "You could put a name on that picture," she would say, "so people will know what it is." When Adi asked how to spell the word, Becky would say, "How does it sound to you?" On one occasion, Becky suggested that Adi might put little labels on her dresser drawers to help her remember where things went.

Becky and her husband, John, wanted to avoid pushing Adi, so they let her interests and enthusiasm guide them. If she had balked at the suggestion of labeling a picture, for example, they would have dropped the idea and waited awhile. But she had already shown an interest in writing by putting single letters on her own pictures, and she responded eagerly to their suggestion. "She liked writing, and it was something we could do together," Becky says.

Before long, Adi was labeling pictures on her own and putting up signs around the house such as "WET PANT," "KEEP OUT," and "NO MEN ULUWD." Becky made little message boxes for everyone in the family, and Adi exchanged notes with her parents. As time went by, Adi's writing improved with very little direction from her mother. When she got to the point where she could write sentences, the two of them would sometimes write stories together. "I'll write a page, if you'll write a page," Becky would say.

When Adi was four-and-a-half, she began to read in much the same way as she had begun to write. Her parents had read to her regularly from infancy on. Every night, John would read to her for half an hour to an hour. Since Adi loved books and knew her letter sounds from writing, Becky began to play around a little with words in the books she read aloud. She would often point to each word as she read. In a book with a rhyme scheme, she would stop reading at the end of a line so that Adi could fill in the rhyming word. After a while, Becky tried it with nonrhyming words, just to see what Adi could do. Other times, Becky would read a line and then point to a word and ask, "Can you tell me what that word spells?"

These occasions were relatively rare; mostly the Rules read aloud just for fun. Becky wasn't expecting, or urging, Adi to start reading yet. They were just playing with words. But before long,

Adi was trying to read on her own, and succeeding. She offered to read to household guests. She read road signs in the car, and she caught her mother if she skipped words in the books she read aloud. When the book was fairly simple, Becky could now say, "I'll read a page if you'll read a page," and they would read together.

By the time she turned five, Adi was writing and reading well—almost as if by magic, it seemed to her parents. They hadn't really done very much (much less than most teachers do in their efforts to get children to read and write in school). But even though it seemed that they had done little, the Rules had done a few very important things. They had demonstrated their own interest in writing and love of reading. They had made reading and writing part of their daily lives, a special and playful part of the time they spent with Adi. They had read enjoyable children's books, which, unlike basal readers, often have the rhymes and predictable patterns that help children start identifying words with ease. And they had provided Adi with opportunities for trying to read and write on her own, always watching to make sure she was enjoying the activities.

> *There would be a real danger if this method were used as a way to help your children get ahead earlier or sooner than other kids in the neighborhood. There's an enormous push in this country to make kids sprint ahead on skills. Too often, the reason for writing, or doing other activities, is entirely lost.*

Adi Rule is not an average child (partly because of the way her parents have raised her). And no two children are alike in the steps they take and the pace they maintain on their way to literacy. So parents should not take her experience as any kind of timetable to be followed by their own children. Nevertheless, children are capable of doing much more than adults have realized. Many children in kindergarten write voluminously when given the chance. Aside from the speed with which she progressed, Adi had done the same things teachers have seen thousands of other children do—children of all abilities and backgrounds. Even for the Rule family, speed wasn't the point anyway; Adi's interests and enjoyment were. So parents can help their children develop a love for reading and writing if they, like the Rules, provide opportunities without pushing and then watch the child's reaction closely.

> *Raising a family, like writing or teaching, is a craft. You try a lot of different things. You have an inkling of something that might work, so you try it and then observe. After trying an experiment, you must have the confidence to abandon it or extend it further. If it doesn't work, you ask yourself, "What would be a better way to do that?"*

Perhaps the easiest way to give children the chance to try writing is by making the necessary supplies available. Special-education teacher Susan Stires says, "Make sure that children have all the tools for writing, accessible and not necessarily put away. The more they trip over them, the more they are inclined to use them." She keeps pencils, crayons, and paper with her children's toys.

When young children write at home, they begin with labels, signs, notes, and lists, rather than full-fledged stories. Parents can make suggestions, but children with access to pencil and paper often come up with their own ideas. Stires's two daughters write as part of their play. "My children have always played waitress," she says. "They use writing. They make lists. As a matter of fact, Anne had a friend over today, and she was saying, 'When Amy gets here, we're going to play with the rabbits and swing and watch TV.' Then she said, 'I know! I'll make a list.'" Anne made a list, which showed not only how much writing was a part of her everyday life, but also how far one inventive speller had progressed by the end of first grade. In her list, which follows, she had to approximate the spelling of only one word.

Anne's and Amy's List. □ 12:00 to 3:30

Help my father. □
My father will give us a big
swing! □ change □ go swimming. □
Play in campire [camper] □

Have rabbits out ☐
Watch TV. ☐
read riddles ☐
read jokes ☐
Play ☐

DONE!

Joan Tornow keeps a blackboard in each of her two sons' bedrooms. They like to make lists of their plans for the next day, even plans for playing with certain toys. Her sons use writing when they play, too. One day, a sign appeared on an alligator constructed out of blocks in the living room. "Do not feed the alligator," said one side of the sign. At the appropriate time, it could be flipped to the other side, which said, "Please feed the alligator."

Opportunities to write need not be restricted to playtime. In fact, researchers Jerome Harste, Caroline Burke, and Virginia Woodward have found that children who are constantly "dragged around" on errands and included in everyday chores and activities have an advantage over other children in learning to read and write. In their book *Language Stories and Literacy Lessons,* the researchers explain that the children they found to be at an advantage were the ones "who were reported as always 'under foot,' who naturally got included in cooking and setting the table, who were reported as writing out shopping lists and reading them during shopping, who were given paper and pen to write a letter to grandmother while a parent wrote letters or sent bills, who were given the occupant mail to open and read while the mother opened and read the rest of the mail."

Harste, Burke, and Woodward point out that parents often include children in such activities for practical rather than educational reasons. On the other hand, several researchers have found that those occasions when parents deliberately set out to instruct their children with workbooks or formal lessons often fall flat. Parents who understand the process by which children naturally learn to read and write avoid imitation school lessons. They are also more likely to appreciate their children's efforts at every stage. They may realize, for example, that the activity often referred to as "just scribbling" can reveal a child's budding knowledge of the written word. Harste, Burke, and Woodward compare scribbling from an American child, an Israeli child, and a Saudi Arabian child. The samples look as different as English, Hebrew, and Arabic writing, showing how much an advanced scribbler has already learned about the features of written language. In fact, when the Saudi Arabian four-year-old handed over her mock writing, she said, "Here, but you can't read it, 'cause I wrote it in Arabic and in Arabic we use a lot more dots than you do in English."

When Tornow's older son was in kindergarten, he surprised her with a note he wrote in invented spelling to a friend who had visited. At the time, Tornow was mildly amused. "If I had known what this was all about," she explains, "I would have been paying attention. I didn't see it [the note] as the germ of a larger thing. You get the impression that they're trying to write and that obviously they're not old enough, so you discount it."

Later, when she took a course on teaching writing, just to satisfy her own interest, she realized that she had not understood the importance of that note. "There are so many things children do that are landmarks or part of a progression," she says, "and if you know that, it is more exciting. When a child takes his first step, you know that he's going to run, or when he loses a tooth, you know he's going to get another tooth. You usually have some idea of what this is all leading to, but with writing, most of us don't."

With her new perspective, she found invented spelling charming. "There is something very endearing and cute about the way they spell these things, and I don't see what's wrong with enjoying the cuteness of that the same way you would enjoy it if a baby said *baw-baw* for bottle. I mean, here's *Thanksgiving*," she says, flipping through a folder of her son's writing, "*T-a-c-s-g-v-a-e-g*."

Responding to Children

Once children do take the opportunity to read and write, parents often wonder how to respond to those efforts. Whether the topic under discussion is something the child has read, watched on TV, done, or written, parents can apply the same principle. Their role is to help children become aware of the knowledge they already possess. If the time seems to be right, parents can then use questions or suggestions to nudge children toward the next logical step in pursuit of their own interests. For parents of young children, the first question about when to nudge arises as the child begins using invented spelling.

> *When it comes to helping invented spellers, parents usually have neither experience nor training to draw on. It's hard for teachers, much less parents, to understand the sequences of growth children go through and to know what will help at different points. But someone who isn't acquainted with teaching procedures can never go wrong with letting learners know what they do well.*

In *Understanding Writing,* edited by Thomas Newkirk and Nancie Atwell, Atkinson researcher Susan Sowers points out that children will make progress in invented spelling up to a certain point without any instruction at all. Beyond that point, she notes, teachers need to intervene to help children, and her article gives them suggestions on how to do that. Parents of preschool children, however, need not worry. Like Adi Rule, their children will be able to make rapid progress without much interference. Adi, for example, strung all her words together in one line when she began writing. Her parents never told her she was wrong or even talked about putting spaces between words. She did see conventional writing in books and her parents' notes, and on her own she picked up the idea that each word is a separate entity. First she used hyphens to mark the separations, and eventually she switched to the conventional spaces.

> *Let's say a little boy wants to write the word monster but doesn't know where to begin. I ask whether he can hear the first sound. If he knows the letter from games or reading we've done together, I say, "Put it down." If he doesn't, I may not teach the sound at that point because I want the child to still do more fooling around. He's making marks on*

paper, and those marks are wonderful. I'm in no hurry. If the child is demanding it, that's another story.

If the child does know the first sound, then I may try the last sound. Beginnings and endings are easy to get. Next I try the middle sound, all the while exclaiming over what the child already knows.

If he first writes the word MSTR *(monster) on his own. I show him that I can read the word. "It says* monster. *You know why?" Then I make the sounds of* M-S-T-R. *Depending on the child's readiness and eagerness to go further, I may get into some of the vowels. Let's say he omits the* n. *(The nasal is often missed.) I have him say the word* monster. *If he doesn't put in an* n *sound when he says it slowly, then I have a pronunciation or discrimination problem.*

Above all, the principle that I am working on here is letting the child know what he can do. In this instance, he knew M-S-T-R. *That's a simple way of working. Later, if* monster *appears quite a bit in his writing, I'll give him the full spelling of the word, underlining in red those letters that he already knows and possibly underlining in green the new ones to get.*

Many parents are stumped when a child starts asking them questions. If the little boy writes MSTR *and says, "Is that spelled right?" I ask another question: "Why did you want to know?" It's just like a sex-education lesson; you answer according to what the child wants. If he says, "I just want to spell it right," I say, "Who is going to read this?" If he says, "My mommy," or "Just me," then I say, "Well, you're thinking your mommy can't read what you wrote?" It's all relative, depending on the age. If the child is young, I want him to have enough confidence in his own spelling to keep trying.*

As they grow older, inventive spellers become aware that their spelling is different from that in published books. But thanks to good teaching or just the self-centeredness of childhood, they don't feel bad about it. Ellen Blackburn says her first-graders accept that they still have much to learn, in spelling as in everything else. Parents must be very careful about giving young children the idea that their own spellings are "wrong" or "bad." If children don't have confidence in their own ability to try to spell a word, they'll give up trying. And parents of children of any age do need to worry about destroying self-confidence.

Parents often run amok when criticizing something a child has written or said. Whether responding to a child's writing or a dinner-table conversation, some parents leave the impression that the child can do nothing right. One mother is well aware of the stifling effect of excessive parental criticism. "My father was a perfectionist," she recalls, "and at the dinner table we were not allowed to say, 'I feel pretty good,' because *pretty* was an adjective describing how something appeals to your eye. Therefore, you cannot feel 'pretty good.' With this every-night carping, our dinner tables became very quiet. We used to talk about how free Wednesday nights were, when Dad had Lions' Club meetings. We could tell jokes, and we could sit with our elbows on the table." After volunteering to help out in an Atkinson classroom where children wrote freely, she began to see the connections between stifling criticism at the dinner table and in the classroom.

The mother had some insights into the cause of her own father's behavior. After growing up on a farm, he had gone to Harvard University and eventually became a highly successful business executive. In the process he turned into "pretty much of a snob" as he worked hard to advance himself socially, and it was in fear of any "possible relapse" that he maintained such rigid standards of speech. Fear is often the motivating force behind excessive parental criticism. At best, parental fears may simply have a chilling effect, as the children at the executive's family dinner table discovered. At worst, those fears can turn into self-fulfilling prophecy.

Parents who believe that they themselves were poor learners are afraid their children will be. A classic example is a parent who has had a reading problem and becomes all upset when a child stumbles on one word. He may have read the first three correctly and missed the fourth, but his parent says, "Oh my God, he's just like me!" Another parent whose child made the same error might say, "Look at that! She's almost there!"

In working with writing, the parents' chief role is to let their child know what they understand and what they have learned from the piece. If there are parts that confuse the parent, then the parent should ask plain, honest questions that give the child the responsibility of explaining what the reader needs to know. If a paper is messy, uses confusing language, or is illegible, then the parent says, "I can't figure this out. Help me."

In short, many parents do more harm than good because they feel compelled to behave like an old-fashioned schoolteacher. Both parents and teachers can be of more help by responding as honest readers. First, they can show their interest, and priorities, by responding to the content of a piece of writing. Then by asking for the writer's help, readers can show where more work is needed in the piece, without shaming the writer. Notice the difference in tone between different ways of phrasing the same comment. "This sentence confused me" has quite a different effect from "This sentence is confusing" or, worse, "This sentence is a mess." A statement like "This handwriting is atrocious" condemns the writer. "I can't make this out," on the other hand, demonstrates the true purpose for legible writing. Parents, like teachers, can also help by focusing on one problem at a time. Writers can't attend to all their errors at once, anyway, and if they are forced to try, they're not likely to want to keep writing.

Finally, parents should beware of coming down hard on a child who appears to be regressing, in writing or any other skill. Often it is best to wait and see what happens next. Many an apparent regression has turned out to be just a minor setback on the way to a major breakthrough. It is only natural to grasp the gist of a new concept or rule before learning its refinements and exceptions. A three-year-old who has just discovered that an *-ed* ending puts a verb into the past tense may say *breaked* for *broke*. When Adi Rule first discovered a silent *e*, she began attaching *e*'s to the ends of her words willy-nilly. Even an adult who has just learned that a compound adjective is hyphenated before a noun may write "scantily-clad teenager," unaware that phrases including an adverb ending in *-ly* do not require the hyphen. Thus, an error is often actually a sign of progress.

> *On the other hand, praise can cause problems, as well. I am not saying that praise should not be given. But praise is often used as a substitute for thinking. And if compliments are given indiscriminately, they simply aren't heard when they really are merited. Praise can also be used to manipulate because it makes the receiver overly beholden to the giver.*
>
> *Instead of telling a child "That was very good," I could say, "I notice that when you wrote about the boy and his dog, you showed how the boy would lean down, hug the dog, and nuzzle him. And because of the way you described his face when he did it, I understood how much the dog meant to him." Better still, I might quote the phrase or line I'm referring to. In this case, I don't have to tell the child this is good writing. I have shown that it is with my specific example. Thus, the writer knows that I cared enough to select the details to give back to her as a kind of gift. Good teaching gives the gift of attention in such a way that children are able to give themselves gifts when the teacher is no longer present.*
>
> *Praise can be insulting when it implies that the receivers couldn't figure out for themselves what's good or bad. In the example of the piece about the boy and the dog, the writer will now be able to recognize on her own when her writing is good and therefore be able to give herself a gift of self-praise when the adult isn't there. This approach encourages independence. Unfortunately, in most classrooms or homes, children are constantly seeking out an adult for praise as if they themselves could never tell whether something is good—or as if only an adult's approval could make it good.*

The occasional well-timed question also nudges children a little further in the direction of independence. Good questions challenge children to think, and eventually to think about think-ing—that is, to learn how to learn. When it comes to talking about things children have read, written, or even watched on TV, teachers recommend asking genuine, open-ended questions. The parent must want to know what the child has to say. Children can sense when an adult has an answer ready in advance. Many good questions begin with *why:* "Why do you think the person did that?" a parent might ask about a character in a book or TV show.

Ask questions that get children to evaluate and speculate. When a child has read, seen, or written a story, ask the child's opinion about favorite parts and characters. To-gether, talk about what you think might happen next in the story, based on what has already occurred.

One type of question parents may not be familiar with is the *process question,* which focuses children's attention on what they have done or will do in the process of reading and writing: How many drafts did you go through? How did you choose this topic? What's going to happen next? Was this hard for you to read? How did you figure that out? These questions help children start think-ing about thinking.

Of course, process questions need not be restricted to discus-sions of writing. To me, it's not writing as much as a way of viewing how people learn. In math, if a child gets something right, I say, "That's right. How did you figure that out?" Then children will soon start to ask themselves, "How did I do that?" We're usually saying, "That's wrong. Why did you do that?" That's no fun.

Sometimes the best question gives back to the child re-sponsibility for choosing the next step. I ask, "And what do you need to learn next? What do you need help with now?" I may think I know what the child needs, but I always try to treat children with respect. I ask questions based on the as-sumption that they want to learn. Too many directives and questions are based on the assumption that children do not

*want to learn. After a healthy dose of that, our worst fears
are confirmed: children fight learning. It's the same thing
with lies. Tell children they're liars, and the odds are that the
next time they will lie.*

Parents can safely assume that children do want to learn.
When their work or play receives a warm response and a few
well-timed questions and suggestions, children find their own
ways to challenge themselves. Adi Rule surprised her mother
often with her ability to tackle new projects. One day shortly
before she turned five, Adi disappeared into the study to do some
writing. After a little while, Becky went in to see what she was
doing. Adi had written this:

NASHNL-NOOS-PAPR	National Newspaper
THISWKAND	This weekend
ATTHERULE	at the Rules'
BABDUCK	baby ducks
GRODBIGR	growed bigger.

Becky was thrilled. She and John read the newspaper every night
and Adi enjoyed the comics. Sometimes her parents pointed out
pictures of animals or other things that might interest her. But she
had come up with the idea of doing her own newspaper all by
herself. And her attempt revealed that she had a clear grasp of the
purpose and even, to some extent, the format of newspapers. The
word *National* was somewhat of a mystery, but Becky guessed
that it had come from *National Geographic,* Adi's favorite magazine.

After exclaiming with delight at what Adi had done, Becky
asked her one question: "What else happened?" When Becky
returned, Adi had added a second news item:

OSOTHISWKAND	Also this weekend
THERULESWENT	the Rules went
TOHRMIT	to Hermit
ILEND	Island.

Becky again expressed her pleasure and asked once more, "What else happened?" When she returned to the study, Adi had added her name and a final message at the bottom of the page: *REDMORTMORO* (read more tomorrow).

Adi, too, was pleased with her newspaper. She read it aloud to herself several times, reading *grew* in place of *growed* on the second and third readings. Aware that newspapers come out in many copies, she decided to make her own "copies" on her mother's typewriter. She knew how to replace the expensive single-strike ribbon with the multi-strike cartridge, but she had trouble putting in the paper, so she enlisted her mother's help. Then Adi typed her first "copy," which turned out to be a new draft of the original.

NASHNL-NOOS-PAPR!	National Newspaper!
THISWKAND	This weekend
ATTHERULES	at the Rules
BABDUCKS	baby ducks
WRBORNOSOTHISWKANDTHE	were born. Also this weekend, the
RULESWENT!	Rules went
TO-HRMIT	to Hermit
ILEND	Island.
REDMORTMORO	Read more tomorrow.
IMSOHAPE	I'm so happy
IHATTIM	that I'm
GOING	going
TO-MA-KOPES	to make copies.
THEand	The end.
BY-ADI	By Adi.

Although Adi had occasionally crossed out a letter here and there to change her spelling in the past, Becky was surprised at how much Adi had changed her first "copy." She had not only added punctuation and corrected some spelling, but she had also rewritten one whole sentence about the baby ducks. When asked why, Adi revealed a surprising sensitivity to the needs of "NOOS-

PAPR" readers outside the family: "They didn't know the ducks were born yet," she explained. After Adi had made nine copies, many of which bore no resemblance to the original, Becky suggested that they go into town to make photocopies for friends and relatives.

CHAPTER 12
An Educational Alliance

At Boothbay Region Elementary School (BRES), the fifth-grade class now puts out each year's final issue of the *BRES Reporter*, the quarterly newspaper first started by the children in the resource room several years ago. Producing a newspaper is a large undertaking for any elementary class and their teacher, but when the fifth-graders in Connie Bataller's classroom first tried their hand at it, they found they were not alone. Until May of that year, the paper had been mimeographed. Now for the first time, it would be printed just like a real newspaper.

First, the fifth-graders wrote some of their own articles and solicited others from the rest of the school. Then they made decisions on how to arrange the layout of the paper. One child's mother, the owner of an advertising business, helped the children sell ads. Another mother was a typesetter for the local newspaper; she typeset the articles the children had edited and laid out. The newspaper donated the use of its typesetting equipment. Another local company offered to print the copies, and the publisher of the local newspaper recommended the *BRES Reporter* to his readers. On a class trip to a newspaper in a nearby city, the fifth-graders were thrilled to see that professionals laid out a newspaper in much the same way they had.

In the end, the children made eight hundred dollars, which helped finance an outdoor-education week for their class. But they had gained much more than money. They had learned a lot about how newspapers are made and financed. They'd had the chance not only to write for a larger audience, but also to edit and arrange other people's writing. The *BRES Reporter* could not have come out at all, however, without the cooperation of parents, teachers, and local businesses.

With mutual understanding, respect, and commitment, parents and teachers can work together to produce concrete results such as newspapers, as well as less tangible benefits that may not be immediately apparent. When things go well, parents can have a positive effect on their children's education in school, while teachers can have a similar influence on education in the home. But both parents and teachers need to choose their paths carefully, for few relationships are fraught with more pitfalls than theirs.

Agreeing to Disagree

The children at Boothbay Harbor had experienced education at its best, thanks in part to the collaboration between their teacher and their parents. Unresolved conflicts between parents and teachers, however, sometimes produce education at its worst. Anxieties and insecurities can blossom on both sides of the fence. When things don't go well, both have much to lose.

Parents fear that a misstep may jeopardize their child's position in the eyes of a person with the power to affect that child's intellectual, emotional, and social development for at least a year. That development becomes even more important when it is seen as a reflection of the parents' own genes and abilities, as it almost always is. Teachers fear that a misunderstanding may bring down the wrath of not just one parent but perhaps others, who may in turn complain to administrators. Administrators have the power to make life miserable for a teacher. Matters may become even more complicated when both adults base their conclusions about each other on information from the child, an immature and sometimes unreliable source.

> *After they had exchanged notes, one teacher said to a parent, "I promise to believe half of what he tells me if you promise to believe half of what he tells you."*

A fourth-grade teacher describes what happened to one little boy when she and his mother were working at cross purposes. The child's first draft of a piece about video games had pleased him very much, until he took it home. "And it came back all covered," his teacher recalls, "totally, totally, totally corrected. Not just spelling—she changed his words around and changed his information. After that, it was so hard for him to make any changes in it himself. And when a girl asked him how he liked it, he just made a face."

The teacher understood the child's predicament. "I say all the time, 'Don't worry about the spelling and punctuation yet, not until later in the process,' " she explains. "The mother says, 'But that's not spelled right.' And the child is caught between these two important people in his life. They put their little souls on paper and we say, 'That's okay. These ideas are great,' if they are, and all Mother can do is scold." In another case, a first-grader took home a story he had started at school and proceeded to work on his ending. Convinced that the child was "frustrated," his mother wrote an ending for him and had him copy it onto his own page.

Although such extreme cases are rare, misunderstandings and disagreements are not. Unfortunately, the real loser in most conflicts is neither the teacher nor the parent, but the child. So it's in the interest of both adults to reach an understanding without undercutting each other's authority.

Teachers who use methods unfamiliar to parents need to find

ways to explain what they're doing. Most teachers give presentations on writing and talk with individual parents at school open houses. Many send home newsletters and progress reports explaining the children's work in more detail or hold year-end celebrations for young writers and their families. The New York City Writing Project recommends that teachers invite parents to participate in special evening sessions at school. When parents get a chance to write under a teacher's guidance, they gain insights into their children's experiences with writing, as well as the teacher's methods and standards.

Teachers, however, can do only half the work. The rest is up to parents. One teacher reports that the one or two parents who had complained about her methods did not bother to attend her evening sessions on writing. Before they complain or interfere, parents need to understand what it is they're complaining about. A first-grade teacher suggests that parents visit their children's classrooms before taking any kind of action. Too often parents "come to you with complaints and criticisms on how you can make things better," she says, "and they've never even been in the room."

Even when parents and teachers do understand each other's philosophies, however, differences sometimes remain. Parents who want their children to write, for example, may discover that their schools subscribe to the workbook-and-drill method of teaching. These parents find themselves in a difficult position, knowing that their children could be doing so much more with writing than they are. One solution to the problem is to do nothing about the situation at school while doing plenty to encourage writing at home.

As a parent, I always err in the direction of affirming what my child knows, whether it is in agreement with the teacher or not. After all, writing is a skill people practice over a lifetime. I'm not going to let one year disrupt my child's progress. If the child is having a difficult time in school, why should I make it doubly difficult by taking the same approach at home?

Two different attitudes toward writing can, and often do, coexist side by side. One little girl thrilled her parents when she spontaneously began writing in invented spelling. In the first grade, she met with a more conventional approach to spelling. Since then, she has always had teachers who emphasize splintered "skills," but her parents have continued to encourage her to approximate spellings when necessary at home. Now in the fourth grade, she still loves to write and has consistently done well on spelling tests, averaging in the nineties.

Teachers recommend that parents in this situation make clear to their children that different standards for writing are maintained in school and at home. One first-grade teacher says of component-oriented classrooms: "I would probably try very hard to make sure my child didn't get into that kind of classroom to begin with, but if that happened, I think it's important not to undermine the school. I would say, 'That's what your teacher believes is a good way to do it. She has these reasons. But at home, we can do it this way.' "

Because of the education her own children are getting, special-education teacher Susan Stires understands the dilemma many parents find themselves in. Once when Stires asked her daughter how reading was going, the little girl replied, "Oh, I don't have reading—I have masteries." Stires laughs. "I have just been sure that reading has always been a part of our life. I feel that the education my kids have been getting is one of bits and pieces, of skills and drills. But I feel that we are the real teachers of our children, that I teach them reading and writing and my husband [a high-school science teacher] teaches math and science. My own role is to provide them with opportunities to read and write in their daily lives. That's how we counteract it."

Working for Change

Despite her own success, Susan Stires is aware that many parents do not have the training she does. "If I were a parent without the skills that I have, but I wanted to see my child involved in writing,

I would take action," she says. "It would be a matter of getting a group of parents together, going to the school committee, and saying that we know that this method of teaching writing is here and that we are interested and want this for our children. That is what the school committee is there for, to listen and represent those parents."

Parents who know about successes at other schools may want to change their own school systems, for the sake of other people's children, as well as their own, and even for the sake of teachers. Whatever form such a campaign takes, however, it must be handled with diplomacy. "Parents need to be aware that teachers are being inundated with new programs," says one teacher. "Just barraged. With computers, for example. And at the same time, no one ever takes anything away. Social studies and science are still there." On top of new materials and methods, teachers have also been barraged with criticism for the last decade. As a result, they are likely to be sensitive, if not defensive. "A parent who comes in as an expert—I know how writing should be taught—is going to be shot down," warns Boothbay Writing Project Director Nancie Atwell.

As Stires suggests, parents may want to start by talking with members of the local school board or with school administrators. A school-board member in a district where writing is heavily encouraged suggests that parents go straight to their school principal. They might, for example, arrange for their own principal to talk with an administrator in a district where writing has been going well. Informed administrators can arrange for training programs and generally make life much easier for teachers who want to change their own methods. Once one or two teachers in a building get started, ideas usually begin to spread.

Many teachers, however, have reservations about effecting change via the administrative route. "Anything that's meaningful in the way of change in the classroom has to come from the teachers," one teacher says. "It can't come from the administrators." There are ways to approach teachers directly with new ideas. In some cases, parents have stimulated interest in change by offering teachers books and articles on new developments in writing instruction. Nancie Atwell recommends that parents initiate weekend or after-school writing groups. Then parents and teachers could share their writing and talk about the implications of their own discoveries for classroom instruction.

Most risky, and in some cases most effective, a few teachers recommend that parents actually demonstrate what children can do with writing. First-grade teacher Ellen Blackburn presents this scenario. A child is doing a lot of writing at home, so his parent takes in a piece to share with the teacher at a conference. Blackburn recommends the "We have a mutual interest in this child" approach. "I'd present it this way," she says. " 'You see my child all day at school, and I'm sure you'd be interested in the things he does at home.' I wouldn't present it as, 'Well, this is what they can do at home, and they're not doing it in school.' And I imagine that a teacher who is interested and really cares, would say, 'How do you do that?' "

A mother named Joyce Vining Morgan discovered how successful the direct approach could be when she offered to help with writing instruction in her daughter's second-grade classroom. The teacher was a "white-haired veteran" of the classroom. Her students sat in rows and all worked on the same thing at the same time. According to Morgan, she was the type of teacher who "tends to reprimand her students ahead of time if she thinks they might get out of line." Explaining that another parent in the school system had been volunteering to help teachers handle writing, Morgan offered to do the same and asked the teacher to call if she was interested. In October, Morgan got a call and went to her first class. The teacher had chosen to try the experiment on Friday afternoons, often an unproductive time for any class, but particularly for the unruly bunch she happened to have that year.

On that first day, Morgan took in a poem written by a local poet, including all the drafts that he had gone through. The poem was begun on the back of a church bulletin. It was not clear whether the sermon that day had acted as an inspiration, a kind of muse, or a sedative that drove the poet to create his own intellectual excitement. But the first draft of the poem was intermingled with notes from his wife about inviting another couple to dinner that night. After that, the poem went through numerous drafts, nineteen pages in all, before it was distilled into eight lines. The children were impressed that the poet could be so messy when he wrote and that after all that work the poem was not accepted for publication.

After the children had written a piece on E. T., a topic their teacher had assigned, the two women each took a group of six children. In Morgan's group, the children all took turns reading their piece aloud and then fielded questions from the group. Morgan kept track of the questions and gave each child a list. "Toward the end, it got to be a competition," she recalls. " 'How many questions did you get?' " The children went back to their seats, where some worked on adding information and clarifying things that had confused their readers. Then Morgan started in with another group.

"I carried on like that," she says, "and had no idea of what she was doing until after the class. And then we compared notes." The teacher, Morgan discovered, had taken an entirely different approach with her students. "They'd come up six at a time, and one by one she'd go over the story and correct the punctuation and spelling and make sure the proper letters were capitalized. I was appalled, and when she asked what we were doing, she was clearly appalled. And we were both not saying how appalled we were."

The teacher was very concerned that the children learn editing skills. Morgan, on the other hand, was convinced that those particular pieces of writing were not yet ready for editing. As the teacher and volunteer talked, however, they did find common ground. They settled on a two-stage process. Morgan worked with the children on content questions in early drafts. Then when the writers were ready to edit, they went to their teacher.

Over the course of a year, the teacher was impressed by what her students could do. She discovered that they were able to choose their own topics. Even though they were a particularly boisterous class, they were able to work together in groups without direct supervision. In fact, she was so enthusiastic that she had ideas for other ways in which volunteers could help teachers with writing. It occurred to her that elderly people might make excellent classroom volunteers, willing to listen to children's work and respond to questions. The next year, the teacher invited

City of San Diego Public Library
La Jolla Branch

****

2/4/2013 3:48:18 PM

Title: The European explora
Item ID: 31336085313030
Date Due: 2/25/2013,23:59

Title: The Mohawk
Item ID: 31336033423311
Date Due: 2/25/2013,23:59

Title: Write from the start
Item ID: 31336019118208
Date Due: 2/25/2013,23:59

3 items

Renew at www.sandiegolibrary.org
OR Call 619 236-5800 or 858 484-4440
and press 1 then 3 to RENEW.
Your library card is needed
to renew borrowed items.

Morgan to come back, and several other teachers from the same building invited her to assist in their classrooms.

Joyce Morgan's success demonstrates one instance in which a parent and teacher worked out a way to make the most of each other's strengths. Of course, she is an unusual parent. She has done a lot of writing herself and teaches composition at a university. But there are many ways in which individual teachers and parents can mesh their time, talents, and philosophies to benefit children.

In the same school where Morgan volunteered, for instance, another parent with unusual qualifications found that she took on different roles in different classrooms where she assisted. This mother was also a college writing instructor, as well as a journalist, and she had participated in a summer institute on teaching writing. In the first classroom where she volunteered, she assisted a teacher who had much interest in writing, but little experience in teaching it. In that instance, the parent came in as a kind of expert. But the following year she assisted a teacher who was thoroughly trained in teaching writing. This time, the parent was really more of an aide, experienced and trained, but an aide nevertheless. She conferred with the children and typed their books.

Parents need neither training nor experience, however, to help a teacher in a number of different ways, depending on the level of their own knowledge and the amount of time they have to give. For teachers used to the simplicity of worksheets, just the thought of having every child write every day can seem logistically overwhelming at first. Parents can help make the task more manageable. They can bind the small cardboard books used for publishing and type the children's work. More experienced teachers sometimes train a parent to talk to children about their writing. But the parent must always be conscious that the classroom is the teacher's domain.

The role the parent takes is the role the teacher gives.

Parents often find that a combination of approaches works best. One mother whose child attended a private school spent considerable time talking with both administrators and teachers over a period of about a year. She didn't insist that they change anything; she simply asked them to talk with one of the directors of the New York City Writing Project and to look into what was available. Her efforts paid off when the school decided to offer a series of workshops for their teachers through the Writing Project.

At a public school in a rural area, another mother talked with her son's first-grade teacher, as well as the school reading specialist, who had had some training in writing instruction. The mother also joined a group of parents who were making books for the children. Since her son had done little writing beyond copying and tracing earlier in the year, she suggested that the children be allowed to write in journals regularly. The teacher agreed. By the end of the year, the children were keeping journals, as well as doing other types of writing from time to time. They still did lots of worksheets and often wrote from story starters, but the mother knew that she had been instrumental in providing opportunities for her son and his classmates to write in school.

Learning from Each Other

Teachers often say, "Parents don't know their own kids." But parents could also make the same statement about teachers. Part of that is the two worlds. I'm sure that I don't understand my daughter Laura as she functions at school in the midst of a class of thirty. But the teacher doesn't know the beauty of my child alone. Parents and teachers both possess information that the other doesn't have. We need to bring the two together.

One natural way for parents and teachers to exchange views is through the stories they tell about children. A fifth-grade teacher in Boothbay Harbor enjoys conversations with parents she runs into in the grocery store. In an encounter with one mother, the teacher praised a little boy's piece about an owl. The teacher recalls: "And her response was, 'You know, he wrote that for me. I was the one he wrote it for. And every time I read it, it gives me goose bumps.'" The teacher laughs. "And that gave me goose bumps, for a parent to be so proud of her youngster's writing and to think that it carried that much meaning."

When parents and teachers work together in a spirit of collaboration, they learn from each other, and children inevitably benefit from the exchange. The writing folder itself brings parents and teachers together at periodic meetings in an effort to help each other understand children. Teachers use the folder to illustrate a child's progress. At the same time, parents can often explain things that have puzzled teachers. One second-grader's writing revealed a recurring theme of fires and explosions. What had seemed like a predilection for violent fantasies, however, made sense in the context of information the little boy's mother was able to provide. Three homes had burned in the family's neighborhood in recent months, an airplane had crashed into another house, and a university performed crash tests on cars nearby. On second thought, his tales didn't seem to be fantasies at all.

In other instances, the writing answers parents' questions about their children's behavior at home. Junior-high teacher Nancie Atwell says, "Some of the best moments I've had teaching have been conferences with parents. The kids write about their families so much, but when they're thirteen they don't *talk* at home. They stop talking to their parents for about four years. It's awful. And so the parents see that for their kids the family is still at the core of their lives."

Parents who volunteer to help teachers in the classroom get a glimpse of their children from a new perspective in the midst of a group of peers. The exchange between parent and teacher, however, can go far beyond insight into one child's behavior. They can teach each other about writing in special sessions, and a few parents, like Joyce Vining Morgan, can actually introduce new methods of instruction into the classroom. But more often, parents who volunteer to work in classrooms make some of the same discoveries about learning and writing that teachers do. To make those discoveries, parents need not work in their own child's room. In fact, sometimes they may learn more in another room.

A parent learns most from a teacher when both are compatible in philosophy and temperament. The odds are high for finding a good match if parents are willing to work in any room in the school, just to help out and to learn as much as possible about working with children who write. If parents want to work only in their own child's classroom, however, then the odds are greatly reduced. It may also be difficult for some children to share a parent with other children. There are ways of getting around the problem, but that depends on the individual child's sense of security.

The question remains, however, how can parents find out which teacher they might work with best? First, the parent might do a bit of reading and perhaps even some writing before approaching administrators or teachers. The principal may then be able to make better recommendations, based on what the parent knows and believes. But the job isn't over yet. There is always the matter of personal style in working with children. To find a good match in styles, the parent may have to visit several rooms or talk with several teachers. In spite of all the steps I've recommended, the outcome is largely determined by the school. Some administrators and teachers are more open than others. But the parent can at least be prepared to give the principal appropriate options to choose from.

Whether they go in as apprentices or typists, and whether their own children are present or not, parents will find many rewards in classrooms where children share their writing. One mother who typed many books for her son's class has fond memories of the experience. "There would be a stampede when I would come into the room," she says. "You know, 'Mine first! Mine first! Mine first!' And they'd have a sign-up sheet and see how many I could get to that day. Oh, they loved sitting there and watching it come into print. They had to be right there." A mother who helps children write at a kindergarten tells about a little boy who can't read his own invented spelling yet. Whenever he asks her to read his book to him, she shares his thrill—magically, mysteriously, the words say the same thing every time.

While sharing children's sense of wonder at the power of the written word, parents often pick up skills that they can apply at home. Peg Nichols, mother of the Atkinson fourth-grader named

Debbie, volunteered up to six hours of her time every week to help out at school and found that she learned a lot from one teacher she worked with. Although she had always wanted to help her children become self-reliant, questions she heard in the classroom gave her a new way to encourage independent thinking at home. When her children came to her with a problem, she got into the habit of responding with questions. "What are your alternatives?" she would ask. "How could you solve that problem?"

A mother of two teenagers took a job as an aide at her local school and was mildly surprised to hear that the teacher she was assisting, Susan Porter, planned to have her split transition and first-grade class write every day. On the first day of the new routine, however, the aide was horrified to learn that Porter expected *everyone* in the room to write at the beginning of the period. For many months, the aide enjoyed listening to the children read their work but was uncertain as to how to respond. She wrote dutifully but never showed a word of her work to anyone. By the end of the year, however, she began showing her writing to Porter. During the two following years, she became more and more confident in her abilities. She listened to the children and asked questions with assurance and skill. She continued to write every day but now shared it with the children, as well as with Porter. She wrote about her own children, her work with Porter, and her own experiences. The class was particularly delighted by her description of a meal she ate with her husband at a fancy restaurant where the main course, a fish, arrived whole, complete with eyes and tail.

Looking Ahead

When he examined the status of writing in our schools for the Ford Foundation in 1978, Donald Graves found a sorry state of affairs. For every three thousand dollars our schools spent on reading, only one dollar went for writing. Educational research showed the same lopsided set of priorities. Less than one-tenth of 1 percent of all funds went to studies on writing. In both cases, the lack of dollars reflected lack of interest.

To make matters worse, much of the writing research that had been done up to that point was based on an experimental or "scientific" model. Researchers studied finished pieces of writing or teaching techniques, but the practice of trying to "control variables" produced artificial environments. Thus, the results were often of little use in real classrooms.

The situation had already begun to change in the mid-seventies, when the back-to-basics movement became vocal and *Newsweek* published a cover story called "Why Johnny Can't Write." Writing research began receiving more money. The National Institute of Education supported its first study of writing in 1977. A year later it funded the Atkinson study.

Although the gap between theory and practice in education has often been large, many teachers have been influenced by recent research, for several reasons. For one thing, the late seventies and early eighties saw a trend toward the more natural "descriptive" study in which researchers borrow an anthropologist's skills to observe people intensively over long periods of time in their own environment, at home or at school. Many teachers have found reports from such research projects far more useful than the findings of experimental studies. At Atkinson, results were also reported in readable prose. And teachers were not only heavily involved in the study itself, but also wrote some of the articles that came out of it.

Since Atkinson, Donald Graves has broadened the scope of his work. First, he and his colleague Jane Hansen investigated the link between reading and writing in Ellen Blackburn's classroom, where an innovative approach to teaching reading paralleled recent strides made in teaching writing. Since then, Graves and Hansen have been directing a larger research team studying how teachers change their methods in both reading and writing instruction.

We can speak of the need for children to write, but unless teachers have been moved to write, children won't get the chance. Traditionally, teachers have taught what is important to them. Although they are still in the minority, a growing number of teachers will teach writing because it is impor-

tant to them. The biggest barrier to overcome in many cases is the memory of their own unfortunate histories as writers. Succeeding generations of children who have had more positive experiences in school will be much more inclined to write and, in turn, to teach writing.

The next generation includes an increasing number of students who have found writing to be an important part of their lives. They will be better teachers than we have been. As they become writers, better readers of research, and better teachers of the craft, they will place higher demands on research. These teachers want relevant findings written in understandable English.

Interest in writing will continue to grow in society at large, as well, because so many people from all walks of life have found writing to be an important tool for thought and source of enjoyment. As our civilization speeds up, there is a greater need to reflect, to make sense of the rapid pace of every day. People sort things out by keeping journals, diaries, packets of letters from friends. Of course, the majority of people in the country do not do this. The group I speak of is just a small percentage.

But that is not to say that writing is the exclusive domain of the intelligentsia or of the highly educated. In fact, it is one of the most rapid means of upward mobility in our society. People who can put their thoughts down on paper can have an effect on family, colleagues, and the communities in which they live. A well-written piece can transcend the barriers within a society that demands diplomas and other certificates of achievement. I suspect that as time goes on, more and more people will realize that they have that kind of power. It is our task to help children to understand the power of well-chosen words that reflect a strong voice backed with strong information.

Society's increasing interest in writing has been reflected in school programs, as well as in increasing funding for research. The National Institute of Education now has plans for spending $5 million to establish a national writing center that will combine the research efforts of several universities. Writing projects and institutes have had a profound impact on teaching, both by disseminating research information and by encouraging teachers to write.

To many, writing still means penmanship, spelling, and parts of speech. Yet to an increasing number of teachers, parents, and children, it means much more. When a researcher asked a third-grader how she had changed as a writer during the first six months of the Atkinson project, the little girl said, "I'm much different because I know how hard it is to write, how much you have to tell, how much you have to cross out, how much you have to think what you are going to write." The movement to improve writing instruction will continue to grow as more and more teachers, administrators, and parents gain a new understanding of writing and learning, as well as the courage to apply what they know at home and at school. Then more and more children, like those in Brooklyn and Boothbay and Melbourne and Atkinson, will get a chance to show what they can do.

Suggestions for
Further Reading

BISSEX, GLENDA. *GNYS AT WRK: A Child Learns to Write and Read.* Cambridge: Harvard University Press, 1980.

Bissex documents her son's progress as both a writer and reader between the ages of five and eleven. The book reveals not only one child's development from an inventive to a conventional speller, but also his parents' interaction with him, as well as the contrast between his experiences with written language at home and at school.

BRUNER, JEROME. *On Knowing: Essays for the Left Hand.* Cambridge: Harvard University Press, Belknap Press, 1979.

In a series of essays on various ways in which we develop and act on knowledge, Bruner addresses topics such as the function of myth, the role of surprise in thought, and the elements of creativity. He also considers the questions of what kinds of knowledge are best learned in school and how teachers can lead children to make their own discoveries. The subtitle refers to certain qualities, such as intuition and sentiment, which have long been associated with the left hand and which Bruner considers to play an important role in knowing.

CALKINS, LUCY MCCORMICK. *Lessons from a Child.* Exeter, N.H.: Heinemann Educational Books, 1983.

This book is about a little girl named Susie, some of her third- and fourth-grade classmates, and the teachers who participated in the two-year research project conducted by Donald Graves, Lucy Calkins, and Susan Sowers in Atkinson, New Hampshire. Calkins shows how these students and teachers changed during the course of the study, developing new skills both as writers and readers.

GRAVES, DONALD H. *Writing: Children and Teachers at Work.* Exeter, N.H.: Heinemann Educational Books, 1983.

In his book on the "twin crafts" of teaching and writing, Graves shows teachers how to get a writing class started, confer with young writers, improve skills, understand writing development, and keep records on children's progress.

HARSTE, JEROME, CAROLINE BURKE, and VIRGINIA WOODWARD. *Language Stories and Literacy Lessons.* Portsmouth, N.H.: Heinemann Educational Books, 1984.

If examined within a social context, even scribbling and pretending to read reveal a child's knowledge of language and strategies for applying the knowledge, according to Harste, Burke, and Woodward. Drawing on their research with three-, four-, five-, and six-year-olds from different socioeconomic backgrounds, the authors describe what preschool children already know about the written word, how school assignments ignore that knowledge, and how adults can help children further their growing understanding of the language.

HEATH, SHIRLEY BRICE. *Ways with Words: Ethnography of Communication, Communities, and Classrooms.* Cambridge: Cambridge University Press, 1983.

Anthropologist Heath reports on her findings in an ethnographic study of language use and development in three communities in the Carolina Piedmont: a working-class white community, a working-class black community, and a middle-class "mainstream" community of both blacks and whites. In a highly readable style, Heath shows how social history, family structure, and religious training influence the ways in which language is used within a community. Toward the end of the book, Heath describes how teachers she worked with used her research and their own observations to help children from all three communities get off to a better start in school.

KIMMEL, MARGARET MARY and ELIZABETH SEGEL. *For Reading Out Loud!* New York: Dell Publishing Co., 1984.

In the first part of this book, Kimmel and Segel discuss the value of reading aloud to children of all ages and suggest ways to increase a child's enjoyment of books. But two-thirds of the book consists of an alphabetical list of books, old and new, that are especially suitable for reading aloud to primary- and middle-school children. For each book, the authors include a suggested age range, a description of the story, and tips on parts that parents may want to skip.

LAMME, LINDA LEONARD. *Growing Up Writing: Sharing with Your Children the Joys of Good Writing.* Washington, D.C.: Acropolis Books, 1984.

In a thoroughly practical guide for parents, Lamme offers much advice on how to help children become interested in writing, develop fluency, and sharpen skills like spelling, handwriting, and usage.

MURRAY, DONALD. *Write to Learn.* New York: Holt, Rinehart and Winston, 1984.

This book begins with Murray's vague desire to understand the "dominant figure" of his childhood and ends with a finished piece of writing about his grandmother and her influence on him. In between, he describes his model of the writing process: collect, focus, order, draft, and clarify. At each stage, he offers writers numerous approaches and techniques, illustrated by his own work on the piece about his grandmother. *Write to Learn* would be useful to parents and teachers who want to experience writing as a process of discovery.

PAPERT, SEYMOUR. *Mindstorms: Children, Computers, and Powerful Ideas.* New York: Basic Books, 1980.

Papert explains the philosophy behind LOGO, a computer language he developed at Massachusetts Institute of Technology. He believes that children's ability to learn their native language easily, early, and naturally shows their ability to learn many other things in the same way, under the right circumstances. Just as people best learn French in France, LOGO allows children to learn math in what Papert refers to as "Mathland—where mathematics would become a natural vocabulary." The learning environment he describes resembles the best writing classrooms in many ways: children and teachers collaborate, experiment, tackle complex tasks, enjoy their work, and realize that they should learn from, rather than be ashamed of, errors. Although the book is not an easy read, it is well worth the effort.

SMITH, FRANK. *Writing and the Writer.* New York: Holt, Rinehart and Winston, 1982.

Smith examines what he calls "the psychology of the writing act." He focuses on the differences and connections between composition and transcription, between spoken and written language, between meaning and the conventions used to convey meaning. After addressing these issues, he focuses on how people learn to write and how teachers can help.

TAYLOR, DENNY. *Family Literacy: Young Children Learning to Read and Write.* Portsmouth, N.H.: Heinemann Educational Books, 1983.

Researcher Taylor has made a three-year case study of six middle-class families with children successfully learning to read and write. Writing in plain language, she describes the different ways in which the children she studied were exposed to writing in the context of their everyday family life. She shows how they began to use writing for their own purposes, often in ways that went unnoticed by the adults around them. Taylor is particularly interested in the ways in which certain social events, like read-aloud sessions and secret club meetings, motivate children to read and write. At the end of the book, Taylor discusses the implications of her findings for schools.

TEMPLE, CHARLES, RUTH NATHAN, and NANCY BURRIS. *The Beginnings of Writing.* Boston: Allyn and Bacon, 1982.

Citing research and several hundred samples of children's writing, Temple, Nathan, and Burris analyze children's changing perceptions of written language and their attempts to master it as they progress from scribbles to fluent, conventional writing. The book has good sections on the parallels between oral and written language acquisition, the peculiarities of English spelling, the history of writing, and the strategies children use to communicate in writing.

TURBILL, JANE, ed. *No Better Way to Teach Writing!* Rozelle, N.S.W., Australia: Primary English Teaching Association, 1982.

Twenty-seven Australian primary-school teachers and their language consultant describe what happened when they voluntarily changed their approach to teaching writing. The book demonstrates the difficulties overcome and results achieved when one group of teachers first allowed children to write every day, use invented spelling, choose their own topics, and talk about their work.

ZINSSER, WILLIAM. *On Writing Well: An Informal Guide to Writing Nonfiction.* New York: Harper & Row, 1980.

While Donald Murray focuses on the process of writing, Zinsser concentrates more on the product. With humor, grace, and plenty of examples, he describes the qualities to strive for and the pitfalls to watch for. He discusses usage, style, openings, and closings, as well as different types of writing, such as humorous, critical, scientific, sports, and travel writing.